A Far Cry From Freedom: Gradual Abolition (1799-1827)

New York State's Crime Against Humanity

by
L. Lloyd Stewart

authorHOUSE™

1663 Liberty Drive, Suite 200
Bloomington, Indiana 47403
(800) 839-8640
www.AuthorHouse.com

First published by AuthorHouse 12/27/05

ISBN: 1-4208-8365-8 (sc)

Library of Congress Control Number: 2005908430

Printed in the United States of America
Bloomington, Indiana

This book is printed on acid-free paper.

TABLE OF CONTENTS

ACKNOWLEDGEMENTS xiii

PREFACE xvii

INTRODUCTION xix

CHAPTER I 1

THE GEOPOLITICAL EVOLUTION OF ENSLAVEMENT IN
NEW YORK 1

    AFRICAN ENSLAVEMENT IN NEW NETHERLAND.........2

    THE AFRICAN PRESENCE IN NEW NETHERLAND 13

    RESISTANCE TO ENSLAVEMENT 47

    ENSLAVED AFRICANS REVOLT IN NEW YORK.............50

    ENSLAVEMENT IN NEW YORK STATE 61

CHAPTER II...97

THE PATH TO ABOLITION IN NEW YORK STATE 97

    THE INITIAL EFFORTS AT ABOLITION 99

    THE DUTCH AND ABOLITION 112

    ECONOMIC AND POLITICAL SHIFTS LEAD
    NEW YORK TO GRADUAL ABOLITION 120

CHAPTER III 135

THE GRADUAL ABOLITION ACT 135

CHAPTER IV 191

ALBANY COUNTY AND THE GRADUAL ABOLITION
ACT..191

CHAPTER V 235

NEW YORK STATE'S COMPENSATED ABOLITION
PROGRAM..235

    SUBSIDY PAYMENTS MADE TO NEW YORK
    SLAVEHOLDERS..237

    SUBSIDY PAYMENTS MADE TO LOCAL
    GOVERNMENTS 247

CHAPTER VI..**269**

GRADUAL ABOLITION AND ITS FISCAL IMPACT ON
NEW YORK STATE..269

CHAPTER VII...**287**

GRADUAL ABOLITION LAW HAS NO IMPACT ON THE
STATUS OF ENSLAVEMENT 287

CHAPTER VIII **323**

FINAL ABOLITION IN NEW YORK STATE 323

    THE JIM CROW STATUS OF "FREED" AFRICAN
    DESCENDANTS AFTER EMANCIPATION.......................325

CHAPTER IX **345**

CONCLUSION..345

RECOMMENDATION **355**

A CASE FOR REPARATIONS AGAINST THE STATE OF
NEW YORK 355

SELECTED BIBLIOGRAPHY..**367**

INDEX..**371**

ILLUSTRATIONS

Figure 1 The Dutch Settlements In North America 5

Figure 2 Map Of Triangle Trade 8

Figure 3 1767 Manor Of Rensselaerwick 10

Figure 4 Albany (Fort Orange/beverwyck) 12

Figure 5 Esteban Gomez's Map Of 1529 16

Figure 6 Enslaved Africans Being Landed In North American 21

Figure 7 Stowage of the British Slave Ship Brookes 23

Figure 8 Advertisement To Sell An Enslaved Female 25

Figure 9 Ship Of Enslaved Africans Arrives In New York City 30

Figure 10 Colonial Era, New York City 33

Figure 11 Illustration Of New York City Enslavement Market 35

Figure 12 Adolph Phillipse Probate Inventory 37

Figure 13 Example Of New York City Enslavement Codes 45

Figure 14 1741 Slave Revolt List 54

Figure 15 A List Of White Persons Taken Into Custody On Account Of The 1741 Conspiracy 57

Figure 16 Venture Smith's grave at the First Church Cemetery in East Haddam, Connecticut 60

Figure 17 Free African American Farm Plots – NYC 119

Figure 18 Lloyd Colbert 167

Figure 19 Caesar Nicoll (1737-1852) 231

Figure 20 Sojourner Truth17 1797/1800 -1883 298

Figure 21 Austin Steward27 (1793-1869) 302

DOCUMENTS

Document 1-1 Indenture of Sam for three years to become Shoemaker..70

Document 1-2 Indenture of Sam for three years to become Shoemaker (con't)..71

Document 2 Hire-out Agreement For An African American Family 74

Document 3-1 An Albany Law forbidding enslaved men from being in the Street after 9 PM 110

Document 3-2 An Albany Law forbidding enslaved men from being in the Street after 9 PM 111

Document 4 Bill for Teaching Black man Dick..........................141

Document 5 Record of submission by Town of North Hempstead to the State of New York for Payment to Daniel Whitehead Kissam 145

Document 6 Purchase Of Ester And 2 Mo. Old Child.................164

Document 7 Birth Of Harriet To Phoebe 165

Document 8 Overseers Of The Poor Manumission Of Lloyd Colbert 166

Document 9 Manumission of Bettee or Betsy 168

Document 10 Manumission Certificate Of Thomas Adams 169

Document 11 Affidavit of witness to Freedom of Thomas Adams of Troy..170

Document 12-1 Affidavit Of Freedom Of Prince Williams.........172

Document 12-2 Certificate Of Freedom Of Prince Williams.......173

Document 13-1 Affidavit Of Freedom Of Frisbee Way...............176

Document 13-2 Certificate Of Freedom Of Frisbee Way 177

Document 14 Amariah Paine Vs. Overseer Of The Poor, Town Of Schodack 179

Document 15 Affidavit Of Mariah For Manumission..................180

Document 16 Executors Manumit Three Slaves In Troy.............182

Document 17 Overseers Of The Poor Grant Peggy Freedom......183

Document 18 A slave boy named Jack born of Gin Given to Joseph Duprey from Johannes Hardenburg 184

Document 19 Sale to William Robbins by Gerrit Van Zandt 194

Document 20 Affidavit by Matthew Vischer as witness to sale of slave Antone to William Robbins 195

Document 21 Sale of Slave named Class to Gerrit Van Zandt 196

Document 22 Receipt of sale of slave, Frank, to Gerrit Van Zandt of Albany..197

Document 23 Bill for the advertisement of a Negro wench for sale by Garrit Van Zandt 198

Document 24 Receipt for sale of Dine and her child to Gerrit Van Zandt 199

Document 25-1 Sale of Slave Jacob to Volkert Douw.................200

Document 25-2 Sale of Slave Jacob to Volkert Douw (con't).....201

Document 26 Deed of V. A. Douw to Elsie Fonda for a slave named Dina 212

Document 27-1 Letter from Major Fonda to A. Van Campen to assist in the return of a slave named William formally Leon 214

Document 27-2 Letter from Major Fonda to A. Van Campen (con't)..215

Document 28-1 Sale of Slave to Abraham Ten Eyck.................220

Document 28-2 Sale Of Richard For Six Year Period 221

Document 28-3 Sale Of Richard For Six Year Period 222

Document 29 New York State Gradual Abolition Of Slavery Act
Accounts Of Payments...236

Document 30-1 Payments Made To New Utrecht Slaveholders..246

Document 30-2 Payments Made To New Utrecht Slaveholders..247

Document 31 Certification Of Birth And Abandonment Of
Tempe...248

Document 32 Certification Of Birth And Abandonment Of
Charles 249

Document 33 Request For Payment For Tempe 250

Document 34 Request For Payment For Charles....................252

Document 35 Receipt Of Payment From Overseers For
Charles 253

Document 36 Coversheet For Payment Submission To New York
State...255

Document 37 Certification Of Abandonment For 4 Children......256

Document 38 Request For Payment For George And Harriet 258

Document 39 Request For Payment For Jane And Esther..........260

Document 40 Final Approval Page 261

Document 41 Coversheet For Payment Submission To New York
State...262

Document 42 Request For Payment From NY State 264

Document 43 Request For Assistance From Comptroller 265

Document 44 Town of Oyster Bay's (Queens County) Request for
Payment...275

Document 45 Mamaroneck, NY's Authorization for Payment....276

Document 46 Amounts and Proportions of the Total New York State Budget Spent on Abandoned Black Children 280

Document 47 Certificate of Abandonment, Piscataway Township New Jersey 283

Document 48 Hire Agreement Bill For Negro Pete....................291

Document 49 Notice Of Runaway -- 26th Aug. 1774 311

Document 50 Notice Of Runaway -- 13th June 1809..................312

Document 51 Geneva Gazette 46 Aug. 1, 1810...........................315

Document 52 Population Of The State Of New York, ca. 1800 ..340

TABLES

Table 1 Town Minutes - Salem, NY (1790-1826).........................147

Table 2 Town Minutes Poughkeepsie from 1769 to 1833 154

Table 3 "Yorktown Record of Negro Children Born to Slaves"..162

Table 4-1 Albany Co. Register of Manumitted Slaves
(1800-1805)...203

Table 4-1a Albany Co. Register of Manumitted Slaves
(1800-1805)...206

Table 4-2 Albany Co. Register of Manumitted Slaves
(1800-1805)...209

Table 5 Town of Watervliet Minutes (1793-1844)......................218

Table 6 Town of Guilderland, Records of Birth of Slaves
(1803-1807)...224

Table 7 Records of Bethlehem for the Purpose of Intering Negro
Children born of slaves..226

Table 8 Register of payments to Albany Slave holders
(1800-1803)...239

Table 9 Abandoned Children Recorded for Albany, NY
(1799-1806)...241

Table 10 Land Settlements and Financial Payments to Indigenous
People..363

DEDICATION

This work is dedicated to my Ancestors, those named and unnamed: the Smith family, the Epps family; the Peterman family; the Van Dorn family, the Van Vranken family - **and to those families and their members not yet found** - whose story this history actually became. Moreover, it is dedicated to my Grandchildren: Imani Mylee, Lamine Lloyd, Miyani Nevaeh, Selah Inaya, Kaiya Rene, Azaan Lamar, and Nailah Amira; whose story - thanks to the determination and struggle of their Ancestors - this history will *never* become!

ACKNOWLEDGEMENTS

The author would especially like to give praise and thanksgiving to the Father/Mother God, THE ALL, for the blessings and love provided to pursue this work. In addition, I'd like to also thank my Ancestors, known and unknown, without whose inspiration, instruction and sacrifices this work would not have been accomplished.

Special thanks are given to the following individuals for their support and assistance in finalizing this work: To Dr. Maulana Karenga for his unwavering support, inspiration, direction and counsel and most importantly for his gracious and insightful Preface to this book. To Prof. Hollis Lynch, who was my initial inspiration in pursuing historical research and who provided much needed consultation and willingness to review my original Manuscript. To Lloyd Hogan, Prof. of Economics, for his unwavering support and encouragement, and his assistance with editing and supporting the economic concepts of human enslavement and abolition presented herein; and, to Dr. Asa Hilliard, for his timely support, encouragement and insight.

Most importantly, I'd like to acknowledge and thank my parents, Louis and Elizabeth and my Grandmother, Mamoo, who individually and collectively blessed me with unconditional love and encouragement and who graciously and lovingly allowed me to be my own person.

Special Appreciation and love to my wife, Mitzi Glenn Stewart, for her unconditional love and her willingness at ALL times and hours of the day or night to discuss, argue, proof and edit this work from its very beginning. And special thanks to my Cousin and "Big Sistah" Doris Bedell, whose professional editing skills and timely presence at a difficult period in this work's development allowed me to transcend the last major hurdle to completion. Love and thanks to my Daughter, Malaika Stewart Doumbouya, for her editing assistance and to my children: Yusuf, Rahsaan, Tahirah, Jelani and Jamal and my Godchildren: Salihah Elizabeth and William Austin, for their continued love and support.

Eternal thanks to my sister, Judith-Ann, for her belief and unwavering confidence in my ability to undertake such a project, and to my departed Brother Gary - I know I shall never see his like again! To my Brothers: Timothy, Arthur, Steven; and my entire family related and extended for their continuous love and support. Special thanks also to my spiritual Brothers Norman, Bill and Tambuzi, without whose lifetime support, love and encouragement, I would have never attempted this undertaking. And to my fraternal Brothers Greg and Chas, who have taught me the true meaning of "Eternal Brotherhood". Finally, I'd like to thank my "Best Friend" Elaine, for her spiritual guidance and support throughout my entire life.

Acknowledgement and gratitude is also extended to the State University of New York African American Research Foundation in Albany, New York for a Research Grant (2001-2002), which allowed me to pursue the initial research for a substantial part of this work. Additional acknowledgement is given to the staff at the New York State Archives, the Albany Institute of History and Art and the New York State Historical Society for their willingness to allow me to have access to the many documents and manuscripts included within this work. Finally, I'd like to acknowledge the numerous local historians and their staffs who were willing and instrumental in providing direction and access to local and county documents that addressed both slavery and gradual abolition in their respective counties, cities and towns.

To Rosa, Jim & the Fiona,
Peace & Blessing

A FAR CRY
FROM FREEDOM

L. Lloyd Stewart '06

PREFACE

This is a work that deserves to be read, not only because of the quality and amount of research and thought that went into it, but also because of what it reveals about the history of the state of New York and this country. It also points to their need to come to terms with the immoral, evil and unjust acts committed in the name of race, religion and the "right" to conquest. Brother Lloyd Stewart draws a clear line between his work and many recent works on enslavement which attempt to tone down and sanitize the horror, criminality and human tragedy of African enslavement. Indeed, he is especially concerned with stripping away New York's unofficial masking of the horror of its policies and its pretension of a benevolence impossible in such a violent, degrading and dehumanizing process. As the title suggests, Brother Lloyd is very concerned with exposing the myths, hypocrisy, extended brutality and injustice in the concept and practice of "gradual abolition," which subsidized the enslavement of children and reinforced enslavement while pretending to ease and erase it.

Rich with documents and documentation, Brother Lloyd unveils the state's sanction of enslavement with law, subsidy and ideology, its bloody vengeance for rebellion and resistance and the contradiction between self-congratulatory claims of freedom and democracy and the daily violent dehumanization of enslavement. He concludes with an argument for reparations for both the inhuman practice and its continuing consequences. Moreover, he reaffirms the essential character of enslavement as a crime against humanity which demands remedy and repair as a matter of morality and law. In conclusion, the book is an important contribution to the ongoing discourse on the Holocaust of African enslavement and merits a close and careful reading for its insistence on objective analysis, cogent reasoning, ethical reflection, and a quick and salutary end to the falsification of the history of New York and the United States. For only when a society confronts and concedes the horrors of its past can it build safeguards against their repetition and begin to heal and repair the devastating damage done, not only to the immediate victims, but also to our concept and practice of what it means to be really human and do justice in the world.

-- Dr. Maulana Karenga

Professor, Department of Black Studies

California State University, Long Beach

INTRODUCTION

"The past is never dead. It's not even past."[1]

PREFACE

This work is a byproduct of genealogical research that I began in 2000 as a special gift to my Grandmother, Anabel Puels. As a result of oral family history, my Grandmother - Mamoo was subconsciously aware of our long family history in New York State, and yet her actual conscious memory of our past was limited to three generations. At the time of these very intimate and enlightening conversations with her, she was a vibrant 93 years old. I was able to present her with this labor of love, a preliminary copy of our family history, on Christmas 2001. She, unfortunately for all her family members and the community at large, passed on November 1, 2002, at the age of 95.

As I began the research on this book, it became clear to me that our family history in New York State was indeed extensive. More importantly for this work, it became evident that our family had unfortunately experienced a substantial portion of the chaotic and dehumanizing history of African Americans in New York State during its first two centuries. I have traced our Ancestors back to the late 1700s, and I have been able to identify and document both the life of my Great-Great-Great- Great-Great Grandfather Johannes Van Vranken (1783-1865) and that of his family to the present day. Johannes is recorded on his son, Samuel Van Vranken's death certificate as having been born in Schagticoke (Rensselaer County), New York.[2]

It is safe to say that he and his family were **enslaved** in New York during the time of his birth. In fact, New York State was in the middle of its long history of enslavement during this period. I have not yet been able to document our families' history prior to his birth, so I am unable to identify the individuals and/or families to whom my Ancestors in New York were enslaved. Undoubtedly, the various slave holding Van Vranken families of Albany, Rensselaer,

Schenectady and Saratoga Counties played some role in their bondage and emancipation.

I have found, however, that a migration of recently "freed" families of African descent occurred in the early 1800s. This migration was probably the result of the passage of the Gradual Abolition Act of 1799 by the New York State Legislature after numerous unsuccessful attempts. It allowed for the emancipation of some enslaved African descendants. This migration was directed at Washington County, NY, which is bordered by the State of Vermont and was known for its surplus of accessible farm land. It is believed that these "freed" African descendant families migrated to Washington County from other parts of New York State i.e. Saratoga, Rensselaer, Schenectady, Albany Counties and downstate in an effort to both establish the reunion of family members separated during enslavement and to take advantage of the accessibility of this surplus farmland. The Van Vrankens were one of these families. It can be surmised that the reason for this migration may also have been the passage in 1821 by the state legislature of a law that effectively disenfranchised "free" African descendants of their voting rights and further eliminated their ability to secure these rights through prevailing land value requirements.

This 1821 law, to be discussed later in greater detail, stipulated that African descendants would be eligible to exercise their right to vote only on the legal condition that they owned land that was valued at $250. While at the same time, it eliminated any previous requirements of land ownership placed on white voters. This law was a direct contradiction to previous voting requirement statutes that had set the threshold for voting privileges at $100 in land value for **all** voters, African descendant and white, alike.

During this period of African American history in New York, Johannes Van Vranken and his wife, Hannah / Elizabeth are baptized on 9 February 1812 in the 1st United Presbyterian Congregation Church in Cambridge, (Washington County) NY. Their children are later baptized in the same Church: Samuel and Hannah (25 July 1812), Robert (13 November 1814) and Margaret (1817)[3]. Johannes Van Vranken (John Van Vronk) is later recorded in the 1825 New York

State Census of Salem (Washington County) New York as living on a small farm with his family, which was comprised of ten members. They are listed in this census as a family of "Free Coloureds." However none of the members of the family were eligible to vote due to the provisions of the aforementioned law of 1821. The family is also recorded as owning a number of cattle, six sheep, six hogs and having domestically manufactured fourteen yards of cotton, linen or other cloth.

Johannes Van Vranken, listed as John Van Vronk or Van Bronk in several later state and federal censuses, continued to reside in Washington County for another forty years in the towns of Salem and Argyle. He raises his 7 children into adulthood and probably was accused of spoiling his 13+ grand and numerous great-grandchildren. His life could best be described as that of a subsistence farmer. His daughter Catherine married a member of the Hazzard family, another of the families of African descent who moved to Washington County in the early 1800s along with the Van Vrankens. The point here is that Johannes Van Vranken and his family were typical of the families of African descent who lived in the numerous farming communities throughout New York State.

On 3 January 1865, Johannes Van Vranken (John Van Bronk) and his second wife, Roseanna, were admitted to the Washington County Poor House for conditions listed as "palsied and old age," respectively. Johannes Van Vranken died on 10 April 1865 at the age of 82 years. His wife Roseanna Van Vranken (Susanna Van Bronk) age 70 years, subsequently moves in with her daughter Catherine Hazzard and her family.

Our family's history spans an extremely significant 200 year period of African American history in New York State. It encompasses the state's history of the inhuman practices of African enslavement and the African slave trade; a protracted period of pre-emancipation called Gradual Abolition resulting in the forced bondage of African descendant children; the final abolition of enslavement; and finally, the period encompassing the disenfranchisement of free citizens of African descent and the implementation of a systemic code of discrimination often referred to as "Jim Crow."

With my family's history as the backdrop for my undertaking this work, it became eminently clear that the history of New York State that we all learn about in our history classes is in large measure incomplete, especially with respect to the history of people of African descent. In the following pages, you will be exposed to an analysis of the reasoning behind this distorted interpretation of history and additionally, you will be provided with a more accurate accounting of the facts and events that occurred during the first two centuries of the history of people of African descent in New York State.

HISTORICAL PREMISE

When people remark that there is often some truth concealed in the myths and legends of past history, it is not at all difficult to comprehend the substance of these statements. When students of history attempt to seek the truth about historical events, we first search for the writings of that particular period, the 'historical record.' We then, peruse the writings of later day and contemporary historians. We search for the 'history,' as it is called. However, when we analyze the process of writing history, we realize that history can often become an exercise in personification. That is to say, history can inherit the human characteristics and personality traits of its writers. It can often be molded to reflect the writer's likes and dislikes, cultural worldview and unfortunately, in the instances of people of African descent, his prejudices and fears. We oftentimes, unknowingly find ourselves presented with "His Story" as opposed to true historical fact.

In much the same manner as witnesses to a crime interpret what they have seen according to their own personal frame of reference so too, does the historian interpret history. Consider that it is not uncommon to watch a trial in which testimony seems to be presented as differing versions of the exact same crime or more importantly, differing aspects of the same crime. This is not to say that the resulting testimony is useless. On the contrary, each version enables the complete truth to become clearer to the judge and jury. Much like a puzzle, each assembled piece of testimony brings us closer to the final truth - the complete picture.

So too, is history like a puzzle. Unfortunately, all too often one version of history is allowed to serve as *the* one and only valid or acceptable truth to the suppression, exclusion and disrepute of other contradicting versions or interpretations, regardless of their methodology.

It is not difficult for people of African descent to visualize the barrier that has thus, been constructed with respect to the history of African people worldwide. It embraces the following mantra:

"Academic discipline must be maintained at the expense of direct confrontation and criticism of certain heretofore "established authorities!" [4]

Unfortunately, African people are confronted with the reality that these 'authorities' are, in point of fact, the ones "… who have desecrated African history, solely on the basis that they are fellow historians." There can be no question that there exists "… a sort of gentlemen's agreemen" in their representation of the world history of people of African descent. [5]

This "agreement" has served as the foundation for a majority of the prejudices and stereotyping that have existed for centuries with respect to people of African descent in Africa, America and worldwide. I believe that this 'agreement' has evolved into an institutional practice used by established scholars to label contrary or differing views of historical events as "revisionist history." It is this writer's opinion that in the instances of the history of people of African descent, this practice has been widespread. Furthermore, I would suggest that this 'agreement' has become the accepted or mainstream version of our history. In reality however, its content, interpretation and presentation have proven to be the "revisionist history" that they so vehemently argue against.

In an effort to embellish past deeds, these standardized expressions of history frequently depict a false or half-true history. We thus, begin to diminish our own God-given intellectual capacity for understanding when we fall victim to these conscious and unconscious attempts at this falsification or, more accurately, this beautification of history. This intellectual pretense forces us, all, to become not impeccant students seeking the truth but unwitting conspirators in the crimes of arrogance and deceit perpetrated by these "established historians." Historians whose renderings of historical facts and events are designed to make these purveyors of biased history feel more comfortable with their past deeds and actions.

History then becomes transformed into myth and legend. It assumes the characteristics and degeneracy of modern day "spinning." The end result is that true history suffers for it. It now contains only parts of the truth and it loses the real essence and purpose of historical remembrance.

Interestingly enough, we realize that historians through their individual or collective cultural identities can gain control of history and then twist and shape it to suit their own personal or nationalistic views. History then, assumes the nature of propaganda and is used as a tool to sway and influence 'public memory'. In these instances, people of African descent find themselves "enslaved," a second time by the prejudices, fears and xenophobia of individual writers and national agendas that may have existed centuries in the past. Consequently, we as African people, find ourselves unable to visualize new and insightful directions and aspirations for our people. Generations of African descendants became victims of this flawed and corrupt historical memory. As in the generational story imparted by Randall Robinson in "The Debt: What America Owes To Blacks"[6] this lack of truthful and unbiased history has caused and continues to cause generations of African descendants to search for temporary solutions to endemic social problems which results in underachievement and self-hate.

"Ingrained low expectation, when consciously faced, invites impenetrable gloom."[7]

It is within this social and political paradigm that today's youth of African descent are raised. We have all heard the old adage that "history tends to repeat itself," as a consequence of these corrupt interpretations of history, we are unable to avoid repeating prior mistakes and are limited in our remembrances of past glories. A people cannot exist on fallacy and fiction as a substitute for history, any more then a people can exist on a history manipulated to showcase only good deeds and accomplishments.

> **"History is a clock people use to tell their historical culture and political time of the day. It's a compass that people use to find themselves on the map of human geography. The history tells them where they have been, where they are and what they are. But most importantly history tells a people where they must go and what they still must be."[8]**

I have opened this book with this introduction for two reasons - first, to set the stage for the readers to comprehend what follows with an open mind. And secondly, and most importantly, to state the circumstances under which the history of an entire race of people can be clouded and falsified by myths and fallacies. This corrupted version of history has been used to propitiate the prejudices and fears of a people who only wished the subjugation of another race of people. This is not to say or imply that all historians not of African descent are party to this pretext of history. However, no intelligent human being can deny that prejudice and fear have manifested themselves in untold numbers of untruths and fallacies surrounding the heritage, culture, intelligence, courage, determination, and abilities of people of African descent.

It is within this framework that I will attempt to provide a comprehensive analysis of the period of Gradual Abolition (1799-1827) in New York State with the ultimate goal of furnishing African descendants with a more accurate accounting of their history in New York. This goal could not be accomplished without a brief yet, detailed accounting of enslavement in New York State. After all, how would one believe the devastation of families of African descent in New York State during the period of Gradual Abolition, if they did not believe, as the majority of Americans do not, that New York State was in fact and deed, a "Slave State?"

The purpose than, of this work is to effectively and with scholarly intent address two profoundly inaccurate myths that surround the history of enslavement and its abolition in New York State. Specifically, this work deals with the universal perception that the nature of enslavement in New York State in relation to the corresponding system which flourished in the southern colonies and states of America was comparatively "benign." Secondly, this work is primarily developed to examine the conceptualization, nature, implementation and substance of the little known period of Gradual Abolition from 1799 to 1827 in New York State.

MYTH # 1: **Enslavement in New York is characterized as having a milder and more humane nature than the system of enslavement instituted in the southern states of America**

Much has been written about the horror and depravity of enslavement in the southern region of the United States. However, the northern region, in particular New York, has been depicted as practicing a more humane and less oppressive version of enslavement. Graham Russell Hodges in "*Root & Branch*" quotes an anonymous New Yorker writing in 1796, who exemplifies this misguided way of thinking when he refers to enslavement in New York as,

> *"... mild (if any slave can be said to receive mild treatment), compared with what they receive in the southern states." [In no part of the world] "do slaves live so comfortable as here."*[9]

Despite claims by eighteenth century enslavers that the region's slaves were well-treated and contented - life on such subsistence homesteads was harsh, monotonous, and unrewarding.[10] The truth is that New York State implemented and benefited from a "slave society" which fostered "slave codes," whippings and murders, brutality, the separation of families, and the disenfranchisement and "Jim Crow" status of African descendants that in all aspects and practices mirrored the "slave society" of the southern regions of America.

"... as the northern colonies were more fully incorporated into the Atlantic economy, the significance of slavery grew.

In some places, the North itself took on the trappings of a slave society, with an economy that rested upon the labor of enslaved Africans and African Americans."[11]

Unlike other northern states during the early 19th century, New York State was next to last (New Jersey was last) to abolish enslavement. This was primarily due to the fact that enslaved labor played a more indispensable role in New York State's economy, such that the institution was more strongly entrenched in the society and economy of New York than in the rest of the North. Additionally, New York State never included the abolition of enslavement in its state constitution as other northern states did. This inaction has lead many historians, scholars, statesmen and the general public at large to assume and conclude that enslavement, if it existed at all in New York State, was not extensive enough to require a constitutional ban on its' continuance.

This book will provide a *new* insight into the documented involvement of state and local government in the institution, administration and fiscal support of "chattel slavery" and the forced bondage of children of African descent during Gradual Abolition in New York State. Specifically, through the use of legislative documents, court, county and municipal records, personal narratives, newspaper accounts, manuscripts, books, and journal articles, I plan to document the history of enslavement in New York under the Dutch, as well as its later administrations under the British and within Colonial America.

Most importantly, I will show that the system of enslavement in New York State, particularly from the British occupation to abolition, mirrored in virtually every respect and function the system of enslavement as it was instituted and practiced in the southern regions of the colonies and later in the republic. By example, New York City's huge seaport made it the focal point for the trading of Africans and their descendants on the eastern seaboard and it became the center of the heaviest slaveholding region north of the Mason-Dixon Line.[12]

Another example of this "slave society" is illustrated in the fact that during the Colonial period, the number of those enslaved in New York State totaled only some seven thousand below Georgia's total enslaved population during the same period.[13] In fact, throughout most of the 18th century New York City ranked second to Charleston in the number of enslaved Africans owned by its inhabitants.[14]

Through the use of primary sources including original New York State and town records, this book will further illustrate how the State of New York actively participated in the institutionalization and support of enslavement, both financially and legislatively. It will also present additional documentation to prove that both local and state governments appropriated taxpayers' dollars to support and perpetuate the bondage of men, women *and* children in New York State

MYTH # 2: **It has been articulated that the State of New York was "quick" to abolish enslavement and that this inevitable process further serves to illustrate the humanitarian and unbiased nature of New Yorkers**

This depiction of New Yorkers has been perpetrated for centuries. As recently as 2001, a New York newspaper article espoused the liberal nature of New Yorkers when it exclaimed,

> **"In 1830, the state legislature deemed slaves could be freed once they reached the age of 25, and after 1830, at the advent of the abolitionist movement, slavery in the state faded to a trickle."** [15]

This 21st Century representation of history belies the true history of abolition in New York State. The more astonishing aspect of this aberration of facts is that the statement was made by a New York State town historian. The assumption that Africans and their descendants lived in a state of "quasi-freedom" for a twenty-five year period until their actual emancipation is the prevailing mantra. This perception and the belief that enslavement died an uneventful death in New York, distort actual historic fact.

In fact, the demise of enslavement in New York State was a protracted endeavor with enslavers in the countryside and particularly farmers of Dutch origin maintaining the institution of enslavement to the bitter end.

> **"In 1820, when 95 percent of the black people in New York City were free, only half of the slaves in Kings County had gained their freedom. In the county of Richmond, 600 black people – almost 90 percent of the black population – remained locked in bondage. In a similar fashion, emancipation in the Hudson Valley also lagged behind the arrival of freedom in the city of New York."[16]**

Additionally, the United States Federal Census acknowledges the fact that until 1850, there were still a number of enslaved African descendants in New York State.

The primary reason for enslavement's abolition in New York State was more the expanding availability of a free and cheap labor supply (European immigrants), which began to made bonded labor unprofitable. Indeed, in the first decades of the 19th century, the system of enslavement was collapsing precisely because this capitalist mode of exploiting "free labor" was becoming the dominant form of economy in the northern section of the United States and even more so in New York State.

Through the examination of municipal and state documents, I will attempt to demonstrate how public policy through the use of the legislative process was manipulated in a conscious effort to benefit enslavers, by allocating taxpayer funds for the implementation of an enslaver compensation program. I will also illustrate how the State of New York implemented and financed a "compensated abolition" initiative that was predicated on the forced bondage of African descendant children and the enrichment of New York enslavers under the guise of abolition. These actions and public policy initiatives served to hold a number of African descendant children in bondage well into the 1850s.

My hope is that at the very least, this work will accomplish a two-fold purpose. First, it should provoke a new awareness and understanding of the efforts now being undertaken by Africans and African descendants to advocate for reparations for documented "crimes against humanity." Included within the final chapter of this work, (Recommendation: "A Case for Reparations against the State of New York") is a design to provide an avenue for present and former citizens of African descent in New York State to implement a structure of restitution for these abuses and evil acts. This effort will most certainly include those "crimes against humanity" that were committed during the centuries that New York State was engaged in the forced bondage of African descendant men, women *and* children.

Secondly, a large volume of primary source documentation is embedded in this work. Beyond the obvious reasons of providing definitive support to the positions developed and presented in this work, this historical documentation is primarily included in an effort to assist other African descendants in their quests to identify, locate and reclaim their family members, who were criminally enslaved in New York during the two centuries that it practiced and profited from the inhuman bondage of men, women *and* children of African descent.

It should also be noted that the guidelines for the development of this work are not those promulgated by academicians. That is to say, that this work is not meant to be a conversation between historical scholars. Neither is the substance and content of this work meant to be presented as some type of historical novel. On the contrary, this work should be accepted and read as a documented representation of historical fact - designed to provide people of African descent with an accurate depiction of the periods of Enslavement and Gradual Abolition in New York State and further, it is designed to allow African descendants to examine how the political, social and economic policies of these periods impacted the growth and survival of families of African descent during New York's first two centuries of existence.

Therefore, this work should not be held to the fixed standards of academic discourse but rather to the higher standards exposed by the Ancient African spiritual concept of MAAT (Truth, Justice, Righteousness, Balance, Order, Reciprocity, and Harmony).

Ashe'

ENDNOTES

1 William Faulkner, *"Requiem for a Nun"*, Act I, Scene III,

2 Listed on the Death Certificate of Samuel Van Vranken, 14 March 1891, Lansingburgh, NY, Certificate # 101214

3 Dodge, Roberta (Bobbi), The Van Vranken Genealogy, 1998

4 Dr. Yosef A. A. ben Jochannan, Africa: Mother of Western Civilization , (Baltimore, MD: Black Classic Press, 1988) xi

5 Ibid

6 Randall Robinson, *"The Debt::* What America Owes To Blacks", (Dotton Publishing, 2000)

7 Ibid , 212

8 John Henrik Clarke, *"African People in World History"*, (Black Classic Press, 1993) 11

9 Graham Russell Hodges, *"Root & Branch: African Americans in New York & East Jersey, 1613-1863,* (Chapel Hill: The University of North Carolina Press, 1999) 169

10 Graham Russell Hodges and Alan Eward Brown, "Pretends to be Free", (Garland Publishing, 1994) xxi

11 Berlin, 177

12 **Reshaping the lives of the enslaved:** Berlin, 177; **New York's seaport and the "slave trade"**: Richard Morris, Forward, The History of Negro Enslavement in New York by Edgar J. McManus; Kenneth M. Stampp, The Peculiar Institution, (Vintage Books,1956) 271-272; Richard C. Wade, Enslavement in the Cities (Oxford University Press, 1964) 6

13 1790 United States Census

14 Shane White, *Somewhat more independent: the end of enslavement in New York City, 1770-1810* (Athens, GA: Press-University of Georgia, 1991) 1 and 16.

[15] Theola S. Labbe, *"Slaves' graves thought to be on farm"*, Times Union Newspaper, 4 Sept. 2001, B1

[16] Ira Berlin, "Many Thousand Gone: The First Two Centuries of Enslavement in North America, (The Belknap Press of Harvard University Press, 1998) 237-238

CHAPTER I

THE GEOPOLITICAL EVOLUTION OF ENSLAVEMENT IN NEW YORK

AFRICAN ENSLAVEMENT IN NEW NETHERLAND

> **The invaluable workforce formed by those men and women was employed to give a cheap start to a capitalist economy whose imperialistic character, here [Africa] in the form of colonialism, also crushed their descendants. The slave trade not only sustained the expansion and the dominance of the Euro-American economy by selling the children of Africa, at the same time it exposed the economy of Africa to its further depredations.[1]**

BACKGROUND

The introduction of African labor in the middle colonies finds its origin in the trade rivalry of the Atlantic during the seventeenth century. The rivalry between the Netherlands and Spain placed the former in possession of African captives and also in possession of territory where African labor was profitable. The Dutch sought to increase commerce by enhancing the production of their possessions. Thus, this situation created a need for labor in those places. From the desire to establish firm and absolute control of Atlantic commerce came the elements necessary to make enslavement possible in New Netherland.[2]

At the end of its conflicts with Spain, culminating in the 1609 truce, the Dutch Republic turned its attention to gaining possessions in the New World. With the formation of the Dutch East India Company in 1602, the Dutch had earlier achieved "phenomenal success" in accomplishing this objective in the East Indies. Given this success, merchants and capitalists in the Netherlands obtained permission to establish the Dutch West India Company with visions of markedly similar success and profits. They had hoped to strip Spain of her New World possessions as they had Portugal in the Far East with the Dutch East India Company.[3]

During Henry Hudson's search for a shorter route from Holland to the Far East in 1609, he sailed up what is now the Hudson River and reached Albany. While the river was not the passage the Dutch sought, they did establish themselves on the Hudson, calling the area New Netherland. Its three earliest colonies were Manhattan (New Amsterdam), Albany (Fort Orange/Beverwyck) and Kingston (Wiltwyck).[4]

In 1614 or 1615, only a few years after Henry Hudson's exploration of the area, Dutch traders constructed a fort at what they knew to be the crucial fur-trading nexus on the North River (Hudson River). While this fort called Fort Nassau was short-lived, it has an important role in history. By erecting it on the site of the future city of Albany six years before the Pilgrims founded the Plymouth Colony to the northeast, the Dutch signaled their claim to the area and their intention to establish a presence.

In 1621, the States General of the United Provinces of the Netherlands (Dutch Republic) chose to grant a monopoly to a trading company to colonize the newly discovered lands in North America. There was concern that the new colonies would need a permanent political presence to protect the Dutch commercial and other interests against the possibility of English, French or Spanish challenges. That year the newly incorporated Dutch West India Company (the "Oude" Company)[5] obtained a twenty-four year trading monopoly along the west coast of Africa (below the Tropic of Cancer) and the West Indies and sought to have the New Netherland area formally recognized as a province.[6] The provincial status was granted in June of 1623 and the Dutch West India Company began the process of organizing the first permanent settlement in New Netherland. Their mandate was "to maintain armies and fleets, to build forts and cities, to carry on war, to make treaties of peace and commerce."[7] This charter was renewed in 1647 for another twenty-five years.

The major Dutch colony in North America, New Netherland, had no fixed boundaries. It was roughly comprised of the following:

1- the area of Schenectady and Albany; the Hudson River Valley; and Manhattan and Staten islands;

2- the present-day Bronx, Westchester County, and the villages of Eastchester, Fordham, and Westchester;

3- to the south, Bergen County in New Jersey; the Delaware River Valley including the former New Sweden (which consisted of settlements along both banks of the Delaware River into modern Delaware, and parts of New Jersey, Pennsylvania and Maryland); and

4- the western end of Long Island which was comprised of the villages of Brooklyn, Bushwick, Flatbush, Flatlands, Flushing, Gravesend, Hempstead, Jamaica, Newtown, New Utrecht, and Oyster Bay, (fig.1).

In 1624, the first wave of settlers departed for New Netherland from their home country of Holland. In the following years, additional ships sailed for New Netherland with colonists, livestock and supplies. The uniqueness of this venture was that New Netherland was a company- owned and operated business that functioned on a for-profit basis for the directors of the company. Its mission was to make a profit for the investors who had purchased shares in the company. In its first half–century, it was directed by five "chambers" of shareholders: the Amsterdam chamber held four-ninths of the shares; Zeeland two-ninths; Maas (Rotterdam, Schiedam, etc.) one-ninth; the Northern Quarter one-ninth; and the Chamber of Stad en Landen (Gronigen and Friesland) one-ninth.

Each chamber had a number of directors who in turn elected a council to run the company. The States-General appointed the chairman, making nineteen directors in all. A new charter granted in 1675 reduced the number of the council to ten, now known as the "Assembly of Ten." Each chamber was responsible for a different proportion of the capitalization of the company and enjoyed a corresponding control over the enterprise. The Amsterdam Chamber was most dominant, for it provided most of the capital for the company. In addition, part of the capital for the company's endeavors came from public funds of the Netherlands itself. This same group of Directors also operated the company's colony in Guyana.[8]

Figure 1
The Dutch Settlements In North America[9]

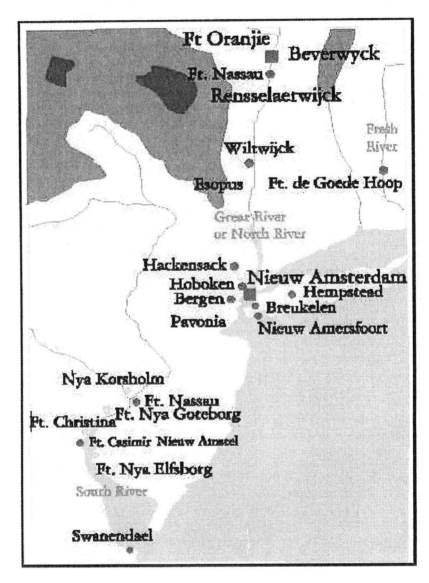

As mentioned earlier, the Dutch West India Company began to send ships loaded with settlers and supplies to New Netherland. The majority of these New World settlers disembarked up the Hudson River from New Amsterdam and in 1624 built a new fort on the banks of the North River (Hudson River), which they called Fort Orange. They built their "crude homes" around the fort and the first trading fort and permanent settlement in what is now Albany (Fort Orange/Beverwyck) was established by eighteen Dutch families some two years before the company "purchased" Manhattan Island from the Native Americans. The town that sprang up around the fort—Beverwijck, later Albany—grew to become the "second city" in New Netherland after New Amsterdam, and eventually the capital of New York State.[10]

Fort Orange located in the northeastern portion of New York State some 150 miles upriver from New York City (New Amsterdam) became the anchor community of upriver New Netherland. In about 1630, a director of the West India Company published an account of the settlement of New Netherland in which he wrote dispassionately and accurately of the fort:

> *They have there, at the uppermost part of the North River, in the latitude of 43 degrees or thereabouts, a small fort, which our people call Fort Orange, round about which several colonizers have settled themselves under the patronage of the aforesaid company. And again another fort of greater importance at the mouth of the same North River, upon an island which they call Manhattes or Manhatans Island...*[11]

The company paid skilled individuals, doctors and craftsmen, to relocate to New Netherland. It sent soldiers for the military protection of the colony, built fortifications, and provided the settlers with provisions. It should be understood that the company's employees carried out all of the activities that one would associate with government or public service but unlike governments, they operated to insure profits for the company and its investors. Given this elaborate corporate structure, the difficulties associated with establishing and expanding a new colony in North America were considerable. In order to increase its profit margin, the company chose to subcontract the responsibilities of colonization to what was referred to as the "Patroonship Scheme of Colonization."[12] Patroons (a title given to this newly created aristocracy in New Netherland) were given large land grants and jurisdictional rights over the colonists within those patents (tracts of land). However, the company retained ultimate authority over the economic, political and social development structures of the colony. At the foundation of this design, the patroons were to receive land lying along a navigable stream for sixteen miles on one side or eight miles on both sides and extending into the interior for an infinite distance. In addition, the company promised generous land grants and privileges to any stockholder who would undertake the "planting" of fifty families in this new colony.

Thus, a landed aristocracy came to control the economic activities of the colony in partnership with the owners of the company.[13] The charter that was granted to the company serves to illustrate the prototype for the "Triangle Slave Trade" paradigm in the sixteenth to nineteenth centuries, (fig. 2). The triangular trade system was so named because ships embarked from European ports loaded with goods from the colonies, stopped in Africa to trade for African captives, after which they set out for the New World to deliver their human cargo, and then returned to their port of origin.

Figure 2
Map Of Triangle Trade[14]

The African dispersion and the "triangle trade"

The company, based in Holland, now with trading and colonization rights in both America and Africa, instituted a process of enslavement that involved the interaction of two major economic systems.[15] The owner class, who represented the company, also owned the infrastructures of shipping and trade controlled the provisions for the colonies, the employees of shipping and the military personnel who implemented and enforced their policies. The slave-owning class (patroons, Southern aristocratic landholders, planters, etc.) exploited and supervised enslavement directly and derived their power from the company.

The company operated by purchasing agricultural products from the slave-owning class and used these products in exchange for acquiring Africans in Africa for their future slave labor force. These Africans were then transported to New Netherland where they were sold to the highest bidders as slave labor for the colony's landowners. The profits were then shared by the owners of the company and the remainder of the profit from these transactions was used to purchase more agricultural products to implement more slave trading. Only in the New World did this transaction of slave trading provide the labor force for a high-pressure profit-making economic system of agriculture production for distant markets. During the 1630s to the 1650s, the company "was unquestionably the dominant European slave trader in Africa."[16]

KILLIAEN VAN RENSSELAER

One of the principal investors in the Dutch West India Company, a Dutch diamond merchant named Killiaen Van Rensselaer, bought a sizable tract of land around Fort Orange from the Mahicans who were indigenous to this area. He proceeded to establish a "Patroonship," or private farming community, which he named Rensselaerswijck, (fig. 3).

Figure 3
1767 Manor Of Rensselaerwick[17]

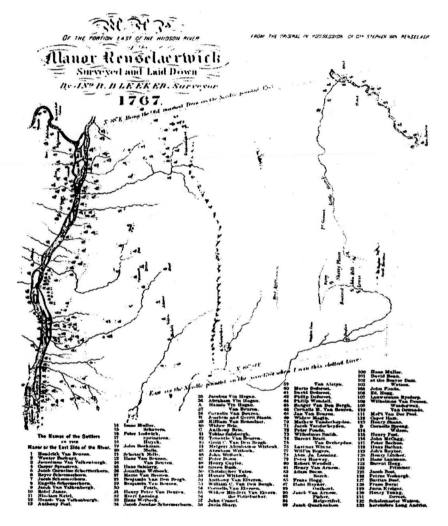

Subsequent to this land purchase, Van Rensselaer had sent representatives to the colony to become friendly with the native Mahican Indians. These relationships gave Van Rensselaer an advantage in any competition to purchase this highly sought-after land claimed by the Native Americans on both sides of the river. On this land he established Rensselaerswijck. Van Rensselaer sponsored the development of Rensselaerswijck and built sawmills, gristmills, homes and barns. Hundreds more settlers soon began coming to the area.

The company, frustrated as to how best to populate its colony, had recently opened it up to private entrepreneurs (patroons), with the condition that in exchange for a piece of land each entrepreneur had to ship fifty colonists to it within four years. Of the number of shareholders who took advantage of this opportunity, Van Rensselaer possessed the only "patroonship" that was even marginally successful—indeed, it lasted into the nineteenth century, passing down through generations of the Van Rensselaer family.

It wasn't long before friction began to develop between the new community of Rensselaerswijck and the established community in Fort Orange, run by the Dutch West India Company. In 1652, Peter Stuyvesant, director general of New Netherland colony, in his resolution of the conflict chose to expand the area around Fort Orange, calling the area Beverwyck and prohibiting Van Rensselaer from building within the new boundaries. (See fig. 4 map of Fort Oragne/Beverwick)

Figure 4
Albany (Fort Orange/beverwyck)[18]

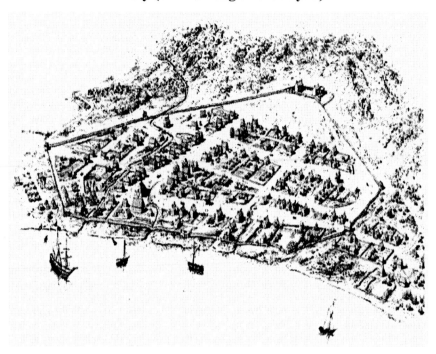

Considering the fact that Kiliaen Van Rensselaer never visited New Netherland, he devoted a considerable portion of his attention and energy to his domain, which he fully intended to see turn a profit. It never did in his lifetime. Van Rensselaer died in 1643, at the age of sixty-three. However, his patroonship did grow, with a steady stream of immigrant farmers and tradesmen coming from Europe. Van Rensselaer's idea had been that Fort Orange and Rensselaerswijck (later called Bethlehem) would be mutually supporting. The fort would provide protection, and the "patroonship" would supply the fort with various goods.[19]

Even under English rule, the Van Rensselaers continued to hold much influence in the area and in 1685, the Patroonship was converted to an English manor with the family retaining title to the area with the second Killiaen Van Rensselaer , grandson of the first Patroon, becoming lord of the new manor.

Albany (Fort Orange/Beverwyck) began to emerge as the focal point of settlement and commerce in the upstate region of New Netherland. Agriculture and fur trading were the primary sources of its economy. Albany farmers bartered their crops and forest products for imports. Its merchants rivaled in many ways the more established merchant community in New York City (New Amsterdam). In fact, several prominent New Amsterdam merchants managed operations in both locations.[20]

THE AFRICAN PRESENCE IN NEW NETHERLAND

The irony of world history is that the presence and role of Africans and their descendants in the founding and settling of New Netherland has been confined to their enslavement and bondage.

Africa was once the home of a number of great civilizations known for their wealth, technology and learning. While these civilizations were ultimately destroyed by the slave trade and European colonialism, there is evidence that a number of the first explorers of the New World came from this so-called "Dark Continent." They left their mark upon the New World before, during and after Columbus made his famous "discoveries."

African explorers from the Empire of Mali outfitted ships and ventured across the Atlantic Ocean many centuries before Columbus and had an impact on the development of civilization in the New World, most particularly the Olmecs of Central America. Several scholars including Leo Wiener, "Africa and the Discovery of America (1922) and Ivan Van Sertima, "They came before Columbus" (1975) have extensively researched these influences of African civilizations on the early civilizations of Central and South America. Additionally, scientists have discovered trace elements of nicotine from tobacco in the remains of ancient Kemetic (Egyptian) Pharaohs. And, last but not least Christopher Columbus, himself, documented in his diaries and ship logs the sightings of Africans navigating the Caribbean.

When most people think of Africa, they imagine the millions stolen from their villages, enslaved and sent directly to work the huge plantations of the Americas. Before the insatiable labor demands of the plantation reached a peak in the 17th and 18th centuries, however, there were the Atlantic Creoles, a group of Africans who led quite different lives from the unfortunate masses caught in the throes of the New World slave economy.

Atlantic Creoles were worldly Africans, who built a tradition of sailing and exploration on centuries of expertise. They traveled to find work in the great ports of the Atlantic; such as London, Lisbon, Cadiz, Seville and Boston. They often spoke more than one language, and they were familiar with the traditions and religions of Europe. Atlantic Creoles were often literate and able to negotiate the legal systems of the day. Knowledgeable in trade and seamanship many of these cosmopolitan citizens of the World worked on ships as translators, seamen and pilots. Historians refer to these men as "Atlantic Creoles" because they lived on both the east and west shores of the Atlantic Ocean and, as a group, were of African or mixed ancestry. Middlemen in trade between Europe, Africa, and North and South America, they served as merchants, translators, and sailors. Their tongue served as the common language of trade.

The very first Africans who arrived in New Netherland may not have come directly from Africa, nor were they necessarily enslaved. Africans had traversed the Atlantic basin for centuries. Doubtless there were some among the many fishermen, pirates, and anonymous explorers who visited North America long before colonization.

One of the first of these African Creoles to be documented in World History was Pedro Alonso Nino. Nino, called the Negro, was born in Spain in 1468 and died about 1505. He traveled the coasts of Africa, and was a pilot to Christopher Columbus on some of his voyages to the New World. He returned to Spain and resolved to go to the East Indies on his own account. The Council of Castile gave him permission to discover new countries, on the condition that he should not touch those that had been already discovered by Columbus. Nino left the Port of San Lucas toward the end of May, 1499. After a rapid passage of twenty-three days, he arrived on the north coast of America. Nino, now sailed up the coast to Punta Araya, where he discovered the famous salt-mines that are still called by the same name. He then returned to Spain.

ESTEBAN GOMEZ

Probably, the best known of these African Creoles was Esteban Gomez, an African-Portuguese naval pilot, who sailed up the Hudson River and named it Deer River in 1525 some eighty-four years before Hendrick Hudson "discovered" the exact same river. Esteban Gomez, was born in Cadiz, Spain, in 1474. He had served in the Portuguese East India fleet, acquired a reputation as a skilled pilot, and was pilot of the "San Antonio" on Magellan's expedition in 1519. In 1523, Gomez scouted the North American coast from Nova Scotia to the most southern tip of Florida.

In 1524, when difficulties between Spain and Portugal arose with respect to the limits of their colonial discoveries, Gomez was one of the Council of Pilots appointed to decide this question. Gomez proposed to the King to avoid these difficulties by seeking a western passage to the East Indies by way of the new continent. His proposal was accepted and, in command of a ship, he left San Lucas in November, 1524.

He reached the coast of Florida in January, 1525, and continued his voyage north, exploring every inlet in quest of the desired passage. Without discovering any western passage, he was resolved to return home but chose to explore the continent further from Cape Charles to Cape Cod and the Hudson - where he entered New York harbor and charted the lower Hudson, and then up into Canada.

In 1529, Gomez spent ten months sailing up the east coast of North America as far as what are now New Brunswick and Nova Scotia in Canada. He then sailed south to Cuba, sighting along the way Cape Cod, Nantucket Island, and the mouths of the Connecticut, Hudson and Delaware rivers. He is believed to have been the first non-indigenous person to have set foot on land in what is now Maryland.

Based on Gomez' reports, the cartographer for King Charles I of Spain was able to produce his famous map of 1529, which was the first ever to show the east coast of the Western Hemisphere almost perfectly outlined (fig. 5). It also showed that missionaries arrived as far north as present-day Maryland, New York, and New England.

Figure 5
Esteban Gomez's Map Of 1529[21]

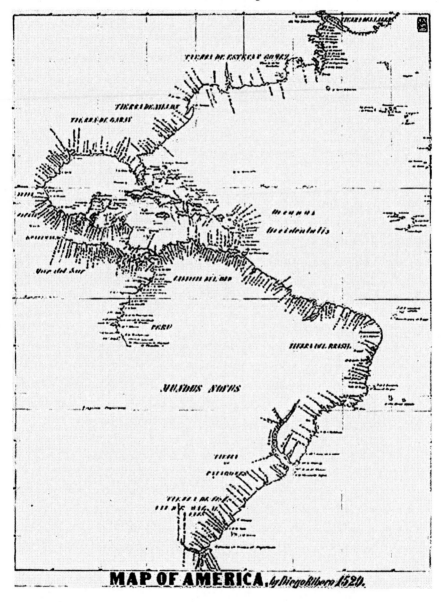

JAN RODRIGUES

The first non-indigenous settler on Manhattan Island, Jan Rodriguez of San Domingo, was also of African descent, a free man and sailor. In June 1613, Captain Thijs Volchertz Mossel an experienced Dutch explorer, and his crew of the vessel the *Jonge Tobias,* journeyed from the West Indies up the coast of North America, into the harbor of the Hudson River and along the island of Manhattan. When Mossel and his ship sailed away from Manhattan in 1613, he left behind one crew member, Jan Rodriguez.[22]

Apparently their parting was caused by a dispute between crew members and Rodriguez.

However, Rodriguez received "wages of eighty hatchets, some knives, a musket, and a sword" from Captain Mossel.[23] While these commodities suggest that he had past experience as a soldier, they may have been an advance on future services because it was common for sea captains to leave a man behind on new territories in order to sustain land claims. Mossel then returned to Amsterdam to claim monopoly rights to explore the Hudson River.

A month or so later in August 1613, a second vessel captained by Hendricks Christiansen, landed on Manhattan Island. On shore he encountered Rodriguez, who informed Christiansen that he was "a free man and had nothing to do with anybody."[24] Rodriguez then entered Christiansen's service as an interpreter with local Rockaway Native Americans and facilitated a trade agreement between the Native Americans and Christiansen. In April, the *Jonge Tobias* returned. Angry at Rodriguez' perceived disloyalty Captain Mossel called him a "black rascal."[25] A fight ensued in which Mossel's crew wounded Rodriguez, but Christiansen's crew was able to save him from further harm. After the two vessels departed, Rodriguez remained behind and fathered several children with Rockaway American Indian women.

Rodriguez had become fluent in Native American languages, and when European explorers and traders arrived at Manhattan in subsequent years, he facilitated trade relations between them and the local Native Americans. Rodriguez eventually married into the Rockaway Nation. He participated in all aspects of trade and began the commercial and cultural exchanges for which Manhattan Island would become famous. He negotiated with avaricious ship captains and proved critically important for commercial relations with the Native Americans. Alone among these early explorers, he is known to have acculturated into both European and Native American life.

Rodriguez was the first non-indigenous resident of Manhattan Island, as well as the earliest known African descendant on the island. He is significant to history for several reasons. First, Rodriguez' origins epitomize those of the cosmopolitan African seamen working in the Atlantic basin during the seventeenth century. Rodriguez' mixture of West Indian and African heritage was common in the men known as the Atlantic Creoles and his survival skills and those of other African Creoles were impressive.

Second, he declared himself a free man, though his employer regarded him as no more than a servant, a conflict that signaled the first of many such cultural collisions to come between Africans and Europeans. Rodriguez was a prime example of the multiple talents displayed by the first generation of immigrants of African descent to New Netherland.[26]

Another example of the African presence in New Netherland is the account of Francisko, a man of African descent who was one of the founders of Bushwick, in what is today Brooklyn.[27]

The force of the Diaspora of the Atlantic Creoles remained very much alive even as the plantation tried to seal the doors of the Atlantic to them. Jan Rodriguez and a handful of other documented Atlantic Creoles in New Netherland were free, but not all were.

ENSLAVEMENT OF AFRICANS IN NEW NETHERLAND

The second generation of African descendants in the history of New Netherland began with the Dutch colonization of North America, and the introduction and enslavement of eleven Africans in New

Netherland in 1625 to 1626.[28] Under the Dutch "patroonship" system, New Netherland continued to expand with more colonists, settlements, and slaves. The "Freedoms and Exemptions" granted by the company to all "Patroons, Masters, or Private Persons who will plant Colonies in New Netherland" passed on 7 June 1629,[29] and included the following proviso:

> *"In like manner, the incorporated West India Company shall allot to each patron twelve men and women out of the prize in which Negroes shall be found, for the advancement of the colonies of New Netherland."[30]*

According to the Colonial Records of New York, this number was increased several times until it finally reached "as many as possible."[31] By 1640, there were 1,600 Africans in North America, with almost a third of them in Dutch New Netherland. From the time of the Dutch occupation, when it was called New Amsterdam, virtually until the end of the American Revolution, New York City was identified as the enslavement capital of Colonial America.

The Dutch settlers in New Netherland insisted on the right to import slaves from the very start of their settlement in 1626.[32] They were upset that they had to use indentured servants rather than slaves in 1644, precisely because they recognized the legal impediments to the fullest long-term use of the labor of their indentured servants.[33]

The Dutch had first realized the profit-making advantages of large numbers of Africans in 1646, when a shipload of Africans was purchased from Tamandar'e, off the coast of Brazil. These African innocents were sold for pork and peas on the company's account. The majority of these Africans did not remain in New Netherland but were sold to the Middle Colonies and the South. The company was quick to realize the favorable circumstances of this "foreign" labor base as a means of coping with the growing labor shortage in New Netherland.[34] Thus, with these single events the fate of millions of Africans and their descendants was cast.

At the same time, the Dutch expulsion from Brazil in 1644 may have cheapened slaves for North America and the Caribbean as the

Dutch sought to dispose of their slaves from African sources more cheaply.[35] Between 1659 and 1664, the company rerouted to New Amsterdam several shiploads of Africans that had been bound for Pernambuco in Brazil.[36] A company director's communiqué from Amsterdam expresses the rationale for the expansion of enslavement in the New World:

> *We have seen that more Negroes could be advantageously employed and sold there [New Amsterdam] than the ship Tamandar'e brought. We shall take care, that in future a greater number of negroes be taken there [New Amsterdam].[37]*

Figure 6
Enslaved Africans Being Landed In North American [38]

The demand for labor during the colonial period far outran the supply. The strategy of the company to meet this shortage was to send more shipments of farm produce to Angola, their primary resource for Africans, and after the exchange they then transported these Africans back to New Netherland to work in the cultivation of the colony. Governor Pieter Stuyvesant of New Netherland seeing the tremendous opportunity for increased profit in this slave trade requested that Dutch slave traders import their human cargoes directly from the west coast of Africa to New Amsterdam in order to supply local farmers and English colonies north and south of the port of New York.[39]

The horrendous journey of the "Middle Passage" from Africa to the New World, the beginnings of the Maafa[40] was replete with chains, torture, hunger, starvation disease and death was but an inkling of the fate that awaited these African "innocents" in the New World. Vomit, urine, feces, and perspiration made the holds of the ships intolerable by the end of the voyage, even on such ships that took precautions to clean them. Indeed, it was the foul smell that wafted over New Amsterdam in 1655 that announced to the inhabitants that a slave ship had arrived.[41]

Figure 7
Stowage of the British Slave Ship Brookes[42]

(Under the Regulated Slave Trade Act of 1788)

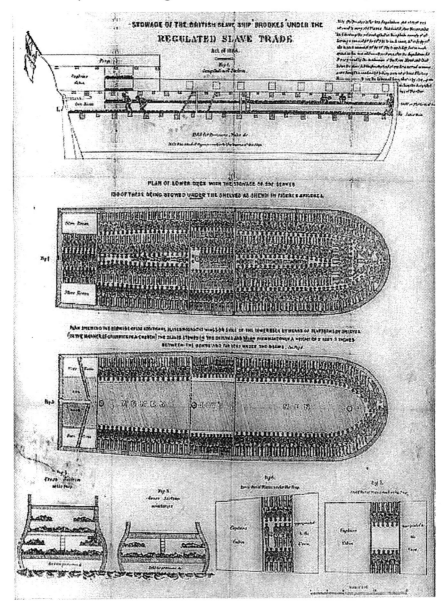

With the arrival of these slave ships, whether in the West Indies or Colonial America (North and South), scholars agree that life for these first Africans in the New World was harsh and full of isolation and alienation. Separation from their culturally grounded families, religion, history, and traditions were the circumstances that awaited them, not to mention the horrendous and protracted life sentence to hard labor.[43]

Interesting enough, Europeans imported Africans partly for demographic reasons. As a result of epidemic diseases, which reduced the native populations of the Americas by 50 to 90 percent, the native labor supply was insufficient to meet the colonists' ever-increasing demands for more and more specialized labor. Consequently, Africans who were experienced in intensive agriculture, raising livestock and had an expediential knowledge of how to raise crops such as rice, with which Europeans were unfamiliar, became valued "commodities" to the colony's development.

Additionally, African descendants spent years in the Caribbean on sweltering plantations that seasoned them to the rigors of "New World" enslavement. Once exposed to the diseases of the Europeans, they became physically conditioned to survive in their colonies. Figure 8 illustrates the advantages such conditioning had with prospective slaveholders. Notice the reference to her having had smallpox as a child.

Figure 8
Advertisement To Sell An Enslaved Female

15 April 1734

TO be Sold, a Young Negro Woman, about 20 Year old, fhe dos all fortr of Houfe werk; fhe can Brew, Bake, boyle foaft Soap, Wafh, Iron & Starch; and is a good darey Women fhe can Card and Spin at the great Wheel, Cotten, Lennen and Wollen, fhe has another good Property fhe neither drinks Rum nor fmoaks Tobacco, and fhe is a ftrong hale healthy Wench, fhe can Cook pretty well for Roft and Boyld; fhe can fpeak no other Language but Englifh; fhe had the fmall Pox in *Barbados* when a Child. Enquire of the Printer here of and know the Purchafe.
N.B. She is well Clothed.

Advertisement Offering a Slave for Sale
New York Weekly-Journal April 15, 1734
New York Historical Society

Africans worked as farmers, builders and in the fur trade of the company. Their involvement in the fur trade yielded immediate and substantial profits. Some of these Africans also helped build the wall intended to keep settlers safe from the Native American populations at the location of today's Wall Street. The Dutch governor of New Amsterdam told the heads of settler families in 1641 that he would use the "strongest and fleetest Negroes" to fight the Native Americans with hatchets and the half pike.

Pieter Stuyvesant, the governor of New Netherland requested in 1652 that the Dutch West India Company send "clever and strong Negroes" to work and to fight Native Americans, either directly or as adjuncts in carrying supplies.[44] Likewise, in 1652 the Massachusetts Assembly ordered that all the inhabitants of the colony, including

"Scots and Negroes," be armed and trained for war.[45] They also became New York City's first maintenance workers.[46] In the mid-seventeenth century, New Netherland's welfare and survival rested squarely upon the institution of slave labor.

The company's specific strategy for colonial development involved the importing of parcels of ten to twenty Africans at a time to work on the farms, build public buildings and military works for which free workers were not available. The company also guaranteed the safety and stability of slave labor by passing fugitive slave ordinances. Even with these assurances the Dutch settlers did not readily become slaveholders at the rate anticipated by the company. This led to the company, by default, becoming the largest slaveholder in New Netherland. The Company, always directed by the need to increase profits, chose to address its slave-owning position by creating a new profit center for its shareholders by way of leasing its many enslaved Africans to surrounding farmers and businesses. In so doing, the company had established a new labor market for the more then 300 Africans that it owned.[47]

With the initial arrival of Africans around 1625 to 1626, Colonial laws and codes did not establish their legal status within the colony. Africans seemed to exist in a "twilight zone between indentured servant and clear-cut enslavement." In the 1620s and 1630s, Africans were referred to as slaves but the 1640s saw the appearance of "half-slaves" and "free Blacks."[48] The Dutch were also very protective of their investment in human capital and often used the political powers of their colony to discourage any attempts to alter their monopoly on African labor. One example of this resolve took place in New Amsterdam, where the Dutch initiated the first sales tax wherein "an import tax of 10 percent was imposed to discourage merchants from selling 'human cargo' outside of the colony.[49]

It was during this period that the company chose to abandon its monopoly on trade in goods deciding to share the expenses and risks associated with trade by opening up commerce to merchants of all friendly nations. However, this gesture was subject to a 10 percent import duty, a 15 percent export duty and the restricting of all shipping to company ships. Chief among these trading commodities were Africans. "This strategy resulted in expansion and the establishment of settlements in New Jersey, on Staten Island and in what is now the Bronx." [50]

NEW NETHERLAND'S ECONOMIC SYSTEM

Unlike the British settlements in New England, the individuals largely responsible for the exploitation of New Netherland's resources were merchants from the home country who controlled the colony's lifeline to Holland. Profits from their enterprises flowed into Amsterdam, thus depriving New Netherland of capital and the ability to develop a viable colony-based merchant community. This lack of economic independence was one of the reasons the Dutch colony on Manhattan "was headed toward failure from its very beginning."[51] Since profit making was the major focus of the Colonial [Dutch] administration, the fluctuating fortunes of the company's imperial interests rather than the particular needs of New Amsterdam's economy and community guided the formation of policy.[52]

Essentially the difference between the Dutch New Netherland merchants and the merchants in the British colonies centered around the fact that New Netherland merchants primarily worked at the local level and never controlled foreign trade. The company's control of the participation of New Amsterdam merchants in the slave trade similarly was geared toward reaping advantage for the company. The ability to independently trade with one's sovereign nation is a critical factor of economic competitiveness and independence. New Netherland merchants did trade on their own, when it was possible, but more frequently they were employed as agents or suppliers for the major Dutch trading firms.[53]

Despite the substantial increase in the price of slaves between 1636 and 1664, the company did not profit greatly from the New Netherland slave trade. This was primarily due to the fact that higher prices prevailed in the plantation colonies, and slaves supplied to New Netherland sold at a discount (10 percent) below the international market. It represented the same amount as the export duty levied in 1655 to prevent the diversion of Africans to the plantation colonies.[54]

By 1656, the company had reversed its attitude toward the existing land-grant policy of patroonships. The patroons had become more interested in the profits derived from money lending and trade than the potential profits of land development and colonial expansion. Their own agendas began to take precedence over the interests of the company. The company acted swiftly. It now viewed the granting of patroonships as inadvisable and injurious to increasing the population of the colony. It subsequently decided to grant private individuals as much land as they could cultivate, without giving them patroon privileges.

The result of this action was an increase in the population of New Netherland from an estimated 2,000 to 3,500 in 1655 to 9,000 in 1664.[55] During this period of Dutch rule, New Netherland, as had been initially planned, was transformed from a trading post into a full-fledged colony. As colonial wealth and its economy grew, so did the requirements for a correspondingly larger labor force. Unlike Southern colonial provinces, New Netherland had a need for a highly diversified slave force geared to the needs of a mixed economy. Africans, consequently, populated the entire colony.

Private settlers were soon importing Africans as well, with the encouragement of the company. The company was even willing to forgo profit for the sake of spreading enslavement in New Netherland and stabilizing the colony. Consequently, the company allowed private owners to exchange Africans they were dissatisfied with for those Africans owned by the company.

Local artisans, merchants, and frontier farmers eagerly bought the slaves, spreading the popularity of the slave system throughout Dutch colonial society. Africans became essential to the economic survival of New Netherland due to the fact that "newcomers (Europeans) did little to sate the colony's need for farm workers."[56] An official of the company reported in 1647 that "agricultural laborers, who are conveyed thither at great expense…sooner or later apply themselves to trade, and neglect agriculture altogether."[57] From this perspective, African labor was absolutely essential to their way of thinking.

> **In 1644 alone, it [the Company] bought 6,900 captives on the African coast. From its stations in Angola, the company imported slaves to New Netherland to clear the forests, lay roads, build houses and public buildings, and grow food. It was company owned slave labor that laid the foundations of modern New York, built its fortifications, and made agriculture flourish in the colony so that later white immigrants had an incentive to turn from fur trapping to farming.**[58]

This first *and* second generation of Africans in New World America tended to be remarkably cosmopolitan. Few of this second generation came directly from Africa. Instead, they arrived from the West Indies and other areas of European settlement, where they were first "broken" to meet the requirements of slave life. These imported Africans were often multilingual and had Spanish or Portuguese names. Dutch slaveholders in New Netherland eventually favored "Negroes who had been twelve or thirteen years in the West Indies," deeming them "a better sort of Negroes" than "Negroes directly from Africa.[59]

Until the middle of the eighteenth century, the majority of Africans were to be found in the counties, that bordered New York harbor, Queens, Kings, Richmond, New York—and Westchester. The upper Hudson Valley colonists' preference for fur trading rather than agriculture accounts for their lagging behind in both overall population and its slave population during this period. However, when the large land grant policies of the company became the norm, the Hudson Valley, where the land was monopolized in huge patron estates that discouraged free immigration, began also to rely heavily on African labor.

Figure 9
Ship Of Enslaved Africans Arrives In New York City[60]

Great Britain and the Dutch Republic emerged as the principle maritime powers of the seventeenth century. Their rivalry led them into several wars, in which the issues at stake were ultimately the freedom of the seas and the control of the slave trade.

The first Anglo-Dutch war was fought entirely at sea and ended in a compromise after two years of fighting. It was related to the English Navigation Act of 1651 that was directed against Dutch trade with British possessions. The second war, 1665 to 67, was directed at English commercial supremacy especially in the East Indian trade and the West African slave trade. This war involved raids on Dutch colonies in Africa, the disruption of shipping along the Dutch coast and an attack on British ships on the Thames River. In response to Dutch actions, Charles II of England formally annexed New Netherland as a British province. A fleet of British ships was sent to seize the colony. The resulting British takeover was a function of these international wars among emerging European capitalist states to conquer the "New World" as a basis for the accumulation of "primitive" capital. New Netherland became one of the major properties in this worldwide "Monopoly Game of Colonization."

New Netherland's ability to determine its own fate had been denied them from the very beginning. Their existence and survival lay in the hands of the "winner" of this real-life, international game of intrigue. Governor Pieter Stuyvesant of New Netherland surrendered Fort Amsterdam, and Fort Orange capitulated in September of 1664. The loss of the New Netherland province led to the second Anglo-Dutch war during 1665 to1667.

This conflict ended with the Treaty of Breda in August of 1667 in which the Dutch relinquished their claim to New Netherland, now New York, and Delaware, in exchange for Surinam, off the coast of Brazil.[61] After a number of additional skirmishes for control of the colony, the Treaty of Westminster in 1674 put an end to the conflict and the British remained in control of New York.

For African New Yorkers, both enslaved and free, British occupation meant severe change. Under Dutch rule, some Africans had gained half or full freedom, even if enslaved, they had some legal and social rights. Yet given these accomplishments, the Dutch could not be described as completely colorblind. "Free" Africans and African descendants who could not produce proof of their status, on demand, were always in danger of being re-enslaved. These freedom and other social policies changed under British rule. The legalization of enslavement in 1665 was the first example of this "New World Order" shift in colonial policy, with enslavement now redefined as an inherited, racial status. The British brand of enslavement would soon result in terms of life enslavement as the rule and not the exception. It was during this period that Africans and their descendants were either free or slave. As far as the English were concerned there was no middle ground by which Africans and their descendants could be protected by common law. Slaves thereafter became outright property with no rights and they were governed as such.

The British "conquest" of New Netherland found the groundwork well laid for making New York its' most important slave-holding colony north of Maryland for a century and a half.

Figure 10
Colonial Era, New York City[62]

Everything north of what is now the city hall area in the borough of Manhattan, for instance, was forest and outside city limits.

THE DEVELOPMENT OF BRITISH ENSLAVEMENT

The English occupation of New Netherland fostered the establishment of a commercially profitable slave system. Unlike the Dutch West India Company which used enslavement to implement colonial policy, the Royal African Company used the colony to implement enslavement.

The West India Company never tried to develop or implement a profitable slave trade but strove instead to promote the economic progress of the colony by keeping slave costs down. The purpose of enslavement, as Governor Pieter Stuyvesant saw it, was "to promote and advance the population and agriculture of the province."[63] However, under British rule and the directives of the Duke of York, the steady importation of Africans, by every possible means, served to stabilize the economy of the colony by expanding production and increasing profit.

The cornerstone of British policy was to encourage the importing of African labor to develop the colony. The British administration extended little effort to attract European free workers or indentured servants to the colony. The British viewed the institution of enslavement as the most effective means of increasing profits and simultaneously developing the colony. As a result, few Europeans entered the New York labor market.

The British continued their reliance on African slave labor as the foundation of New York's colonial work force. Between 1698 and 1738, the African population increased at a faster rate than did the white population in the colony. The increased demand for African labor also increased their value. In 1687, a healthy male sold for ten pounds; in 1700, forty pounds; and by 1720, sixty pounds. By 1760, a healthy male sold for one hundred pounds.[64] In 1709, the British established New York City's first slave market, the Meal Market, at Wall Street and the East River (fig. 11).

Figure 11
Illustration Of New York City Enslavement Market[65]

THE MEAL MARKET, 1711

This market was the site where enslaved blacks were auctioned to new owners or hired out for a period of time.

In the early 1700s under British rule, there were some 800 African men, women, and children in the city of New York, representing about 15 percent of the total population. Local and state documents did not distinguish between free and enslaved Africans until 1756. Before then the term "slave" was used to describe all Africans and their descendants, who were all looked upon as valuable sources of labor.[66] In 1706, the Colonial Assembly passed a law stating that "Negroes only shall be slaves" and in the same law, the British insured the hereditary nature of enslavement by having children inherit their mothers' condition of enslavement or freedom.[67]

The British desire to legalize the enslavement of Africans reflected a greater sense among the British that Africans were an inferior race of people. By the first decade of the eighteenth century, the British had affirmed "Hereditary African Enslavement" in law in the New York colony.

The English even established, in the first years after the capture of Manhattan, a fruitful relationship with the pirates who infested the East India routes and had their headquarters in Madagascar. Dutch privateers seized a group of thirty Africans and Indian Africans off the coast of New Spain in 1704 and delivered them to New York. How many Africans were brought to the colony by way of this formidable journey may never be known, for these "importers" never made a legal entry. Adolphus Philipse, a former Dutch patroon turned privateer, was described at the end of the century as returning in a ship from Madagascar with "nothing but Negroes."[68]

Adolphus Phillpse had acquired a large portion of land from the Wekquaesgeeks and Sint Sink Native American nations. He began his personal empire by securing both Dutch loans and a Dutch commission business in the fur, lumber, and slave trades. Adolphus Phillipse and his brother Frederick understood the European system of exporting raw materials from the far-flung colonies for manufactured goods and other commodities and used slave labor as a means to increase production and expand their profits. Adolphus' brother, Frederick also entered into the slave trade and speculated in land. He had migrated to New Netherland in 1653 as a foreman of construction for the Dutch West India Company and became one of the richest men in the Colony. As a result of these slave-trading "excursions" between 1680 and 1750, most of the people that lived at Phillipsburg Manor were of African descent. These Africans and their descendants constructed, operated, and resided on a complex that consisted of a mill, manor house, bake house, slave house, wharves, and a church.

These enslaved Africans and their descendants labored as millers, bakers, sailors, dairy workers, coopers, and servants.[69] Figure 12 is a reproduction of Adolph Phillipse's probate inventory; notice in the first column the listing of his African slaves and their descendants as property "on the Manor of Phillipsburgh." This document lists seven men, five women, three "men not fit for work" seven boys, and one girl among his "possessions" at the time of his death.[70]

Figure 12
Adolph Phillipse Probate Inventory

On the mannour of Phillipsburgh

Negros Viz:

Ceaser ..		Susan .	
Dimond .		Abigal .	
Sampson .		Massy .	Women
Keiser ...	Men	Dina ..	
Flip		Sue ...	
Tom			
Venture .			

James .. | Charles . | Men not fit for work
Billy ...

Tom abt 9 years old ...
Charles 9 Do ....
Sam 8 Do ....
Dimond 7 Do .... Boys
Hendrick 5 Do ....
Ceaser 2 Do ....
Harry 1 & 4 months
Betty 3 years old A girl

Cattle Viz:
6 worken oxen
12 Milch cows (old)

2 Silver Tankards ..
1 Do Mugg ......
6 New Silver spoons
6 old Ditto ....
1 Silver teapott ....
6 Silver forks .....
1 Do pepper box ..

(In the Garrett) April 19th 1750
6 flax Spinning wheels
2 Woll ... Do
1 old gun
Some wool & Tow
a Miners pick Ax
4 Sithes & 2 handles
a flax Reel
a pr of old Scales and weights
Some old baskets and old Cask
a tin Cullender
1 small old brass kettle
1 do skillett
1 old chafin dish & a small mortar

THE AFRICAN LABOR FORCE

In New York City, in the early 1700s, Africans constituted nearly 20 percent of the male work force. These highly skilled workers proved extremely proficient in virtually every field of colonial and economic development.

Africans and their descendants in the various towns and villages of New York very often worked as: coopers, tailors, sailors, bakers, tanners, goldsmiths, naval carpenters, blacksmiths, spinners, weavers, bolters, sail makers, millers, masons, candle makers, tobacconists, caulkers, carpenters, shoemakers, brush makers, glaziers, wheelwrights, tailors, butchers, metal workers, silversmiths and in the frame construction of houses. Their skills and experience in these trades matched in all areas those of white artisans. On Long Island, Africans were concentrated in production agriculture. Their ability to keep "plantations" in the north operating fully and efficiently was well documented.[71]

Fort Orange/Albany

From the earliest days of its establishment enslaved and free African and African descendants were part of the upstate Albany community. The Van Rensselaers of the area utilized "slaves much as the Southern planters did, as farm workers, house servants and in the many trades necessary to a self-sufficient manor."[72] They were also used to meet the tremendously laborious requirements of an agrarian economy. African descendant females were also employed as domestics and personal servants to the aristocratic hierarchy of the city. They "were also employed as nursemaids, companions, shop assistants, tradesmen, scouts and woodsmen as well as laborers."[73] In upstate counties such as Saratoga "most households had neither the acreage nor the range of duties particularly in winter to support more than a few slaves."

For example, the two African matrons in the Flatts' household of Saratoga had children, but were husbandless and could expect their children to be sold. Most married women of African descent lived in separate households from their husbands, depending upon their spouses' visits to sustain expectations of family life."[74]

The kitchen was the domain of the slave, where women of African descent served as cooks, seamstresses and laundresses. Men of African descent were skilled in caring for livestock, cutting wood, and serving as field hands. There was a seasonal house to the outdoors, sometimes in a permanent structure as at the Schuyler House in Old Saratoga, but often in a temporary wooden hut where the slaves lived until the weather became cold. Wheat cultivation required field hands during spring planting and summer harvesting, the other seasons being devoted to cutting trees for lumber or barrel staves and the transport of produce to market. Hudson Valley slaves thus performed a variety of tasks, rather than the steady field labor of their Southern counterparts.[75]

New Amsterdam/New York City

Approximately 74 per cent of the Africans in the colony of New York in 1703 resided in New York City and its surrounding areas, while more than sixty per cent 60 percent of Africans and their descendants were located there a half century later.[76] In this region of the colony, farmers became prosperous by the presence of a nearby market (New York City) and began to invest in slaves. The development of large "plantations" in and around the New York City area led to the development of a resident slave-owning class. This new aristocracy used enslavement to stabilize their station in life. The result of this ontogeny caused a close relationship to develop between this aristocracy and enslavement in colonial New York.

In the marginal, barter society of New Netherland's first decades, Africans could be exchanged for beaver skins or for provisions such as pork and peas. As the colony progressed to a specie economy, slaves took on an additional value related to but partly independent of the value of their services.[77]

It can be argued that the more significant stimulant to slaveholding by this aristocracy was the social prestige derived from the ownership of a large number of Africans. In its history New York was perhaps the most aristocratic of all the colonies.[78]

Even in the areas where African descendants were not the largest demographic element, they tended to be well placed in the society. In North America, for example, slaves were most likely to be found in the largest estates and wealthiest households. William Byrd, living in Virginia in the 1680s on land occupied by his estate and the smaller farms of former indentured servants, still felt that he was living in a "great family of Negro's [*sic*]." Byrd's slaves not only worked the fields but also provided domestic service in close proximity to the European master.[79]

This same situation prevailed in New Netherland. The wealthiest had large estates of slaves, where everywhere else European indentured servants prevailed. Thus, only the company officials and the governors had as many as forty slaves each in New Netherland. Slaves also provided most of the domestic service in the homes of the elite, even though some visitors may have preferred Europeans, believing that "Angolan slave women are thievish, lazy and useless trash." But whatever the overall Dutch opinion of them, Africans and their descendants were virtually ubiquitous in domestic service among the better households. Slaveholders could also engage in large-scale nonagricultural enterprises without the problems contingent upon using indentured servants, especially in some skilled tasks, where the loss of a trained servant might be hard to make up.[80]

In technical skill and versatility African and African descendant workers spanned the entire range of free labor and were a vital component in transforming an unstable Dutch outpost into a rich and powerful state.[81] Thirty years after the first settlement at New Amsterdam, the population of some 1,000 proved surprisingly heterogeneous with one-fifth of the total Africans enslaved and free.[82]

EARLY ATTITUDES ON ENSLAVEMENT

Any knowledgeable scholar of this period would support the contention that with the occasional outbursts of honest indignation against enslavement and the slave trade there existed a great deal of moral indifference and unconcern of enslavement which allowed this great social problem to develop and grow.

During the first century and a half of the African's presence in Colonial New York, whether ruled by the Dutch, the British or Americans, few whites voiced public concern about the practice of chattel enslavement. This attitude was directly linked to the fact that early colonists in New York and the other colonies "thought that the great natural resources of America were meant to be consumed and exploited as quickly and ruthlessly as possible."[83] It should also be noted that prior to 1750, *no* church condemned slave ownership or slave trading.

One fact seems certain, the church as an institution played a small role in obtaining freedom for Blacks.[84]

In addition, throughout most of the colonial period, opposition to enslavement among white colonists was virtually nonexistent. Settlers in the seventeenth and early eighteenth centuries came from a sharply stratified society in which the upper classes savagely exploited members of the "lower classes." They, therefore, saw little reason to question the enslavement of Africans. Although whites may have become uneasy over the prospect of a slave revolution, real or imagined, few were moved to publicly denounce enslavement. It is widely contended that one of the motivations of early American laws was "a desire to justify to the civilized world the glaring incongruity of legal enslavement existing in a land which boasted that "all men were created equal."[85]

Africans did what they could to free themselves of this oppressive system, sometimes by escaping[86] and also by other rudimentary as well as more sophisticated means, both individually and collectively. Enslaved Africans learned to work slowly, break tools, steal from their masters, poison animals, told stories of resistance, and in some cases rebelled sometimes with violence.

Whatever the effort, it was continuously thwarted by the society that bound them.

Even though there were very few laws passed in the first twenty years of British occupation regulating the activity of Africans and their descendants, it soon changed. Under British control, enslavement in New York and the other colonies grew at a tremendous and unprecedented rate. In 1698, there were 2,170 Africans in the colony of New York. The year 1723 saw the African population by way of internal population growth and importations reached 6,171; of this total some 2,395 had been imported from Africa and the West Indies. By 1746, this number had grown to over 9,000 adults, the largest labor force of Africans in any English colony north of Maryland. In New York City, the enslaved African population had grown to an all-time high of 20.9 percent of the city's total population. Also, in 1746, in upriver New York, Africans in Ulster County alone accounted for one of every five inhabitants.[87]

Slave Codes

> *And be it further ordained by the Authority aforesaid that no Negro or Indian slaves above the number of three do assemble to meet together on the Lord's day or any other time, at any place from their master's service, within the city and the liberties thereof, and that no such slave to go armed at any time with gun, sword, club or any other kind of weapon whatsoever penalty being whipt at the public whipping post fifteen lashes unless master or owner of such slave will pay six shillings to excuse the slave.*[88]

With this growth of enslavement in all the British colonies, lawmakers turned their attention to the regulation of the lives of enslaved Africans. The resulting "slave codes" routinely forbade teaching Africans and their descendants to read and write, outlawed group gatherings outside of church, restricted contact with free Africans, and required enslaved Africans to carry passes. The early laws were also designed to restrict the contact of Africans with other whites particularly with respect to socialization and the exercise of commerce.[89] As early as 1695, the Kingston court (Ulster County) "[o]rdered that if three or more Negroes gather at unseasonable hours, except upon a master's business, such Negroes shall be whipped or each master must pay a piece of eight for his Negro's freedom."[90]

The year 1702 seemed to mark the beginning of the categorizing of Africans as legally separate from the mainstream colonial community. It was in this year that a new law passed in the New Jersey Assembly illustrated the attitude of colonial lawmakers. It clarified the rights of enslavers over their enslaved Africans and expressly established the institutional acceptance of slaveholders' rights. It further allowed enslavers to punish their slaves at their own discretion, thus placing "slaves" outside of the rule of British law.

Many of the laws that were passed in the early days of the republic were stimulated primarily by a fear of slave insurrections.[91] In Colonial New York, a highly visible and powerful example of these efforts to end individual inspired emancipation (escapes) was highlighted in 1705, when the Colonial Assembly passed a law titled "An Act to Prevent the Running away of Negro Slaves out of the city and county of Albany to the French at Canada." This law mandated the penalty for being recaptured beyond forty miles north of Albany (Albany County) at or near Saratoga (Saratoga County) to be execution. This Law was enacted under the guise of protecting the colony during their conflict with French Canada by insuring that intelligence on the disposition of the colony not be communicated to the French. It appears that the colonists were so afraid of the possibility that "slaves" would defect to the French that they enacted legislation with a death penalty to discourage its possibility and/or continuance.[92]

It would appear that the true purpose of this law becomes clearer when certain facts are considered. For example, the governing officials of the city and county of Albany had already convened to discuss this issue with its interesting proviso that addressed the fears that slaves would continue to leave their "owners" and seek refuge with the French. The law further requires that "the slave(s), once recaptured", should be appraised and their value determined prior to trial by an appraiser with the express purpose of assessing, levying and collecting a tax to be paid to the treasurer of Albany County by enslavers within the city and county. The treasurer was then charged with defraying the expenses of the prosecution (not to exceed ten pounds) and the owner was then given the full value of his/her executed slave or slaves in accordance with the findings of the appraiser. This provision was an effort to compensate the owners for their loss of property (the execution of a slave).[93]

This law provides an unimpeachable example of governmental complicity in the administration of enslavement in New York State. This policy is further exemplified by the fact that in 1715 after the war with the French (as stated specifically in the legislation), this law was "revived" because the 1705 law had served the city and county of Albany so well.[94]

This continuing state of fear of subversion by African descendants also manifested itself during the Revolutionary War with the British. Similar British policies during the Revolutionary War seriously handicapped the American war effort. An especially dangerous situation existed in Northern New York, where British sympathizers encouraged American desertions. The American authorities feared that the slaves would revolt if soldiers left their home districts. The Albany Committee of Safety repeatedly refused to release its militia as unrest continued among their enslaved African descendants. The committee clamped a tight curfew on enslaved African descendants and deported unruly enslaved African descendants to New England, where the threat of subversion was less immediate. Similar measures were taken at Schenectady, where the Committee of Correspondence treated even minor offenses committed by enslaved African descendants as evidence of British subversion. Additionally, slaves venturing into the streets of Schenectady at night were severely flogged.

Figure 13
Example Of New York City Enslavement Codes

22ND APRIL 1731

City of New-York, ſſ.

A L A W

For Regulating Negroes and Slaves in the Night Time.

BE It Ordained by the Mayor, Recorder, Aldermen and Aſſiſtants of the City of New-York, convened in Common-Council, and it is hereby Ordained by the Authority of the ſame, That from hence-forth no Negro, Mulatto or Indian Slave, above the Age of Fourteen Years, do preſume to be or appear in any of the Streets of this City, on the South-ſide of the Freſh-Water, in the Night time, above an hour after Sun-ſet; And that if any ſuch Negro, Mulatto or Indian Slave or Slaves, as aforeſaid, ſhall be found in any of the Streets of this City, or in any other Place, on the South ſide of the Freſh-Water, in the Night-time, above one hour after Sun-ſet, without a Lanthorn and lighted Candle in it, ſo as the light thereof may be plainly ſeen (and not in company with his, her or their Maſter or Miſtreſs, or ſome White Perſon or White Servant belonging to the Family whoſe Slave he or ſhe is, or in whoſe Service he or ſhe then are) That then and in ſuch caſe it ſhall and may be lawful for any of his Majeſty's Subjects within the ſaid City to apprehend ſuch Slave or Slaves, not having ſuch Lanthorn and Candle, and forth-with carry him, her or them before the Mayor or Recorder, or any one of the Aldermen of the ſaid City (if at a ſeaſonable hour) and if at an unſeaſonable hour, to the Watch-houſe, there to be confined until the next Morning) who are hereby authorized, upon Proof of the Offence, to commit ſuch Slave or Slaves to the common Goal, for ſuch his, her or their Contempt, and there to remain until the Maſter, Miſtreſs or Owner of every ſuch Slave or Slaves, ſhall pay to the Perſon or Perſons who apprehended and committed every ſuch Slave or Slaves, the Sum of Four Shillings current Money of New-York, for his, her or their pains and Trouble therein, with Reaſonable Charges of Proſecution.

And be it further Ordained by the Authority aforeſaid, That every Slave or Slaves that ſhall be convicted of the Offence aforeſaid, before he, ſhe or they be diſcharged out of Cuſtody, ſhall be Whipped at the Publick Whipping-Poſt (not exceeding Forty Laſhes) if deſired by the Maſter or Owner of ſuch Slave or Slaves.

Provided always, and it is the intent hereof, That if two or more Slaves (Not exceeding the Number of Three) be together in any lawful Employ or Labour for the Service of their Maſter or Miſtreſs (and not otherwiſe) and only one of them have and carry ſuch Lanthorn with a lighted Candle therein, the other Slaves in ſuch Compay not carrying a Lanthorn and lighted Candle, ſhall not be conſtrued and intended to be within the meaning and Penalty of this Law, any thing in this Law contained to the contrary hereof in any wiſe notwithſtanding. *Dated at the City-Hall this Two and Twentieth Day of April, in the fourth year of His Majeſty's Reign, Annoq; Domini* 1731.

By Order of Common Council,

Will. Sharpas, *Cl.*

45

An Act passed on 24 October 1706 stipulated:

> *III. PROVIDED ALWAYS, AND BE IT DECLARED AND ENACTED, by the said Authority, That no Slave, whatsoever, in this Colony, shall at any Time, be admitted as a Witness for, or against, any Freeman, in any Case, Matter, or Cause, civil or criminal, whatsoever.*

C. M. Woolsey interprets this provision to mean that "no matter what cruelties or inhuman treatment they [slaves] might receive from any white or black man, provided the black man was a freeman, he could not be a witness, to tell what they had suffered at the hands, or to tell what property had been taken from them."[95]

It should be noted that these "slave codes" were not restricted to New York City and its surrounding area. Upstate towns and villages actively participated in regulating the lives of their enslaved Africans and their descendants as well. In Albany, it seems that keeping Africans off the streets was a serious problem for the "town fathers." In 1686, an ordinance was passed that banned Africans from driving carts within the city limits. (Interestingly enough, this ban did not apply to Africans who drove beer wagons within the city limits.) In 1733, the Common Council of Albany passed another ordinance designed "to prevent Negroes and Indians slaves from appearing in the streets after eight at night without lantern and lighted candle in it."[96]

These "slave codes" also restricted where enslaved Africans could be employed and how slaveholders could free them. Additional laws were passed to prevent free Africans from aiding runaway slaves.

> **To control a growing, disorderly slave population, the English colonial governors of New York and New Jersey gradually established a slave code comparable in severity to ordinances in South Carolina or the West Indies.**[97]

Additionally, these "slave codes" grew so numerous in New York City that they are seen as a major cause of the 1712 slave revolt.[98]

RESISTANCE TO ENSLAVEMENT

The rarity of manumissions, the lack of sympathy for abolition displayed by colonial legislatures, churches, and citizens insured that freedom-minded Africans and their descendants could look only to occasional rebellions and conspiracies, or, less dangerously, to individual flight.

Under British rule, slaves stole more cash, clothing, and food from masters' households and ran away more frequently than they had under the Dutch. During British rule, Africans in New York also responded to bondage by implementing traditional African forms of resistance and "warfare." Consequently, and throughout this period of enslavement, New York's officials were concerned with the safety of their colonists. Their fears were inspired by the evidence of African cultural influences that existed within the African slave community. Their reaction to this developing culture of interpersonal obligations and dependencies that could best be described as "slave unity," was violent.

This survival-oriented network of West African cultures represented complex interrelationship that were based on the interaction between various cultural subsets that were defined by age, gender, and lineage. These communities were grounded in ancestral and spiritual beliefs, and regulated by complicated ethical systems. Enslaved Africans had used West African models to pattern a new African-American cultural collective. Operating from a position of fear and bias, the legal and political machinery of eighteenth-century New York constantly reacted with brutality toward this evolving network.

Certainly every assemblage of Africans and their descendants did not constitute a borrowing on African tradition, but several did. Sometimes peaceful, sometimes not, these associations drew considerable official attention. The colonial administration repeatedly attempted to outlaw such public and private rendezvous, and with good reason, African uprisings always troubled those engaged in "mastery" and their unfamiliar patterns made white New Yorkers tremble at the news of revolts in other places. European colonials spent little time trying to understand the West African heritage. They rather attempted to punish it, control it, and curse it. Nevertheless, "Africanisms" set the stage of their nightmares.[99]

COLLECTIVE RESISTANCE

In the summer of 1706, white New Yorkers sought organized actions to control and destroy the African collective's ability to resist enslavement. On July 22 1706, Edward Lord Viscount Cornbury, the provincial governor, armed justices of the peace in Kings County (today's Brooklyn)and Long Island with the death penalty in order to deal with African maroons who, after freeing themselves, were striking fear among the local colonists:

> *Whereas, I am informed that several negroes in Kings County have assembled themselves in a riotous manner, which, if not prevented, may prove of ill consequence; you and every [one] of you are therefore hereby required and commanded to take all proper methods for seizing and apprehending all such negroes in the said county as shall be found to be assembled in such manner as aforesaid, or have run away or absconded from their masters or owners, whereby there may be reason to suspect them of ill practices or designs, and to secure them in safe custody, that their crimes and actions may be inquired into; and if any of them refuse to submit themselves, then to fire on them, kill or destroy them, if they cannot otherwise be taken; and for so doing this shall be your sufficient warrant.[100]*

The colonial government's reaction to acts of rebellion and insurrection was swift. "An Act for preventing the Conspiracy of Slaves" was passed by the Colonial Assembly in 1708 it was a direct reaction to the circumstances surrounding the murders of the William Hallet Jr. family of New Town in Queens County, on the evening of 24 January 1708.[101] It is recorded that the family was attacked by an enslaved African, a bondswomen and an enslaved Native American man named Sam, as revenge for Hallet's refusal to allow them to travel on the Sabbath. The bondswoman convinced Sam to kill Hallet, his pregnant wife, and their five children and to seize the estate, Hallet's Cove. After the uprising, the two conspirators and several other Africans were arrested. The *Boston News- Letter* reported evidence of a larger plot in which "several other Families were designed for the like slaughter:"[102]

The Colonial Assembly passed this law in an attempt to deter any future acts of rebellion or insurrection by enslaved Africans against its white citizens. If enslaved African were to murder or attempt to murder any "White citizen or Master," their punishment would be death. It also provides for the protection of colonialists from potential slave rebellions or insurrections and establishes the right of white colonialists to protect themselves and their property from these incidences, including the killing of slaves.

This act was another reversal in the legal status of Africans and their descendants. It was the first decree in New York that made the murder or attempted murder of African and their descendants, not a crime. Interestingly enough, Chapter 149 of the Laws of 1705, mentioned earlier, is referenced in this law with respect to compensating enslavers for the loss of their enslaved men and women, who were executed, as a result of violating this law. This compensation "was not to exceed twenty-five pounds."[103]

Escapes also placed New York City in a state of fear and uneasiness, particularly, around the docks where these escaped African descendants congregated. There were never enough ships to accommodate all the escaped African descendents who fled to New York City. Some of the more desperate runaways seized sloops and ketches in which they attempted to make their escape from the province. "Others skulked along the waterfront, where they were drawn into the gangs of criminal slaves infesting the docks. The most notorious gang was the Geneva Club. Named after the Geneva gin its members were fond of imbibing."[104] There were also gangs known as the Free Masons, the Smith Fly Boys the Long Bridge Boys and many others. "Slaves belonging to such gangs were extremely clannish and often engaged in murderous feuds."[105]

ENSLAVED AFRICANS REVOLT IN NEW YORK

The rebellions and insurrections undertaken by Africans and their descendants in New York State were concerted and sometimes orchestrated efforts that occurred throughout New York State. Whether upstate or downstate, African descendants executed numerous actions and activities designed to gain their freedom from an oppressive system of chattel enslavement equal in every respect to the system instituted in the Southern colonies.

Revolt of 1712

In New York City in 1712 a highly chronicled revolt took place when enslaved Africans and Native Americans gathered in an orchard on Maiden Lane in New York City with hatchets, guns, knives, and hoes and set out to burn and destroy property in the area. The sequence of events follows: The men set fire to a building in the middle of town and the fire spread. While white colonists gathered to extinguish the blaze, the slaves attacked, and then escaped. Several white colonists were killed during the "revolt." Twenty-one enslaved Africans were executed and six were reported to have committed suicide.[106]

The result of this first organized revolt in New York was the enactment of a much stricter "slave code." No longer could more than two or three "slaves" gather together. A salaried "whipper" (oftentimes an African) would be hired to mete out the punishment of whipping to any slave caught gambling in public and any slave handling a firearm. Various other assorted violations would receive similar punishments.[107] Specifically, the involvement in a conspiracy to kill or the rape of a white woman would result in execution. Restrictions and fines were placed on the socialization of "freemen" and slaves. There was even a law passed that discouraged masters from freeing a slave. The master could free his/her slave, but only after posting a bond of 200 pounds. This bond money would be paid to the freed slave over a ten-year period if that slave couldn't support himself or herself.

The law was enacted due to the colonials' belief that "the free Negroes of this Colony are an Idle slothful people and prove very often a charge on the place where they are." More then twenty-eight statutes were included in a massive document entitled "An Act for Preventing Suppressing and Punishing the Conspiracy and Insurrection of Negroes and Slaves." It was passed by the Colonial Assembly on 10 December 1712.[108]

The slave code is a fairly good indicator of the African impact on the colony because-while it was influenced by Dutch experiences in the Caribbean and Brazil and English encounters in Virginia and the West Indies-the laws of bondage in New Netherland and New York typically reacted to the actions of the unfree. The code intended to force Africans to adhere to the socioeconomic culture of bondage; therefore, it specifically targeted African forms of resistance, particularly combinations of the unfree that sought to end or ameliorate their condition.[109]

Notwithstanding government's attempts to further control the lives of "slaves," the congregation of large numbers of "free and enslaved" African descendants in the cities of the North would "nurture movements and agitation for men and women of African descent for certain rights."[110] Interestingly enough, an otherwise forgotten fact concerning the demographics of New York City during the colonial period was that "New York was a biracial city from the outset. Social life and cultural forms reflected African as well as European influences."[111] This dynamic would appear to have laid the groundwork for resistance.

A thorough knowledge of existing norms and culture juxtaposed with their own unique means of communication and culturally inspired survival techniques would seem to place the Africans of New York City in an advantageous position for conspiracy. It has been documented that the harbor of New York City was ripe with roving bands of displaced Africans and other gangs as they were called by the locals, both in the day and night.

This backdrop would seem to inspire fear of rebellion above and beyond the common thinking of the day and the oft-believed stereotypes of the docile and ignorant African people. The white citizens of New York City were seemingly trapped in a mindset that taught and practiced superiority over people of African descent and encouraged hatred and racism. This longstanding view was designed in part to provide colonists with a sense of security. And yet this superiority over people of African descent eventually sowed the seeds of its own downfall.

In fact, New Yorkers identified the majority of the 1712 rebels as Koromantine and Pawpaw Africans, part of the large groups of Africans who arrived in New York City between 1710 and 1712. Koromantine and Pawpaw Africans trained the men in their communities in the conduct of guerrilla warfare. These Africans' knowledge of enslavement in Africa entailed more rights and privileges than accorded to slaves in British North America. In the Akan-Asante society from which these slaves had come, slaves or their children could eventually be absorbed into the community as equals.[112]

"The Great Negro Plot" of 1741

Another well-documented example of African resistance and the true colonial attitude toward preserving the institution of enslavement occurred in New York City in 1741. By this date, approximately one in every five of Manhattan's 11,000 residents was of African descent and, with rare exceptions, enslaved. In the entire colony of New York of the 60,000 residents roughly 9,000 were of African descent.[113]

A demographic this extensive proved to inspire fear in the hearts of and minds of white colonialists. In fact a panic had been created that year when authorities heard that "slaves and free" African descendants, as well as whites, were accused of planning to burn the city and killing all other whites. Calling it the "Great Negro Plot," city leaders arrested 154 blacks and twenty-four whites, accusing them of conspiracy. Thirty-one Africans were executed for being part of a revolutionary plot, thirteen were burned at the stake, seventeen were hanged, and two white men and two white women were also hanged[114] (fig. 14).

Many scholars make a comparison between the "Salem witch-hunt hysteria" and the actions of the city government and citizens of New York City during the trial and immediately preceding and including the initial investigation.[115] It has been conjectured by several writers that the "slave unrest" of both 1712 and 1741 were attributed to the presence of "Spanish Negroes." These African sailors were formally considered "free" in the West Indies however after they were captured in raids on the high seas they were sold as "ordinary" African slaves. No quarter existed with respect to the nationality or status of Africans and their descendants in Colonial America. Skin color dictated status and position in this New World culture. These "Spanish Negroes" petitioned continuously for their freedom as subjects of the king of Spain however, the only evidence was their word and as African slaves it alone had no value.[116]

Figure 14
1741 Slave Revolt List[117]

A LIST OF NEGROES COMMITTED ON ACCOUNT OF THE CONSPIRACY.

NEGROES.	Masters or Owners	Committed	Arraigned	Convicted	Confessed	Burnt.	Hanged.	Transported to	Discharged.
Ancealo,	Peter De Lancey,	April 6,	June 15,	June 17,				Spanish W. Indies	
Augustine, } Spaniards.	Macmulken,	April 1,	June 13,	June 17,				Madeira.	
Antonio,	Sarah Mayaard,	April 1,	June 13,	June 17,					
Albany,	Mrs. Carpenter,	May 12,	June 8,	June 10,		June 12.			
Abraham, a free negro,		June 1,			June 27,			Madeira.	
Adam,	J. Murray, esq,	June 26,	June 25,		June 25.			Madeira.	
Brash,	Peter Jay,	May 9,	June 8,		June 11.			Hispaniola.	
Bastian alias Tom Peal,	Jacobus Vaarck,	May 12,	June 12,	June 10,		June 16.		Madeira.	
Ben,	Capt. Marshall,	June 9,	July 3,	June 13,				Hispaniola.	
Bill alias Will,	C. Ten Eyck,	June 12,	July 5,		June 30,			Madeira.	
Bridgewater,	A. Van Horne,	June 22,	July 1,		June 27.				
Billy,	Mrs. Ellison,	June 25,	July 10,		June 30.		May 11,		July 15.
Braveboy,	Mrs. Kiersiede,	June 27,							
Burlington,	Joseph Haines,	July 3,							
Cesar,	Vaarck,	March 1,	April 24,	May 1,†		May 30,			5.
Cuffee,	A. Phillipse, esq.	April 6,	May 23,	May 29,		May 30,			
Cuba, a wench,	Mrs. C. Lynch,	April 4,							
Curacoa Dick,	Cornelius Tiebool	May 9,	June 8,	June 10,	June 22,	June 12,		Madeira.	
Cato,	Alderman Moore,	May 9,	July 15,		June 22,				
Cesar,	do. Pintard,	May 9,	July 3,						
Cuffee,	Lewis Gomez,	May 24,	June 6,	June 8,		June 9,			
Cesar,	Benjamin Peck,	May 25,	June 6,	June 8,		June 9,			
Cesar,	Joseph Cowley,	May 25,	June 12,	June 13,		9,	June 16,		
Caio,	Gerardus Comfort	May 26,	June 6,	June 8,					
Cook,		July 10,							
Cambridge,	C. Codwise,	May 30,	June 25,		June 30,			Cape Francois.	
Czsar,	Israel Horsefield,	May 30,	June 27,		June 27,		July 3,	St. Thomas.	
Caro,	John Shurmur,	June 2,	June 16,	June 19,	June 27,				

† Of a robbery, but appears to have been a principal negro conspirator.

It is also recorded that several whites were involved and in fact spearheaded the "Great Negro Plot of 1741 (fig. 15). However, the 1741 Manhattan slave conspiracy provided evidence that the enslaved Africans' capacity for collective action was greater than the vigilance of New York lawmakers and that African descendants were capable of their own leadership.

The facts of the plot are more easily separated from the exaggerations that followed its discovery when we scrutinize it against patterns in West Africa and the Diaspora. Historian Thomas J. Davis, in *A Rumor of Revolt*, notes that a healthy sense of self-preservation and a belief in the inferiority of Africans kept white Manhattanites from the thought that people of African descent had masterminded the scheme to set fire to the city and kill its free inhabitants.[118] Instead, they stretched the logical scope of the conspiracy, merging it with their other social phobias and biases. They assigned blame to a great papal plot against the small Protestant colony and then found a core of Irish and Catholic malcontents to charge as corrupters. Some of the condemned Africans who had been introduced to Catholicism in the West Indies kissed crucifixes before going to their deaths and aggravated the fear of a religious conspiracy.[119]

Whatever the motivation, these Africans' crimes necessitated confrontations with an oppressive local structure. Their misdeeds were simultaneously violations of property and acts of subversion. The local Africans and their descendants were quite aware of this fact, as were white New Yorkers. During the investigation of the 1741 conspiracy, groups of militarized Africans and their descendants were again menacing New York and Long Island. African gangs (maroons) were active across the entire region.

Other Acts of Organized Resistance to Enslavement

"Free" and enslaved Africans and their descendants were also used in the various state militias to seek out and capture escaped slaves who resisted the institution of enslavement by becoming "maroons" and preying on white settlers. An early example of maroons surfaced in 1690 when residents of Harlem (of all places) complained of a "band of Negroes," who had escaped from their masters in New York and had committed depredations on the inhabitants of the village.

Other slave conspiracies were uncovered in New York State in the eighteenth century. The first conspiracy of 1708 involved a slave uprising on Long Island. Another slave revolt was recorded in New York City in 1733. One in 1761 in Schenectady mirrored the 1741 plot and another was uncovered in Ulster County, its objective was a mass break to Canada for freedom. In Kingston in 1775, a foiled slave conspiracy to kill the inhabitants and burn the town of Kingston was uncovered. In addition, in Albany in November of 1793, the "Black Arson" involved the burning of slave owner's property by a band of slaves.[120]

These incidents and other acts of organized resistance demonstrated that Africans and their descendants held in bondage had their own definitions of emancipation. It further illustrates the fact that New Yorkers were acutely aware of the dangers inherent in the forced bondage of human beings. Escaped "slaves" were such a concern that even early colonists passed ordinances that decreed that no more than one meal or one night's lodging could be given a stranger without notifying the Director [of New Amsterdam].[121]

Figure 15
A List Of White Persons Taken Into Custody On Account Of The 1741 Conspiracy[122]

	Names of Persons.	Occupations.	When committed.	Arraigned.	Convicted.	Confessed.	Executed.	Discharged.
	Margaret Kerry, *alias* Salingburgh.		4 March.	2 & 4 *June, for receiving stolen Goods.*	4 June,		12 June.	
	John Hughson,	*Shoemaker and Alehouse keeper.*	18 April:					
	Sarah Hughson, *Wife to* John Hughson,		18 April.					
	Sarah Hughson, *the Daughter.*		6 May.			8 *July,*		*Pardoned.*
5	John Romme,	*Shoemaker, and Alehouse-keeper.*	18 May.					*Discharged on Security for his departing the Province.*
	Elizabeth Romme, *his Wife.*		8 May.					
	Peter Connolly,	*Soldier.*	23 June.					31 *August.*
	John Ury,	*A Priest.*	24 June.	15 & 22 *July*	29 July		29 August	
	Edward Kelly,	*Soldier.*	25 June.					31 *August.*
10	William Kane,	*Soldier.*	4 July.			5 *July,*		*December, Enlisted for (West-Indies.*
	John Coffin,	*Pedlar.*	6 July.					
	Edward Murphey,	*Soldier.*	8 July.					
	Andrew Ryan,	*Soldier.*	9 July.					31 *August.*
	David Johnson,	*Hat-maker.*	9 July.					
15	John Corry,	*Dancing-Master*	13 July.					
	Thomas Hughson,	*Yeoman,*	12 and 13 June.					*Pardoned, on Condition of departing the Province.*
	Nathaniel, Walter, William, Richard, — Thomas Hughson's *Sons.*	*Yeomen,*						
20								
	Corker, Fagan, Plommer,	*mentioned in Kane's Evidence in Ury's Trial, and in his Examinations, never found.*						

BENEVOLENT ENSLAVEMENT

> **The entire pattern of African descendant slaveholders across the centuries (1600-1800) in New York may be termed "benevolent" in that clearly more than 97% of the cases involve free males purchasing relatives.**[123]

"Free" African descendants, many of them former slaves themselves, held slaves in New Amsterdam and later in New York City from the first documentation of the practice until its end after 1830.[124] Research chronicles this practice as a form of resistance to enslavement, when African descendants bought wives, children, and other relatives in order to release them from the bondage of whites and to keep families together. Their commitment to the acquisition of enslaved relatives was the result of various factors:

1- many "free" African descendants bought relatives who were slaves to white masters;

2- quite often when marriages occurred between free African descendants and slaves, the free spouse attempted to buy the freedom of the slave spouse and children;

3- additionally, marriages between enslaved couples occasionally saw one spouse emancipated while the other remained in bondage. Consequently, those formerly enslaved tried to obtain the liberty of their enslaved loved ones.[125]

One such example is recorded in Harry P. Yoshpe's article in the *Journal of Negro History* entitled "Records of Slave Manumissions in New York: During the Colonial and Early National Periods":

> *On October 29,1795, John Maranda paid $200 to an intermediary, attorney Samuel Jones Jr., to purchase his liberty from John De Baan. A few months later Maranda freed his four-year-old daughter, Susan, from John Haring of New Jersey for $50. In May 1798, Maranda bought his wife Elizabeth from Dr. Gardner Jones for $150. Dr. Jones threw in Maranda's baby son John for $10 more. Within three years, John Maranda had purchased himself and his entire family out of bondage.[126]*

Sherrill D. Wilson, in her book *New York City's African Slaveholders: A Social and Material Culture History* illustrates that in these instances, family preservation was the motive of these "free" African descendants and that "there is no evidence that they used slaves for commercial purposes."[127] Carter G. Woodson terms this type of enslavement as "benevolent enslavement/enslavement" when he states that "the majority of Negro holders of slaves were such from the point of philanthropy."[128]

Another example of this effort to free family members is illustrated in *A Narrative of the Life and Adventures of Venture, A Native of Africa: But refident above fixty years in the United State of America. Related by Himself.* This narrative was written by Venture Smith, born free in Africa but captured and enslaved at the age of eight.

Venture's great size and unwillingness to suffer insult made him a problem for his holders, and he was sold several times before he was able to purchase his own freedom in 1765 at the age of thirty-six. Venture was eventually able to liberate his two sons, Solomon and Cuff, his daughter Hannah his pregnant wife Meg and their unborn child.[129] In 1798, a narrative of his life, which he related to a local schoolteacher, was published. He describes this effort in the following manner:

> *I was employed in cutting the aforementioned quantity of wood, I never was at the expense of fix-pence worth of spirits. Being after this labour forty years of age, I worked at various places, and in particular on Ram-Island, where I purchased Solomon and Cuff, two sons of mine, for two hundred dollars each.[130]*

With respect to his oldest daughter, Hannah, he writes:

> *Being about forty-six years old, I bought my oldest child Hannah, of Ray Mumford, for forty-four pounds, and she still resided with him. I had already redeemed from enslavement, myself, my wife and three children, besides three negro men. [131]*

Venture Smith died on September 19, 1805, at the age of seventy-seven but his extraordinary efforts to free his family are documented forever in his published narrative.

Figure 16
Venture Smith's grave at the First Church Cemetery in East Haddam, Connecticut

This gravesite was named a site on the state's Freedom Trail in 1997.[132]

EFFORTS TO CONTROL ESCAPES FROM ENSLAVEMENT

Slave owners everywhere (after the Revolutionary War) found their slaves working more slowly and answering more quickly with a tone that chilled. By their formal petitions, frequent absences, willingness to turn fugitive, and acts of insolence and violence, slaves served notice that they took serious the libertarian promise of American independence and would accept nothing less than the end of chattel bondage.[133]

As lifetime "hereditary bondage" was being forged for Africans and their descendants, Dutch colonists almost immediately faced a recurring problem of enslaved Africans escaping. In 1640 and 1642, the Dutch West India Company passed fugitive slave laws to control the damage that absconding Africans did to the colonial economy and social order. In 1654, Peter Stuyvesant revealed that residents of Amersfort (Flatlands), Kings County, were using enslaved Africans to help hunt fugitive slaves.

Additionally, in a concerted effort to curtail successful escapes, a truce, if you will, was implemented among all European countries in Colonial America with respect to returning runaways to their "rightful" owners. Oscar Williams in his book *African Americans and Colonial Legislation in the Middle Colonies*, describes this understanding between colonists, succinctly:

In colonial America, European nationalistic spirit disappeared when it came to the subject of returning runaways. The necessity to return fugitives appeared to be the first American consensus involving Blacks.[134]

ENSLAVEMENT IN NEW YORK STATE

As the Northern colonies were more fully incorporated into the Atlantic economy, the significance of slavery grew. In some places, the North itself took on the trappings of a slave society, with an economy that rested upon the labor of enslaved Africans and their descendants.[135]

THE ENSLAVED POPULATION

New York City and Surrounding Counties

New York City's huge seaport made it the focal point for the trading of Africans and their descendants on the eastern seaboard. And it became the center of the heaviest slaveholding region north of the Mason-Dixon Line.[136] Although the course of enslavement in New Netherland may have stopped short of the transformation initiated by the tobacco and cotton revolutions, it nevertheless reshaped the lives of Africans and their descendants, both deepening the nightmare of enslavement and buffering its worst effects. In the colony of New York, enslaved Africans and their descendants numbered about 2,000 in 1698. By 1720 that number grew to 5,740 enslaved individuals (16 percent of the total population). Subsequently, the number of the colony's Africans swelled to more than 9,000 adults by 1746 and 13,000 by 1756.[137]

Between 1732 and 1754, Africans and their descendants accounted for more than 35 percent of the total immigration through the port of New York. Additionally, many illegal cargoes of Africans unloaded all along the convoluted coast of Long Island to avoid the tariff duties, were not counted. In 1756, enslaved Africans made up about 25 percent of the populations of Kings, Queens, Richmond, New York and Westchester counties.

By 1750, over ten thousand slaves lived within fifty miles of Manhattan Island, the largest such congregation north of Chesapeake, Virginia.[138]

By the mid-eighteenth century, enslavement had become deeply entrenched in New York. In 1750, the enslaved population of New York was 11,014 (14 percent of the total population), nearly double the population figure of 1720.[139] The number of enslaved Africans and their descendants in New York City represented one-fifth to one quarter of all enslaved Africans in Colonial New York.[140] In fact, the New York colony had more slaves than New England, New Jersey, and Pennsylvania combined.

In Richmond and Queens counties bordering New York City, 20 percent of the population was enslaved. Even more strikingly, one in every three residents of Kings County was enslaved, a ratio that would not have been out of place in the South. Additionally, "... in the towns surrounding New York City, 70 to 80 percent of the households held slaves."[141]

Nearly, 40 percent of the households in Kings, Queens and Richmond Counties owned slaves, a higher ratio than in South Carolina, North Carolina, or Maryland.[142]

It would be another fifty years before the number of enslaved Africans and their descendants began to decrease rather than increase.

In 1790, the number of slaves in New York State had grown to some 21,193, according to the first US Census, a figure only some 7,000 below Georgia's total enslaved population during the same period.[143] In fact, through most of the eighteenth century New York City ranked second to Charleston in the number of enslaved Africans owned by its inhabitants[144] and enslavement was as strictly maintained in the Colony of New York as it was in Virginia.[145]

In New York City, of the 3,092 African Americans listed in the 1790 census, about two-thirds were slaves, with about one in every five households in the city owning at least one slave.[146]

These statistics illustrate the extent of the practice of enslavement in New York City and its steady progression of New York State toward a slave-based economic society, especially when we compared this increased reliance on slave labor to the fact that in 1790, only one out of every nine families in Boston owned an enslaved African. The incidence of enslavement was so pervasive in New York City that slaveholding was considerably more evenly distributed than wealth. The bottom 50 per cent of the population owned 6.6 percent of the assessable wealth yet owned 12.1 percent of the slaves. This figure in 1789 was 17.6 percent, a figure three times that of Boston and Philadelphia. In addition, 13 percent of New York slaveholders were women.[147]

By 1790, in upstate New York, specifically in the counties of Columbia, Albany, Orange, Ulster and Dutchess, there were 12,303 Africans, both free and enslaved as compared to 184,491 whites.[148] In the Mid-Hudson Valley, enslavement was a very well-established part of the New Paltz community. The census of 1771 lists twenty-eight slaveholders, who collectively owned seventy-eight slaves over the age of 14 years with the large majority of slaveholders (82%) owning between one and four slaves. By 1790, in New Paltz there were 302 slaves or 13 percent of the population.[149] Additionally, the slave population of the Hudson Valley by 1771, was a little over one-third that of the entire enslaved population of the colony, which then stood at 17,500. By 1790, the enslaved population of the Hudson Valley was 15,000.[150]

Albany County and Upstate

Enslavement had become an integral feature of Albany's first 200 years of existence.[151] In 1771, the enslaved population in Albany numbered 3,877 individuals of African descent. By 1790, Albany County's enslaved population reached 4,099 or 5.4 percent of its total population.[152] Indicators show that enslavement in the city of Albany in 1790 reached its peak when only 238 out of 1,146 heads of families reported that they owned no slaves.[153] In fact, Albany ranked first among counties in New York State in the number of enslaved Africans held (3722) and in the number of slaveholding families (1467) during this period.[154] By 1800, the total of African descendants in the city of Albany was approximately 10 percent of the city's base population.[155]

In the rural communities surrounding New York City and in upstate New York, enslavement persisted more tenaciously. The refusal to part with property was by no means restricted to land; enslavement too died a hard death in New York's hinterland. As late as 1810, a decade after the passage of the Gradual Abolition Act, "more then one in three rural households still owned slaves."[156]

Even smaller upstate communities maintained a dependence on African slave labor. In 1790, in the small upstate town of Easton

(Washington County) census records lists the following residents as slaveholders and the number of held slaves:

Martin Van Buren -2, Gerrit Van Buren -2, Abraham Widedale -3, Daniel Winne -10, Peter Becker -4, Simon DeRidder -5, Walter DeRidder -7, Gerrit Lasing -3, Jacob Van Schaick -6, Peter Van Woort -9, Cornelius Vandenberg -5. All of these slave holders were of Dutch descent and lived on, or very near, the River road.[157]

IMPACT OF ENSLAVEMENT ON FAMILIES OF AFRICAN DESCENT

During the early period of enslavement in New York, the actual numbers of white immigrant workers was not sufficient enough to have a major impact on the labor market. African descendants (free and enslaved) held the majority of the skilled, semi-skilled and manual labor jobs. Yet as the face of enslavement changed in New York, the need for a larger labor force required the importation of more and more Africans directly from Africa.

This readjustment in focus and policy from importations from the West Indies to direct importation from Africa had a debilitating effect on the stability of the enslaved African family in New York City. Indentured servants began to decrease due to wars and the restrictions placed on European immigration, and so the demand for younger male Africans increased, in an effort to supplant this loss and meet the increasing requirements for a larger and larger labor force. With this frenzied need for more and more laborers directly from the African coast came disease and a drop-off in fertility rates. The African family structure, which had been encouraged in the early periods of enslavement in New Netherland began to crumble due to the surplus of newly arriving African males. These new arrivals unaccustomed to the contagious diseases of the New World died in staggering numbers. Stable African descendant families soon followed.

The absence of residential households diminished the chances of black men playing the role of the husband and father and black women the role of wife and mother. The attenuation of familiar ties by distance and time, and the difficulties created by smaller work units, frequent sales, and meddlesome slave holders made it difficult for slaves to maintain a normal family life by contemporary standards.[158]

The nineteenth century would produce an even more devastating restructuring of the lives and status of Africans and their descendants in New York State. Even though New York had lost its preeminence to Charlestown and then to New Orleans as the largest mainland slave city, it remained a major site for "Urban Enslavement" on the North American continent.[159]

URBAN ENSLAVEMENT

Urban enslavement centered primarily on the hiring out of slaves. The "wages of slaves" were recouped by entrepreneurial slaveholders for day(s), week(s), and yearly hires served to enhance their profit margins and considerably reduce their operating expenses and overhead. In most instances, the clothing, feeding and housing of the weekly or longer "hired slaves" was the responsibility of the employer or hirer.

The scope of this "hire system" was considerable. Its financial potential was profitable to both slave owner and employer alike. It also proved a direct attack on the financial stability of white immigrant workers. Slaves could be "hired" by employers or farmers at rates approaching one-half of what a white worker would cost and it provided a source of income for slaveholders during lags in their yearly work schedules. The wages "earned" by these hired enslaved Africans and their descendants were paid directly to their holders.[160]

These rates were profitable to hirers and owners alike. Since white workers commanded a daily wage of about 5.6 shillings by 1760, slave labor cost employers only about half as much as the going rate of free labor. And the rates were sufficient to provide slaveowners with an excellent return on their investment. Although wages fluctuated with changing economic conditions, slaves consistently. returned from 10 to 30 per cent annually on their market value. Slaves valued at £40 in 1695 earned £5 per year plus maintenance-a net return of about 12 per cent on the owner's investment. . And the yield increased considerably in the eighteenth cent. Slaves appraised at £70 in 1725 earned £20 per year –a net return of 29 per cent. When wages and prices soared during the Revolution, slaves could be hired out by the year at from 40 to 60 per cent of market value. .These rates of course were abnormally high and must be discounted accordingly; nevertheless, even the rates prevailing before the war sufficed to make slaves a highly profitable form of investment.[161]

Austin Seward, a slave in Virginia who was brought to New York State by his master, recounts his experiences when he is hired out by his master in Bath, New York:

While I was staying with my master at Bath, he having little necessity for my services, hired me out to a man by the name of Joseph Robinson, for the purpose of learning me to drive a team. Robinson lived about three miles from the village of Bath, on a small farm, and was not only a poor man but a very mean one. He was cross and heartless in his family, as well as tyrannical and cruel to those in his employ; and having hired me as a "slave boy", he appeared to feel at full liberty to wreak his brutal passion on me at any time, whether I deserved rebuke or not; nor did his terrible outbreaks of anger vent themselves in oaths, curses and threatening only, but he would frequently draw from the cart-tongue a heavy iron pin, and beat me over the head with it, so unmercifully that he frequently sent the

> ***blood flowing over my scanty apparel, and from that to the ground, before he could feel satisfied.***[162]

Steward's master, Capt. Helm no longer had the labor requirements for the slaves he brought with him from Virginia.

> ***Capt. Helm, not having demand for slave labor as much as formerly, was in the practice of hiring out his slaves to different persons, both in and out of the village; and among others, my only sister was hired out to a professed gentleman living in Bath. She had become the mother of two or three children, and was considered a good servant.***[163]

African movement, however, went untracked during this period, since the hiring of Africans naturally would require the mitigating of slave codes, which restricted the assemblage of Africans. In order to combat this "danger to the welfare of the community," the Common Council of New York City passed a law appointing a place for the more convenient hiring of slaves. "All Negroes, Mulattoes and Indian slaves that are let out to hire within the city, do take up their standing, in order to be hired, whereby all persons may know where to hire slaves as their occasion shall require, and also owners of slaves discovered when their slaves are hired."[164]

Even slaveholders in upstate New York understood the economic benefit derived from hiring out their African descendant slaves. One ingenious slaveholder in Albany, Peter Van Bergen indentured one of his slaves "a Negro Boy named Sam" to William Brown, a shoemaker in Albany, for a period of three years "to learn the art, trade and occupation of shoemaker and Boot maker" (doc. 1-1, 1-2). Upon the completion of this "apprenticeship," Van Bergen would have a slave trained and experienced in shoemaking that could be used to increase his own profits. In addition, the contract provided that "whenever the said Peter Van Bergen or his family shall want the said Negro Boy Sam … to fetch water and to clean shoes or any such things in and about the House that then the said Negro Boy Sam is to do it."[165]

Brown would receive an "apprentice" who would for three years provide him with help and assistance in operating his shoemaking business. In addition, as a prerequisite to limiting Brown's overhead costs, by undertaking the instruction of Sam, Van Bergen, according to the contract, "shall and will provide to his said Negro Boy named Sam "… meat, Drink, washing, lodging, clothing (except shoes) during the said Term of three years."[166]

The contract also has an unusual caveat that states, "And for the punctual performance hereof the Parties bind themselves each to the other in the sum of Forty Pounds." This writer is unsure as to whether this sum of forty pounds is a performance guarantee or some type of insurance bond. At any rate, the contract ends with the two "gentlemen" agreeing that, "the Parties… have herewith interchangeable at their Hands and seals the day and year above written (15 October 1789).[167]

This "hire" system also spurred a new economy in New York City. Insurers, lawyers, clerks, and newspapers were all actively engaged in the establishment and operation of this new vendue, the "hire market" in New York City.[168] This market's operation involved the participation of all of these professionals by way of direct performance or by contracts, advertisements, and risk management. Their participation assisted in elevating this fundamental need for skilled and unskilled labor to a new level of "investment management."

Document 1-1
Indenture of Sam for three years to become Shoemaker[169]

15 October 1789

Document 1-2
Indenture of Sam for three years to become Shoemaker (con't)[170]

15 October 1789

New York State Profits from Sales and Hires of Enslaved African Descendants

The income from the "duty on sales" at vendue provided substantial income to the treasury of the State of New York. Its influence as a positive revenue stream allowed the state to undertake the numerous activities of governance from a sounder fiscal position. In 1804, the duty on sales at vendue (slave sales, hires, etc.) amounted to a major portion of the $56,322.69 in vendue duty revenue to the State of New York. This figure was almost equal to the state's interest payments on the debt due to the Bank of New York.[171]

In 1804, Elisha Jenkins, New York State comptroller, warned in his report to the legislature that:

> *[t]he duty received on sales at public vendue is considerably less than during the preceding year; this may in part be attributed to the derangement of business in the city of New York in consequence of the prevalence of the epidemic [Yellow Fever or Small Pox] during the last autumn. A similar cause may again affect the sales at public vendue, the estimate is therefore reduced to 35,000 Dollars.[172]*

This reduction in estimated revenue over a two-year period would have significantly reduced the state's ability to provide basic services to New Yorkers. In fact, the estimated loss of $35,000 in vendue income in 1805 would constitute a loss of approximately 1 percent of the entire revenue anticipated by the State of New York in 1805.[173] It could be argued that the epidemic that caused this reduction in potential revenue to the state was affecting not only the sale of slaves themselves but additionally the "hire market."

The skills of enslaved Africans were of such value that their "masters" even rented (hired) them out to non-slaveholders as a means of helping neighbors meet their labor requirements. This aspect of enslavement in the north (the hiring out of one's slaves) and particularly in New York was the cornerstone upon which the slave system in New York continued to grow and impact every aspect of the state's economy. This labor system in eighteenth-century New York City resembled that of the Southern colonies, which also encouraged the arrival of a large number of slaves at the expense of European immigration. With the establishment of the Market House at Wall Street, New York's implementation of this "hiring" system grew to the point that it was unequaled in any of the other colonies, with returns on "hires" of between 10 to 30 percent annually on their market value.[174]

In upstate New York, on the large estates and manors, the estates' holders rented out enslaved Africans to the tenants of their estates. This process was established in an effort to increase tenant production and share the maintenance costs of the slaves themselves.[175] An example of this practice follows:

> *In 1755 John Langdon, Sr. rented his slave Pomp and six oxen to a Mr. Clarkson, for two days at £14, two more days at £20, one day for £12, one more day for £12, then rented Pomp alone (without the oxen) for 2 days for "a holing[hauling] of dong" for £24.*[176]

As commerce in humans gradually came more and more under the control of independent New York businessmen, there existed in the first half of the eighteenth century a 100-percent markup on retailed slaves. Between a third and a quarter of New York's 400 merchants were concerned in one way or another in the slave trade in the mid-eighteenth century.[177]

Once New Yorkers established linkages to correspondents who could offer Africans in return for northern grain and provisions, they acquired a steady, if small, stream of seasoned island enslaved labor as partial payment for cargoes. Indeed, in those years, one-third of New York City's vessels returned home with slaves from the West Indies.[178] The slave trade became one of the cornerstones of New York's commercial prosperity in the eighteenth century.[179]

Document 2
Hire-out Agreement For An African American Family[180]

31 December 1821

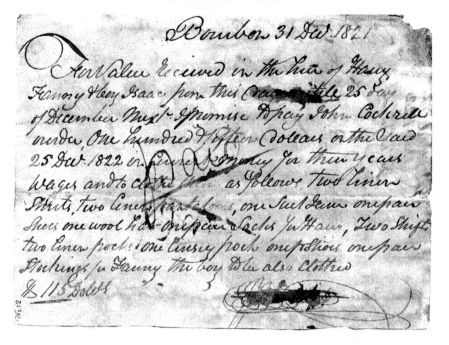

This is a one-year hire-out agreement for an African-American family (Harry, Fanny, and Isaac) for $115. The agreement specifies the clothes and other essentials are to be provided to the family

Numerous accounts record that in the mid-eighteenth century in the midst of pre- revolutionary war rhetoric with respect to British controls on trade, "…at least 130 voyages to various parts of West Africa took place between 1748 and 1772, returning to New York City with greater numbers of slaves than previously. By the eve of the Revolution, city merchants could make the dubious claim of having imported or smuggled at least 3,000 slaves."[181]

Apparently, no social stigma was attached to being a slave trader in colonial New York, as it was in the South. It was considered another business venture open to men with capital to invest, perhaps if anything more likely to produce quick profits. By 1747, most of the city's Africans entered from Africa on the vessels of a very few successful transatlantic importers.[182] New York was the developing center of incipient American capitalism with merchant capital resources residing there. In later years, the "Report on Manufactures" by Alexander Hamilton as secretary of the treasury would indicate that New York's hegemony in the traditional capitalist enterprises was well understood. Enslavement flourished in New York because of this redirected approach to slave labor and manufacturing and the scarcity of immigrant white workers.

As an example of the enormity of the impact of enslavement on New Yorkers, slaveholders very often used enslaved "human property" to pay debts of every kind. They (slaves) stood as security for the purchase of land and other commodities; were taxed and branded like other property; and were even given to relatives as wedding gifts or willed to assorted family members upon the death of their master.[183]

OTHER REVENUE DERIVED FROM AFRICAN ENSLAVEMENT

Enslavement was also viewed as a "cash cow" to the fiscal viability of Colonial New York. In 1734, the Colonial Assembly enacted a law that required a duty for every "Negro, Indian and Malatta Slave" owned in the colony of New York to be used to build fortifications in anticipation of war[184]. In November 1740, to further support the colonial government, it placed a duty on the importation of slaves.

> *For every Negro, Mulatto, or other slave, of four years old and upwards, imported directly from Africa, five Ounces of Sevil, Pillar, or Mexico Plate, or Forty Shillings, in Bills of Credit made current in this Colony. For every such Slave, as aforesaid, of four Years old and upwards, imported from all other places, by Land or Water, the Sum of Four Pounds, in like money.[185]*

Effect on Upstate New York

Enslavement and its degrading tenets of "buying and selling" innocent men, women and children had a significant impact on other areas of New York State, including the mid-Hudson region. Slave ships landed at Poughkeepsie (Dutchess County), New York and the slaves were taken to Katherine Street., where a slave market was located. In addition, the docks at the lower end of Kingston (Ulster County), New York housed a slave market. Another existed in front of the old Lutheran Church on Washington Ave. in Athens (Greene County), New York. [186]

While most upstate cities and towns began to experience the "curse of enslavement," small local towns like Waterford, New York, had been involved in enslavement for centuries. Sydney Ernest Hammersly in *The History of Waterford* speaks of its existence in Waterford. Hammersley recounts the first arrival of Africans to Waterford as follows: "These unfortunates first came to our shores in the West India Company's slave ship in 1647. They were sold for peas and pork."[187]

Historians have surmised that enslavement was so central to the economy in the early days of America that almost every business benefited from it. Eric Foner, professor of history at Columbia University has stated that "[t]he entire economy of this country was based on slavery, north as well as south." In addition, he informs us that, "New York had a stranglehold on the cotton trade which made up half the total value of U.S. exports in 1850" and "Brooks Brothers supplied a lot of clothing to plantation owners. Merchants, manufacturers, everyone felt the economic ripples."[188]

URBAN ENSLAVEMENT AND WASHINGTON, D.C.

This practice of "urban enslavement," the hiring market for slaves existed in all of the major cities in the east as well as in the south. Washington, D.C., the nation's Capitol, was literally built with "hired" enslaved labor. When the newly formed United States government embarked on public works, it hired slave labor. In fact, the Treasury Department paid the absentee masters for the use of their human chattel with federal funds.

In order to protect slaveholders in the city, a special tax was levied on nonresident slave labor. Wedged between two slave states

(Maryland and Virginia), the District of Columbia was ideally situated to become the hub of the domestic slave trade. With the increased demand for enslaved African descendants caused by the expansion of cotton cultivation in the lower South and the slow but steady reduction of tobacco cultivation in Maryland and Virginia, a growing "surplus" of enslaved African descendants developed in the vicinity of the capital.[189]

In his narrative *Twelve years a slave. Narrative of Solomon Northup, a citizen of New York, kidnapped in Washington City in 1841 and rescued in 1853, from a cotton plantation near the Red River in Louisiana* Solomon Northrup recounts his first experiences after being kidnapped in Washington, D. C. He also describes the shocking proximity of his initial holding pen to the United States Capitol.

The building to which the yard was attached, was two stories high, fronting on one of the public streets of Washington. Its outside presented only the appearance of a quiet private residence. A stranger looking at it, would never have dreamed of its execrable uses. Strange as it may seem, within plain sight of this same house, looking down from its commanding height upon it, was the Capitol. The voices of patriotic representatives boasting of freedom and equality, and the rattling of the poor slave's chains, almost commingled. A slave pen within the very shadow of the Capitol!

Such is a correct description as it was in 1841, of Williams' slave pen in Washington, in one of the cellars of which I found myself so unaccountably confined.[190]

He continues by describing his first encounter with his new "slave master," James H. Burch:

Well, my boy, how do you feel now?" said Burch, as he entered through the open door. I replied that I was sick, and inquired the cause of my imprisonment. He answered that I was his slave— that he had bought me, and that he was about to send me to New-Orleans. I asserted, aloud and boldly, that I was a freeman—a resident of Saratoga, where I had a wife and children, who were also free, and that my name was Northup.

I complained bitterly of the strange treatment I had received, and threatened, upon my liberation, to have satisfaction for the wrong. He denied that I was free, and with an emphatic oath, declared that I came from Georgia. Again and again I asserted I was no man's slave, and insisted upon his taking off my chains at once. He endeavored to hush me, as if he feared my voice would be overheard. But I would not be silent, and denounced the authors of my imprisonment, whoever they might be, as unmitigated villains. Finding he could not quiet me, he flew into a towering passion. With blasphemous oaths, he called me a black liar, a runaway from Georgia, and every other profane and vulgar epithet that the most indecent fancy could conceive.[191]

The erratic returns from the tobacco culture and the increasing diversification of crops in the western counties of Maryland and Virginia made slaveholders only happy to meet the labor demands for building the United State's Capitol by hiring out their surplus enslaved African descendants. A great portion of the labor on public works in Washington, D.C. was performed by enslaved African descendants. The workforce which built the Capitol, itself was made up for the most part of a group of ninety enslaved African descendants hired for that purpose.[192] Enslaved African descendants hired from their masters by Pierre L'Enfant began the work on the construction of the White House.

Since much was accomplished very quickly there must have been many; the conditions of their labor from daybreak to dark under the command of tough, hard-drinking James Dermott can only be imagined.[193]

In September 1794, the cornerstone of the White House was laid. While real work would not begin until the next April, masons began preparing stone, which enslaved African descendants hauled up from boats that came from Virginia quarries. Due to the lack of skilled labor in Washington, DC, the White House master stonemason, Collen Williamson, had to train "hired slaves" on the spot at the quarry to cut the stone to build the foundation of the White House.[194]

At year's end the commissioners bragged that they "could not have done without slaves. They were a check on the white laborers, and by 1797 they would rent 125 slaves to work in the city."[195]

The major supplier of slaves was Edmund Plowden, who lived in St. Mary County and owned sixty-four enslaved African descendants. His Moses, Len, Jim, and Arnold worked at the White House. His enslaved African descendants named Gerard, Tony and Jack worked at the Capitol. In December 1794, laborers were paid forty-five shillings a month, about six dollars. So Plowden made forty-two dollars a month without obligation except to provide his enslaved workers a blanket.

There were also middlemen who formed crews of enslaved workers and offered them to the commissioners. In November 1794, John Slye applied to be an overseer claiming "his friends... have engaged to hire to the city thirty valuable Negro men slaves." Slye had previously worked for the Potomac Company and had brought twenty enslaved workers to work for that company. The Commissioners did not pass up Slye's offer and hired him to oversee laborers at the White House for fifteen dollars a month. What percentage Slye took of the annual rental made by the thirty enslaved workers he brought to the city is not known.[196] Enslaved African descendants who labored on these projects did not work out of sight of their "masters" for they also worked for the city. Middleton Belt who supervised the overseers rented two enslaved workers that he owned, Peter at the Capitol and Jack at the White House. Even one of the commissioners, Gustavus Scott, rented two of his enslaved African descendants, Bob and Kitt who worked at the White House.[197] Surely these attempts at illegal profit making violated some federal code of ethics. And yet during this period in American history profits and not ethics were the prevailing standards. It would seem that not much has changed over the centuries since enslavement was abolished; profit at the expense of ethics is still the standard in America.

Between 1795 and 1797, funds for continued construction of the Capitol were in short supply. Commissioner Thornton came up with an idea to get obedient and cheap masons: buy "50 intelligent Negroes" and train them to do the stonework. Two of three experienced men could be induced with a wage of up to four dollars a day to train and supervise the slaves. As an incentive for the enslaved workers, who would not only get room, board and clothing, the Commissioners would give them their freedom in five or six years.

Although nothing came of the idea, it highlights how uncomfortable the commissioners were with free labor. They preferred workers who could make no demands and who were beholden to them for everything they knew.[198]

ENDNOTES

1   Claude Meillassoux, The Slave Route, UNESCO

2   Oscar Williams, *African Americans and Colonial Legislation in the Middle Colonies,* (Garland Publishing, 1998). 3

3   IBID

4   *http://www.nnp.org/newvtour/regions/Albany/*

5   Hereafter referred to as simply: the company

6   New Netherland was a Dutch colony in North America along the Hudson and lower Delaware rivers. The first settlement was made at Fort Orange (now Albany, NY) in 1624, although the colony centered on New Amsterdam at the tip of Manhattan Island after 1625-1626. New Netherland was annexed by the English and renamed New York in 1664.

7   Williams, *African Americans and Colonial Legislation in the Middle Colonies, .4*

8   See: Hugh Thomas, *The Slave Trade,* (Touchstone; 1997); Oliver A. Rink, *Holland on the Hudson: An Economic and Social History of Dutch New York,* Ithaca: Cornell University Press, 1986); Dennis J. Maika, *Commerce and Community: Manhattan Merchants in the Seventeenth Century,* (New York: NYU Press, 1995); John Franklin Jameson, *Narratives of New Netherland, 1609-1664,* (Scribner 1909).

9   Map by Marco Ramerini (*http://www.geocities.com/Athens/Styx/6497/ newnether.html)*

10 New Netherland Project, (*www.nnp.or*g)

11 Ibid

12 Kim, Sung Bok *Landlord and Tenant in Colonial New York,* (Chapel Hill: The University of North Carolina Press, 1978) 6

13 Hugh Thomas, The Slave Trade, (Touchstone; 1997); Oliver A. Rink, Holland on the Hudson: An Economic and Social History of Dutch New York, Ithaca: Cornell University Press, 1986); Dennis J. Maika, Commerce and Community: Manhattan Merchants in the Seventeenth

Century, (New York: NYU Press, 1995); John Franklin Jameson, Narratives of New Netherland, 1609-1664, (Scribner 1909). **For description of Patroon Benefits**: see Kim, 6,

[14] Jonathan Earle, *The Routledge Atlas of African American History,* New York and London: Routledge, 2000),25

[15] **NOTE:** The Triangle trade was not a tidy loop connecting Europe, Africa and the New World. The multiple land and sea paths that took millions of Africans from their homelands to slavery in the New World did not fit into any neat triangle but did include manufactured goods from Europe being sent to Africa to trade for slaves, who were sent to the Caribbean and the colonies which in turn sent foodstuff, furs and raw materials to Europe, which again sent manufactured goods to Africa to trade for slaves.

[16] Herbert S. Klein, *The Atlantic Slave Trade,* (Boston, MA:Cambridge University Press, 1999) 76-77

[17] *www.nysm.nysed.gov/albanyrensselaerswyck.html#map#map.*

[18] The Albany Project

[19] Ibid

[20] **NOTE**: In 1683, after New Netherland was acquired by England, the British Governor Thomas Dongan divided colonial New York (New Netherland) into twelve counties with Albany County becoming one of the original counties. Until the later part of the 18th century, Albany County was thought to be the entire upriver region of the province. In fact, its land mass encompassed the greater part of upriver colonial New York. In 1774, Albany was the most populated county in colonial New York with 42,706 settlers. By 1790, the population had reached 75,921 inhabitants and it was still the most populated county in what was now New York State. During the period from 1772 to 1809, the county was divided, resulting in the establishment of Charlotte (Washington); Montgomery; Tryon (Montgomery); Columbia; Rensselaer; Saratoga; Schoharie; Greene; and Schenectady Counties. The resulting population of Albany County was thereby reduced to 25,155 inhabitants by 1800. See Colonial Albany Social History Project, Albany County, nysed.gov/Albany/albanycounty.html

[21] *http://www.loc.gov/rr/hispanic/portam/img/ribero1.jpg*

22 Simon Hart, *The Prehistory of the New Netherland Company,* Amsterdam Notarial Records of the first Dutch voyagers to the Hudson, (City of Amsterdam Press 1959)

23 Ibid, 26

24 Ibid, 80

25 Ibid, 82

26 Hodges, 6-7;: Edwin G Burrows and Mike Wallace. *Gotham: A History of New York City to 1898,* 19; Leslie M. Harris, *In the Shadow of Slavery: African Americans in New York City, 1626 –1863,* (Chicago: The University of Chicago Press, 2003) 12-13. Also see: Manus, Negro Slavery in New York, 3-4; Rink, Holland on the Hudson, 79-81.

27 Gibbs, C.R., *Black Explorers,* (Three Dimensional Publishing Co, 1992).

28 E. B. O'Callaghan, ed., *Voyage of the Slavers St. John and Arms of Amsterdam,* 1867, J. Munsell, xiii; also see Oscar Williams, *African Americans and Colonial Legislation in the Middle Colonies,* see "An Act of the Director and Council of New Netherlands" passed 25 February 1644.

29 E.B. O'Callaghan, Laws and Ordinances of New Netherland, 1638-1674, (Albany, NY : Weed,Parsons and Company, 1968)

30 E.B. O'Callaghan, *Colonial Records of New York*, Vol.I, 99

31 IBID,154, 364

32 E. B. O'Callaghan, ed., *Voyage of the Slavers St. John and Arms of Amsterdam*, Albany, 1967,. xiii

33 E. B. O'Callaghan, *Documents* 2:213-14

34 Henry Wysham Lanier, *Greenwich Village: Today and Yesterday,* (Harper and Brothers, 1949), 79

35 Richard S. Dunn, Sugar and Slaves, (Chapel Hill: University of North Carolina Press, 1972), 60-6.

36 Berlin, 49

37 Lanier, 79

[38] Isabelle Aguet, A Pictorial History of the Slave Trade (Geneva: Editions Minerva, 1971), plate 79, 82; original source not identified.

[39] E. B. O'Callaghan, 101-102

[40] Refers to the "African Holocaust"

[41] Herren XIX to Pieter Stuyvesant, 23 March 1654, in O'Callaghan, ed., Documents Relative to Colonial New York 14:304-5.

[42] Library of Congress Rare Book and Special Collections Division

[43] Stanley M. Elkins, *Slavery*, (Chicago: University of Chicago Press, 1968), 96-97

[44] John Thornton, *African and Africans in the Making of the Atlantic World, 1400-1800*; (Cambridge University Press, 1998), 149-150

[45] Ibid, 150

[46] Curtis P. Nettels, *The Roots of American Civilization*, (Appleton-Century-Crofts1963), 200-201; also see

Oliver A. Rink; Dennis J. Maika; John Franklin Jameson

[47] Edgar J. McManus, *A History of Negro Slavery in New York*, (Syracuse, NY: Syracuse University Press, 1966), 4

[48] See Williams, *African Americans and Colonial Legislation in the Middle Colonies.*, 14

[49] *African Burial Grounds*, History Statement, General Services Administration, *gsa.gov*, hereafter referred to as: *African Burial Grounds*; McManus, 6,

[50] See: Oliver A. Rink, *Holland on the Hudson: An Economic and Social History of Dutch New York*, , (Ithaca, NY: Cornell University Press,1986); Dennis J. Maika, *Commerce and Community: Manhattan Merchants in the Seventeenth Century*, (New York: NYU Press, 1995;) John Franklin Jameson, *Narratives of New Netherland*, 1609-1664, (Scribner Publishing, 1909)

[51] Oliver A. Rink, *Holland on the Hudson*, 7, 212-213; Lanier, 79

[52] Joyce D. Goodfriend, *Before the Melting Pot*, (Princeton, NJ: Princeton University Press, 1992), 8

53   Ibid, 9

Oliver Rink in <u>Holland on the Hudson</u> has identified four firms that controlled more that 50% of the New Netherland to Holland trade during the period from 1640 throughout the Dutch era. These four firms were the merchant houses of Kiliaen van Rensselaer, Gilles and Seth Verbrugge, Dirck and Abel de Wolff and Gillis van Hoornbeeck. These four companies worked together to control most of the profits from the New Netherlands trade.

54   Maritime History of New York, Federal Writer's Project: Philadelphia, (Doubleday, Doran & Co., 1937) 27

55   See Sung Bok Kim, *Landlord and Tenant in Colonial New York*

56   Graham Russell Hodges, *Slavery, Freedom & Culture*, (M. E. Sharpe, Inc., 1998) 32

57   Berlin, 51

58   *Slavery in the Mid-Atlantic*, New York, *www.geocities.com/etymonline/ cw/northstate2.htm*

59   Ira Berlin, Many Thousands Gone, (Boston: The Belknap Press of Harvard University Press, 1998) 48

60   Columbia University Library, *http://projects.ilt.columbia.edu/Seneca/ AfAMNYC/01bAfAmNYC.html*

61   See C. H. Wilson, *Profit and Power*, 1957; P. Geyl, *Orange and Stuart, 1641-1672*, 1970

62   (*http://projects.ilt.columbia.edu/Seneca/AfAMNYC/03aAfAmNYC. html*)

63   E. B. O'Callaghan, 202

64   Michael Kammen, *Colonial New York,*: A History, (Oxford University Press, 1975), 179; McManus, Negro Slavery in New York, 41-43.

65   Charles Swain, A History of African Americans in Early New York, 4; Also see: Bruce, The Empire State in Three Centuries, 244

66   *African Burial Grounds*

[67] Davis, "Slavery in Colonial New York City," 72-80; Graham Hodges, Root and Branch, 36-38.

NOTE: Chapter 160 of the Laws of 1706 of the Colony of New York stated that, "be it declar'd and Enacted by the Governr, Council & Assembly and by the Authority of the same, That all and every Negro, Indian Mulatto and Mestee Bastard Child & Children who is, are and shall be born of any Negro, Indian, Mulatto or Mestee, shall follow ye State and Condition of the Mother & be esteemed reputed taken & adjudged a Slave & Slaves to all intents & purposes whatsoever." ; also see Sherrill D. Wilson, New York City's African Slaveholders: A Social and Material Culture History, (Garland Publishing, 1994) 38

[68] Hugh Thomas, *The Slave Trade*, (NYC: Touchstone, 1997), 203; also see Ira Berlin, Many Thousands Gone, , (Boston: The Belknap Press of Harvard University Press, 1998) 48

[69] *The Dutch Imprint,* Cross Roads & Cross Rivers: Africans at Phillipsburg Manor, Upper Mills, (*www.hudsonvalley.org*)

[70] Adolph Phillipse's Probate Inventory, 2 February 1750, New York Public Library

[71] **Workforce population**: See Peter Charles Hoffer, Law and People in Colonial America, (Baltimore, MD: The John Hopkins University Press, 1998) 124; **Slave skills and experience**: See Elkins, 94-95; Phillips, 98-114, McManus, 47-48; also see New York Gazette and Weekly Post Boy, March 26, 1749 and July 20, 1747; White, 10-12, A. J. Williams-Myers, Long Hammering, (Trenton, NJ: Black World Press, 1994) 7, Goodfriend, 118-119

[72] Charles B. Swain, "Black's roots in Albany: Old as Fort Orange", Viewpoint, Times Union Newspaper, Feb. 19, 1983

[73] Ibid

[74] Theodore Corbett, Saratoga County Blacks, 1720-1870, *The GRIST MILL*, Quarterly Journal of the Saratoga County Historical Society, vol. XX, no. 3, 1986, 2

[75] Ibid

[76] Evanrt Greene and Virginia Harrington, American Population before the Federal Census of 1790, (New York: Columbia University Press, 1932) 95, 100-101

[77] Graham Russell Hodges, *Slavery and Freedom in the Rural North* , (Madison House Publishers, Inc., 1997) 20

[78] E. Wilder Spaulding, *New York in the Critical Period,* ,New York,1932, 45; also see McManus, Lanier

[79] Thornton, 148-149

[80] Ibid

[81] **Concerning skills of Africans**: See McManus, xi - xii; Ulrich B. Phillips, American Negro Slavery, (New York, 1918,) 98-114; **For Transformation role**: See Arthur Zilversmit, The First Emancipation: The Abolition of Slavery in the North, (Chicago: The University of Chicago Press, 1967) 34

[82] McManus, pg. 197-200

[83] Matthew T. Mellon, *Early American Views on Negro Slavery,* ,(New York: Bergman Publishers, 1969) 165; also see McManus, 3

[84] Williams,17

[85] Mellon, 167

[86] **Escaping from slavery**; over a third of the advertisements in local newspapers indicated that fugitive slaves left their holders to visit a spouse, a child, or other relatives. **Rebellion:** Benjamin Quarles, Black Abolitionists, (Oxford University Press; 1969); McManus, 139-140; White 49

[87] **Growth of slavery**: See A. J. Williams-Myers, "Long Hammering, 21; Greene and Harrison, 92, 95-102; McManus, 25; Thomas J. Davis, A Rumor of Revolt: The 'Great Negro Plot' in Colonial New York, , (NYC: Free Press, , (Macmillan Inc.), 1985) 252; **For Ulster County**: See Williams-Myers, 3

[88] The Albany Common Council twice passed this ordinance.

[89] Jonathan Earle, "The Routledge Atlas of African American History,",(New York Routledge, , 2000) 26; McManus, 123

90   Scott, Kenneth. "Ulster County, NY: Court Records 1693 - 1775." Washington, DC: *National Genealogical Society Quarterly*, volume 60 (Dec. 1972), 277

91   **Slaves outside of British Law**: Williams, 46; **Fear of Insurrection**: Mellon, 166-167, also see 32, 89; Herbert Aptheker, American Negro Slave Revolts, (International Publishers, Co., 1969) 18-52

92   Chapter 149 of the Laws of 1705 of the Colony of New York

93   Ibid; Similar policies existed in New Jersey and Pennsylvania, see Edward R. Turner, The Negro in Pennsylvania, (Washington, D.C., 1911) 26-29

94   Chapter 308 of the Laws of 1715 of the Colony of New York

95   C. M. Woolsey, *The History of the Town of Marlborough, Ulster County, New York from Its Earliest Discovery,* 225

96   Albany Common Council Law of 1733

97   Graham Russell Hodges and Alan Eward Brown, Editors, "Pretends to Be Free" Runaway Slave

Announcements, (New York and London: Garland Publishing, Inc., 1994) xix

98   *African Burial Grounds*

99   Wilder, 17

100   See Wilder, 222, Notes to Chapter 1, No.16 - Letter reprinted in Gabriel Furman, *Antiquities of Long Island* (1874; Port Washington, NY: Ira J. Friedman, 1968) 221-22. (Emphasis Wilder's).

101   Chapter 181 of the Laws of 1708

102   Wilder, 16

103   Chapter 181 of the Laws of 1708; also see Williams, 49

104   Edgar Mc Manus, *A History of Negro Slavery in New York,* (Syracuse, NY: Syracuse University Press, 2001), 106

105   Ibid

[106] **For details of this rebellion see**: Benjamin Quarles, Black Abolitionists, (Oxford University Press, 1969); Herbert Aptheker, American Negro Slave Revolts, International Publishers, Co., pg. 172; Africans in America, Narrative- The Growth of Slavery in North America, pbs. org; Kenneth Scott, "The Slave Insurrection in New York in 1712", New York Historical Quarterly, 1961, XLV, pg. 45; Herbert Aptheker, Essays on the History of the Negro, (NY: International Publishers, 1945) pg. 19; Thomas J. Davis, A Rumor of Revolt: The "Great Negro Plot" in Colonial New York., (NYC: Free Press Macmillian Inc., 1985) 54-55

[107] Edgar Mayhew Bacon, *Chronicles of Tarrytown and Sleepy Hollow,* (G.P. Putmans's Sons, 1897), 142

[108] Chapter 250 of the Laws of 1712 of the Colony of New York

[109] Craig Steven Wilder, *In the Company of Men: The African Influence on African American Culture in New York City,*(New York: New York University Press, 2001) 14

[110] Earle, 27

[111] Joyce D. Goodfriend, *Before the Melting Pot*, Princeton Princeton, NJ: University Press, 1992) Introduction, 6

[112] Graham Hodges, Root and Branch, 100-102,115-119; also see Harris, *In the Shadow of Slavery*

[113] Thomas J. Davis,. ix

[114] Earle, 27; T. Wood Clarke, "The Negro Plot of 1741", *New York History*, 1944, 167-181, Thomas J. Davis, ix; George Ellis, *The Puritan Age and Rule in the Colony of Massachusetts Bay 1629-1685*, 3rd ed. (Boston: Houghton, Mifflin, 1891), 563; Mrs. John King Van Rensselaer, *The Goede Vrouw of Mana-ha-ta at Home and in Society, 1609-1760,* (Charles Scribner's Sons, 1898) Chapter XX; also see William Smith, *The History of the Province of New York*, ed. Michael Kammen, (Boston: Harvard University Press, 1972)

[115] See Thomas J. Davis, A Rumor of Revolt: The 'Great Negro Plot' in Colonial New York, (NYC: Free Press, (Macmillan Inc.) 1985)

[116] Williams, note 45, 79

[117] Reproduced from Daniel Horsmanden - New York Conspiracy, 1744, reprinted 1810,

   http://www.hudsonvalley.org/crossroads/image/image31.html

[118] Davis,250-263

[119] Wilder, 23

[120] See McManus, 139; Thomas, 462 and A. J. Williams-Myers,6, 56-60

[121] O'Callaghan, Laws of New Netherlands, 7

[122] Africans in America/Part 1, *www.pbs.org/wgbh/aia/part1/1h302.html*

[123] Wilson, 28

[124] The year 1830 represents the U.S. Federal Census' cutoff date that this is the last year in which there is documentation, which lists Africans as holders of enslaved Africans in New York City. Also See Sherrill D. Wilson, *New York City's African Slaveholders: A Social and Material Culture History,* 1994, Garland Publishing, xi; also see 1830 Federal census; Carter G. Woodson; Eichholz and Rose, *NY State Manumissions*, Yosphe, for more information on this practice of African American Slave holders, and Goodfriend, *Before the Melting Pot*, 117

[125] See Larry Kroger, *Black Slaveholders: Free Black Masters in South Carolina*, 1985

[126] Harry P. Yoshpe "Records of Slave Manumission in New York During the Colonial and Early National Periods", *Journal of Negro History,* vol. XXVI, 1941, 81,84,85

[127] See Sherrill D. Wilson, *New York City's African Slaveholders: A Social and Material Culture History,* (Garland Publishing,1994)

[128] Carter G. Woodson, v

[129] Africans in America, *www.pbs.org*

[130] Venture Smith, A Narrative of the Life and Adventures of Venture, A Native of Africa: But refident above fixty years in the United State of America. Related by Himself, New London: printed by C. Holt, at the BEE-Office, 1798 (Africans in America: www.pbs.org) **This**

passage has been modified from the original to make it easier to read. Colonial 'f'' changed to modern day 's'.

[131] Ibid   **This passage has also been modified from the original to make it easier to read. Colonial 'f' changed to modern day 's'.**

[132] The Courant Newspaper (COURANT FILE PHOTO), Copyright 2005

[133] Berlin,. 233

[134] Williams, 20

[135] Berlin, 177

[136] **Reshaping the lives of Slaves:** Berlin, 177; **New York's seaport and the slave trade:** Richard Morris, Forward, The History of Negro Slavery in New York by Edgar J. McManus; Kenneth M. Stampp, The Peculiar Institution, (Vintage Books, 1956) 271-272; Richard C. Wade, Slavery in the Cities, (Oxford University Press, 1964) 6

[137] Graham Russell Hodges and Alan Eward Brown, eds. *"Pretends to be Free": Runaway Slave Advertisements from Colonial and Revolutionary New York and New Jersey* (New York and London: Garland Publishing,1994) xxi

[138] Hodges and Brown, xix

[139] Graham Russell Hodges and Alan Eward Brown, eds, xxi

[140] See Gilbert S. Bahn, *Slaves and Nonwhite Free persons in the 1790 Federal Census of New York (* Baltimore: Clearfield Press, 2000)

[141] Shane White, *Somewhat more independent: the end of slavery in New York City, 1770-1810*, (Athens Press-University of Georgia, 1991), 1 and 16; Thomas J. White, ix

[142] Hodges, 164

[143] 1790 United States Census

[144] Shane White, *Somewhat more independent: the end of slavery in New York City, 1770-1810* (Athens Press-University of Georgia, 1991) 1 and 16.

[145] Ibid, 19

[146]   White, 5-6

[147]   Ibid

[148]   McManus, A History of Negro Slavery, 97-100; Thomas J. David, "New York's Long Black Line: A note on the Growing Slave Population, 1626-1790, "Afro-Americans in New York Life and History, 2 (January 1978) :46-51

[149]   O'Callaghan, E.B. The Documentary History of the State of New York. 4 volumes. Albany, NY: Weed, Parsons & Co., Public Printers, 1850, . 849

[150]   Greene and Harrington, 105

[151]   Colonial Albany Social History Project

[152]   Greene and Harrington, 105

[153]   1790 United States Census Data, *1790 County Level Census Data – Sorted by State/County Name, (http://fisher.lib.virginia.edu/cgi-local/ censusbin/census/cen.pl)*

[154]   Ibid

[155]   1800 United States Federal Census

[156]   White, 52

[157]   Washington County Historical Society, *History of Washington County, New York; Some Chapters in the History of the Town of Easton, N.Y.,* 1959, 07-112

Note: A few of these Easton slaves remained in the town for three and four generations. As late as 1957 the remains of two of their descendants were sent from a distant city for burial in the family lot in the Greenwich Cemetery.

[158]   Berlin,186-187

[159]   Shane White, *Somewhat more independent: the end of slavery in New York City, 1770-1810,* Athens Press-University of Georgia, 3-4 and 25-27 also see Berlin, 55

[160]   McManus, 53, Williams-Myers,3

[161] McManus, 53

[162] Austin Steward, Twenty-Two Years a Slave, and Forty Years a Freeman; Embracing a Correspondence of Several Years, While President of Wilberforce Colony, London, Canada West., (Rochester, N.Y.: William Alling, 1857),92

[163] Ibid,96

[164] Williams quoting NY City Common Council Ordinance of 1731

[165] Single folder, EV749/*Slave Documents - 1775-282*, Collections, Albany Institute of History and Art

[166] Ibid

[167] Ibid

[168] Note: Webster's Dictionary defines 'vendue' as: Auction, a public sale of anything by outcry to the highest bidder.

[169] Single folder, EV749/*Slave Documents - 1775-282*, Collections, Albany Institute of History and Art

[170] Ibid

[171] Journal of the Assembly of the State of New York, 1804, 39-45

Note: It is difficult to ascertain, at this time, what percentage of these collected duties were directly related to slave sales, due to the lack of specificity in the Budget documents, themselves.

[172] Ibid, 24

[173] Ibid, 19

[174] McManus, 54; **For increased reliance on slave labor:** See Berlin, Many Thousand Gone, 82, 109-114

[175] Harris, 31; also see A. J. Williams-Myers, 49

[176] Valerie Cunningham, "Slaves & The Langdon Family"; *www. seacoastnh.com*

[177] Thomas, 271

[178] Cathy Matson, *Merchants & Empire: Trading in Colonial New York*, (The John Hopkins University Press, 1998) 202; New York City importers

[179] John R. Spears, The American Slave Trade, 1901, Scribner's Sons, 90-91

[180] Corlis-Respess Family Papers, Filson Special Collections, Filson Historical Society:

[181] Matson, 203

[182] See Swain, 4 and Matson, 203

[183] Sherrill D. Wilson, *New York City African Slaveholders: A social and material culture history*, 1994, Garland Publishing, ix; A. J. F. Van Laer, *Early records of the City and County of Albany and Colony of Rensselaerswyck*, 1916-1919, Albany: University of the State of New York, 149

[184] Chapter 624 of the Laws of 1734 of the Colony of New York

[185] C. M. Woolsey, *History of the Town of Marlborough, Ulster County, New York from Its Earliest Discovery*, (J. B. Lyon, 1908) 226

[186] Charles Swain, *A History of African-Americans in Early New York State*, Introduction

[187] Sydney Ernest Hammersly, *The History of Waterford*, 1957, Published by Col. Sydney E. Hammersley, Waterford, NY, Chapter Twenty-two, "Slavery in Waterford,195

[188] Eric Foner quoted in "Honoring Slaves: Calls for Slavery Restitution Getting Louder", *loper.org*

[189] *Timeline: History of Slavery and Racism, 1790 – 1829*, http://innercity. org/holt/slavechron.html

[190] Solomon Northrup, "*Twelve years a slave. Narrative of Solomon Northup, a citizen of New York, kidnapped in Washington City in 1841and rescued in 1853, from a cotton plantation near the Red River in Louisiana*", (Auburn: Derby and Miller, Buffalo: Derby, Orton and Mulligan, London: Sampson Low, Sons& Co., 1853), 42-43

[191] Ibid, 43-44

192   Captain Basil Hall, *Travels in North America in the Years 1827-1828* (Edinburgh, 1829)vol. II 46; Robert Sutcliff, *Travels in Some Parts of North America, In the Years 1804, 1805 and 1806* (York, 1815), 112, as cited by Letitia W Brown, Residence Patterns of Negroes in the District of Columbia, 1800-1860, *Records of the Columbia Historical Society of Washington DC*, 1969-70, 67-68

193   Ibid

194   Ibid

195   Bob Arnebeck, *Slaves at the Founding.* Early Washington History (*http://members.aol.com/_ht_a/swamp1800/slaves.html*)

196   Ibid

197   Ibid

198   Bob Arnebeck, "Through A Fiery Trial, Building Washington, 1790-1800," (Madison Books, MD. 1991) Thornton to Commissioners, July 18, 1795. Proceedings, July 22, 1795. Cited on 302

CHAPTER II

THE PATH TO ABOLITION IN NEW YORK STATE

THE PATH TO ABOLITION

By 1784, the states of New England as well as Pennsylvania had adopted measures, which either abolished slavery outright or provided for its gradual abolition. However, New York State balked at resolving the issue of slavery. [1]

INTRODUCTION

Deep-rooted white prejudices, the fear of large numbers of free African descendants, the impossibility of assimilating them into white society, and the need for a large and cheap servile labor force had combined to frustrate and defeat any plan for gradual abolition or immediate emancipation for that matter.

Human enslavement was deeply entrenched in the Dutch communities of the southern portion of New York State and these communities' primary source of position and wealth derived essentially from the forced labor of enslaved Africans and their descendants. Various books have spoken of the vast involvement of Dutch farmers and businesses in the institution of enslavement in New York State and its continued proliferation.[2] Perhaps because of their early attachment, Dutch farmers in New York were particularly wedded to African bonded labor.[3] William Strickland in his *Journal of a Tour of the United States of America 1794-1795,* observed that in the 1790s, "many of the old Dutch farmers… have 20-30 slaves [and] to their care and management everything is left."[4] Dutch interests in prolonging the existence of enslavement and the financial position that this economic system afforded them will be discussed in this chapter.

As the various states in the North began to focus their litigious and legislative energies on the issue of emancipation beginning with Vermont constitutionally banning enslavement in 1777, New York presented an important exception. Slave labor played a much more indispensable role in New York than in the rest of the North and the institution emerged more strongly entrenched in the society and economy of the state after the Revolution than it had before.

THE INITIAL EFFORTS AT ABOLITION

During the first century and a half of the African presence in Colonial New York, whether ruled by the Dutch or the British, few Whites voiced a public critique of the practice of chattel slavery.

The rhetoric and fanfare of the struggle for independence, in fact, the Revolution itself, created the "problem of enslavement." Having accepted liberty as a fundamental tenet of American society, newly initiated Americans were faced with the prospect of no longer viewing enslavement with the same equanimity of mind as previous generations. The inconsistencies in the ornate nature of the rhetoric of independence and the actual existence of enslavement within America's new democratic society became a troubling proposition for these newly constituted defender s of liberty and justice. In response, a number of states and territories organized abolition societies, including Rhode Island (1785), New York (1785), Illinois (1785), Delaware (1788), Maryland (1789), Connecticut (1790), and New Jersey (1793). In 1794, the American Convention of Abolition Societies was established in Philadelphia to unite the various state societies.[5]

Neither the American Revolution nor the United States Constitution were inspired or conceptualized around the issue or resolution of the "problem of enslavement" in either the United States or New York State. In reality, these two lessons on the value and cost of liberty served to heighten the nagging questions of enslavement in a free society. During the colonial era, very few whites considered enslavement to be a major social problem. During the last decades of the 1700s, very few could deny that it was.

The first formal protest against enslavement in Colonial New York had come at a 1767 meeting in Purchase (Westchester County) when Quakers made a good faith effort to rid their communities of enslavement and the "shadows of sin" they believe it nurtured. Several Quaker congregations even compensated individuals formerly held as slaves by their members.

And yet, even the great intentions of the American Revolution to preserve the rights of all men and establish freedom and equality as the hallmarks of a developing nation began to retreat to the farthermost recesses of historical memory. And, those who had been willing to sacrifice private interest for the common good had long since resumed the individual and basic challenges of their own rigorous existence. If any of them had concerns about enslavement, it did not seem to bother them.[6] Future governor and abolitionist John Jay, himself, explained the simple logic of this reaction, when he said,

> *"... prior to the great revolution, the great majority ... of the people had been so long accustomed to the practice and convenience of having slaves, that very few among them even doubted the propriety and rectitude of it."*[7]

Most of the Revolutionary leaders who came to power in New York in 1777 had anti-enslavement sentiments, yet, as elsewhere in the North, the urgency of the war with Britain made them delay, and they restricted their activity to a policy statement and an appeal to future legislatures "to take the most effective measures consistent with public safety for abolishing domestic enslavement." This resolution passed in the state Constitutional Convention by a vote of 29 to 5.[8]

The war proved particularly destructive in the case of New York, and the state was a battleground from one end to the other. Little was done during the war towards ending enslavement, except that in 1781 the legislature voted to manumit slaves serving in the armed forces.[9] However, the war itself wrought havoc with the institution of enslavement. Many slaves ran off to the British during the occupation of the state. Others achieved freedom by taking up the rebels' offer of manumission in exchange for military service. The slave population of New York City was permanently reduced, when the British and the American Loyalists pulled out of New York at the end of the war, some 3,000 formerly enslaved Africans left with them.

Along with John Jay, Rufus King, Governor Lewis Morris of New York State, and others like Alexander Hamilton who approached the problem of race through a natural rights philosophical lens, insistently arguing that all men were by nature free and equal. If there were inequalities between the races, it was "probably" due to environmental factors that led to a want of cultivation on the part of African descendants.

Hamilton's position on the cause of the abolition of enslavement had been consistent throughout the revolutionary period. On March 14, 1779, he wrote to John Jay, president of the Continental Congress, concerning the conscription of soldiers of African descent into the Revolutionary Army. The letter was delivered by Colonel Henry Laurens, who was en route to his native South Carolina to enlist the support of the state's governor and legislature for arming African descendants to fight the British. Hamilton reasoned that Revolutionary leaders should make a broad appeal to the slave population of South Carolina before the British beat them to it. In exchange for taking up arms against the Crown, African descendants would be "given their freedom with their muskets."[10]

He argued that "this will secure their fidelity, animate their courage, and I believe will have a good influence upon those who remain, by opening a door to their emancipation." While asserting the dire need for new troops against the British onslaught, Hamilton also felt compelled to assure Jay that African descendants were up to the task. "I have not the least doubt that the negroes will make very excellent soldiers, with proper management." He went further and defended the mental capabilities of African descendants. "I frequently hear it objected to the scheme of embodying negroes that they are too stupid to make soldiers. This is so far from appearing to me a valid objection that I think their want of cultivation for their natural faculties are probably as good as ours joined to that habit of subordination which they acquire from a life of servitude, will make them sooner became soldiers than our white inhabitants."[11] For Hamilton, granting slaves their freedom along with their muskets was both a moral and strategic decision, a blend of ideology and political expediency, "for the dictates of humanity and true policy equally interest me in favour of this unfortunate class of men."[12]

In the last quarter of the eighteenth century, this cadre of Federalist leaders at the forefront of the Revolutionary cause in New York shaped the dominant racial discourse of the state, and thereby the politics associated with race. All were staunch abolitionists, and nowhere are the paternalistic views of this generation of New York leaders expressed more clearly than in the words and deeds of Jay himself. Before becoming co-author of *The Federalist*, Supreme Court Chief Justice, or Governor of New York, Jay was the first president of the New York Manumission Society, founded in 1785 with Hamilton as his vice president. Jay was the author of the Society's constitution and wrote in the preamble that

> *"It is our duty...to endeavor, by lawful ways and means, to enable [African descendants] to share equally with us in...civil and religious liberty...to which our brethren are, by nature, as much entitled as to ourselves."*

Throughout the Revolutionary and Confederation years, Jay fought for gradual abolition of enslavement in New York. He also argued vigorously for an abolition clause in the first state constitution drafted in 1777.

The Birth of the Abolition Movement in New York

New York State's abolition movement developed and progressed in concert with the national movement for abolition. However, not all New Yorkers supported the emancipation of their enslaved people of African descent and northern Abolitionists had remarkably little influence over the public at large. Very few, Northerners were abolitionists, and many regarded abolitionists as dangerous fanatics. What made their case telling was the south's violent reaction to the concept of abolition.

The earliest attempts at abolition in New York State began in 1777, when the first New York Constitutional Convention was held and the drafters of the Constitution made no mention of race, creed, or previous condition of servitude as an impediment to suffrage. The suffrage qualification was offered to "every male inhabitant of full age" who met the property and residence requirements. In this initial Constitution of 1777, framers instituted two forms of franchise in this peculiar democratic document:

1- any man owning a freehold worth twenty pounds or paying rent to the value of forty shillings, could vote for the members of the Assembly; but

2- a freeholder whose freehold was worth one hundred pounds could vote for senator or governor.[13]

The unusual circumstances for the election of other office-holders, both statewide and local were vested in a curious structure identified as the Council of Appointments. This Council consisted of the governor and one senator chosen annually from each of the four senatorial districts. It was given the authority to appoint judges, mayors, coroners, district attorney, etc. In short, all the statewide and local government offices, that are currently popularly elected.

At the Constitutional Convention of 1777, abolitionists, primarily composed of Federalists, were in the clear majority. While the constitution did not explicitly abolish enslavement, the Convention did adopt a resolution proposed by Governor Lewis Morris urging future legislatures to take measures committed to the principle that "every human being who breathes the air of the state shall enjoy the privileges of a freeman."[14] The resolution won temporary support from the constitutional convention by a vote of 31-5, but did not survive the final version of the document. Building on the success of this action, in 1785, the State of New York attempted to pass a gradual abolition law.

Ever present, at both of these attempts to incorporate the abolition of enslavement within the framework of New York life, were the Republican representatives of the Dutch dominated counties of Kings, Richmond, Ulster and, Long Island, who maintained a vigorous campaign against the passage of any abolition or emancipation laws. It had become evident that this third resident generation of Euro-Americans had, as their preceding generations of Dutch and British forefathers before them, chosen to develop and enforce a political system and societal structure that was shaped by the politics of race.

This oppressive ideology had already been ardently stitched into the political fabric of life in New York State. The political realities of race in New York as a backdrop to the development and implementation of political and economic policy was a manifestation of the doctrines of these preceding generations and their present day elected Republican enforcers.

And yet, this new generation of New York Revolutionary leaders was for the most part, staunchly abolitionist. John Jay and his colleagues all understood that the Revolutionary rhetoric of freedom rang hollow if the natural rights it espoused did not extend to ending hereditary enslavement. Jay wrote in 1780, from Europe to his friend Egbert Benson, a native New Yorker, a Delegate and a Representative from New York, concerning the continuation of enslavement in New York,

> *"till America comes into this measure [for abolition], her prayers to Heaven for liberty will be impious...I believe God governs this world, and I believe it to be a maxim in his as in our court, that those who ask for equity ought to do it."* [15]

Momentum thus, began to build throughout New York State to end enslavement in the early 1780s as pressures were placed on political leaders to follow the lead of its neighboring northern states. In 1784, the *New York Journal* published a letter from an abolitionist in Pennsylvania to a friend in New York. Pennsylvania was one of the first states to pass and implement a gradual abolition of enslavement in 1780. The Pennsylvanian attacked any type of personal enslavement, saying that,

> *"... the argument in favour of personal slavery are so few, and those few so weak, those in behalf of liberty, and the equal right all men have to freedom, so numerous and*

cogent, that it is really embarrassing to advocate for the latter, to arrange them and apply them." [16]

In 1785, the New York State Legislature sought to make good on the 1777 Convention's resolution on abolition and moved to pass a gradual abolition law. Within the state legislature, "the opponents of abolition were clearly identified; representatives of Kings, Richmond, and Ulster Counties, where there were many slaves and where Dutch slave holders were zealous of their property", human though it may be.[17] In their view property rights took precedence over human rights. They therefore, made several attempts to postpone any vote on emancipation during legislative debates on the 1785 gradual abolition bill.[18]

"It was argued that the measure was 'class legislation' unfairly aimed at the established Dutch community of rural New York amongst whom there were many slaveholders."[19]

This legislation followed a recurring theme in northern abolition laws of the period for it allowed for the "freedom of slaves" after a period of what amounted to "statutory servitude." However, this legislation also denied "freed" African descendants the right to vote, hold public office, intermarry with white persons and testify against white defendants in court.

Aaron Burr, a prominent Federalist politician, led a group of militant abolitionists and proposed the immediate abolition of all enslavement in the state. The Assembly rejected Burr's proposal 33-13, but approved a more moderate plan of abolition by a majority of 36-11.[20] In actuality, all but one member of the Assembly voted for some form of abolition, since ten (10) of the members that voted against the moderate bill voted with Burr on the more radical measure.[21] The bill that emerged from the Assembly stopped short of granting African descendants full political equality. It denied the right to vote or hold political office, forbade African descendants to intermarry with whites or give testimony against whites in a court of law, and it barred them from serving on juries. The Senate rejected the bill and went on record against the Assembly's measure, arguing that racial restrictions were not only unfair but also dangerous, and could result in civic disorder if a portion of the electorate was denied the rights of citizenship.[22]

The "stake in society" argument on voting fell on deaf ears in the Assembly. While the Senate revised the bill to allow for intermarriage, the holding of public office and the admissibility of evidence in courts; the Assembly would not budge on the Senate's action. Fearing that a gradual abolition bill would not be passed, the Senate nonetheless signed off on the measure that denied the right to vote to African descendants and sent it to the Council of Revision for consideration.[23]

COUNCIL OF REVISION

The New York Constitution had also established another unique body that, in effect and practice, usurped certain powers we now assume to be granted to the executive branch alone. The Council of Revision was granted the power of the veto over legislation. It was composed of the Governor, the Chancellor, and the judges of the Supreme Court. The Council had the power to return bills to the legislature for revision and further review - essentially giving it veto power over the legislature – however, the legislature could override the Council's veto with a two-thirds majority in both houses.[24]

With Federalist Robert Livingston presiding over the Council of Revision as Chancellor, the 1785 Gradual Abolition bill was rejected and sent back to the legislature. In issuing the veto, Livingston made a total of five objections concluding that:

1- Because the bill enacted the disenfranchisement of Negroes, mulattoes, and mustees, it excluded persons of this description from all share in the legislature, and those offices in which a vote may be necessary;

2- Because it holds up a doctrine that is repugnant to the principles on which the United States justified their separation from Great Britain;

3- Because this class of disenfranchised and discontented citizens, who at some period may be both numerous and wealthy may, under the direction of ambitious and factious leaders, become dangerous to the State and effect the ruin of the Constitution whose benefits they are not able to enjoy;

4- Because the creation of an order of citizens who are to have no legislative or representative share in the government, necessarily lays the foundation of an aristocracy of the most dangerous and malignant kind, rendering power permanent and hereditary in the hands of those persons who deduce their origin through white ancestors, only; and,

5- Because the last clause of the bill, being general, deprives those black, mulatto, and mustee citizens who have heretofore been entitled to a vote. Further, the Constitution does not support that the legislature may arbitrarily dispose of the dearest rights of their constituents.[25]

In returning the bill to the legislature, Livingston and the Council offered to New York's political leaders a vision of society which sought to integrate African descendants by ostensibly giving them a political stake in that society. The alternative was not only political instability and possible insurrection, but also a violation of the natural rights of citizens of African descent. Since some African descendants had already exercised the right to vote in New York, depriving them now of this essential privilege under the idea of political expediency, without their having been charged with any offence, served to disfranchise African descendants in direct violation of established rules of justice."[26]

Upon resubmission of the bill however, the Senate was now unwavering in its support for the original abolition bill, disenfranchising citizens of African descent. Apparently its members wanted an emancipation bill more than the suffrage measure. The Senate passed the original bill in un-amended form and sent it on to the Assembly.[27] By now, the Assembly had also changed its collective mind. Heeding Livingston's veto message, a majority of the Assembly now strongly favored both emancipation and voting rights, and voted down the unrevised bill forwarded by the Senate by a vote of 23-17.[28]

The bill however, died on the floor and abolition for the tens of thousands of African descendants criminally enslaved within the boundaries of the state was again delayed in New York.[29] The legislature did however enact a law that banned the importation of slaves to New York.[30] Not an insignificant undertaking, it was diminished however, by the legislature's inability to endorse a truly heterogeneous society.

The Re-Introduction of Enslavement Codes

While some [states] pressed for abolition, in 1788, the New York Legislature enacted a comprehensive enslavement code, systematizing and strengthening the regulations underlying the system of enslavement.

Laws such as: "An Act concerning slaves" in 1788, allowed slave holders to free a slave if that individual could become self-supporting. [31] Provisions were also made for the registration of "freed" slaves, the requirement that children would follow the condition of their mothers and "be esteemed, reputed, taken and adjudged slaves to all intents and purposes whatsoever."[32]

Additionally, the baptism of slaves was not considered to affect their status as slaves and the law included several "Slave Code" provisions restricting and regulating the conduct and rights of slaves. This Law further stipulated that the manumission of a slave by his/her owner would require the posting of a "security bond" to be approved by the court, "in a sum, not less than two hundred pounds," a new deterrent to the possibility of emancipation. [33] How this law impacted the emancipation of African descendants in New York is unclear? No records exist regarding the overall effect of this specific legislative action.

Ironically, this recent enactment of "Slave Codes" was directed as much to the conduct and requirements of slave holders as it was towards slaves. Slave holders were required to "punish his runaways, prevent assemblages of slaves, enforce the curfews, sit on the special courts and ride the patrols."[34] Newly introduced abolition legislation and resulting deliberations in 1796 seemed to have very little affect on the status and inner workings of New York's slave owning aristocracy. Examples of this inherent disregard for abolition existed throughout New York State.

Individual localities like the city of Albany also instituted regressive 'slave codes,' an example of such laws was passed in 1793, doc. 3-1 and 3-2. This law forbade enslaved men from walking in the streets and lanes of the city after 9 o'clock pm. It stipulated that:

> *"Be it ordained that from and after this Day, no Negroes or Mulatto slave, of any description whatever, be permitted and they are hereby forbid, under the penalties hereafter mentioned, to walk or be seen in the Streets and Lanes of this city, after the hour of nine o'clock in the evening. And in case any Slave or Slaves as aforesaid, shall be found in the said <u>illegible</u> or in any Tavern or Tipling (?) house, or any disorderly house or improper place, after the hour above said, such slave or slaves shall forthwith be committed to the Goal of this City and county, there to remain close custody, for the space of twenty-four hours; and further, that after the expiration of such confinement, such salve or slaves shall, previous to a discharge, be liable and obligated to pay the usual Goal fees."[35]*

Document 3-1
An Albany Law forbidding enslaved men from being in the Street after 9 PM [36]

25 November 1793

Document 3-2
An Albany Law forbidding enslaved men from being in the Street after 9 PM[37]

25 November 1793

they are hereby forbid, under the penalties herein after mentioned, to walk in the streets and lanes of this city, after the hour of Nine O'Clock in the evening. And in case any slave or slaves as aforesaid, shall be found in the said streets or in any tavern or Tipling house, or any disorderly house or any improper places, after the hour above said, such slave or slaves shall forthwith be committed to the Gaol of this City and County, therein to remain, in close custody, for the space of Twenty-four hours; and further, that after the expiration of such confinement, such slave or slaves shall, previous to a Discharge be liable and obliged to pay the usual Gaol Fees. Provided always, that if the master or mistress of such slave or slaves, shall prove to the satisfaction of the mayor, Recorder, or any one of the Aldermen of this City, that by his or her own such his or her slave or slaves was or were on the lawful and necessary business of his, her or their master or mistress; then, and in such case, the said mayor, Recorder or Aldermen before whom such hearing and enquiry to be had shall in his discretion, order such slave or slaves to be discharged upon payment of the Gaol fees.

THE DUTCH AND ABOLITION

Many Dutch homesteaders particularly along the Hudson River were dependent upon African labor to eke out a modest standard of living. The truth of the matter is that for the vast majority of slave holders in New York, enslaved Africans were not simply servants but an economic investment.

It is imperative to our understanding of the state's unwillingness to implement abolition legislation that we examine the mind-set by which the opposition to emancipation was defended so vehemently in New York State, especially given the fact that remnants of emancipation had existed in New York's not so distant past.

In modern terms, Dutch slave holders could accurately be described as "property rights advocates."[38] Their position on the right to remain in dominant control of "human property" was passed down from generation to generation as a 'time-honored tradition'. This aggressive slave owning tradition contradicts the description of Dutch enslavement by historians as being of a "benign nature". One need only to remember that it was the Dutch colonists of New Netherland who instituted a version of "half-freedom" that was designed to "conditionally free" enslaved men and women, while at the same time keeping their children, both born and unborn, locked in perpetual bondage.

DUTCH FREEDOM POLICES

Therefore we, the Director and Council do release, for the term of their natural lives, the above named and their wives from Slavery, hereby setting them free and at liberty, on the same footing as other free people here in New Netherlands. [39]

In 1644, the Dutch West India Company granted "conditional freedom" to a number of enslaved Africans on condition that they make an annual fixed payment of farm produce. They were also required to provide specific services to the colony on demand.

"... where they shall be able to earn their livelihood by Agriculture, on the land shown and granted to them, on condition that they, the above named Negroes, shall be bound to pay for the freedom they receive each man for himself annually, as long as he lives, to the West India Company for its Deputy here, thirty skepels (barn baskets-22 ½ bushels) of Maize, or Wheat, Pease or Beans. And one Fat Hog, valued at twenty guilders, which thirty skepels and the hog they, the Negroes, each for himself, promises to pay annually, beginning from the date hereof, on pain, if anyone of them shall fail to pay the yearly tribute, he shall forfeit his freedom and return back into the said Company's slavery."[40]

Notwithstanding this policy, the motives of the company officers who crafted the law were transparent. They sought to relieve themselves of the burden of supporting aging slaves, yet wished to reserve the right to command the labor of young and vigorous African youth.

This "conditional freedom" also stipulated that children born and unborn, would remain the property of the Company forever. The reasoning inherent in the implementation of this tyrannical policy, with respect to the children of formerly enslaved, was to allow the company to retain an effective and replenishing potential supply of enslaved labor.

"The Dutch West India Company's officers envisioned Africans born in New Amsterdam as a fresh and continuously available source of labor. Such children would make especially desirable slaves, since they would be acculturated and would have roots in the city. With their kinfolk nearby, they would not pose a risk of flight. Company administrators did not hesitate to exert their authority over these youngsters." [41]

It is arguable that this practice was also related to a Dutch custom of giving their children their own personal slaves once they reached the age of six or eight years of age; usually these slave children were of a similar age to their youthful masters/mistresses.[42] Whatever the reasoning, this practice of enslaving the children of former slaves by the company was consistent throughout their entire presence in New Netherland and later in New York State. This practice would reappear in a modified form once again when the issue of gradual abolition was debated in the legislature in the later part of the 18th century.

During the Dutch period of enslavement (1624-1664) in New Netherland, at least twenty-four enslaved Africans were manumitted at either a "half-free" or full freedom status. Almost all of these manumissions involved some conditions imposed upon those freed. "Half freedom" benefited the masters as much or more than the freed Africans themselves. In many cases, "half-freedom" proved a more efficient system of labor in New Netherland than chattel enslavement. It provided the Dutch West Indies Company with an "on call" work force, which would be used on fortifications and other public works whenever the need arose. [43]

It should be noted that this manumission act by the Dutch and the eventual manumission of these enslaved Africans was the result of continued petitioning and protests by these Africans and some whites for emancipation. Eventually, the company grudgingly gave in to their protests for freedom. On 25 February 1644, twenty men were manumitted; eleven of whom received "half freedom" status. These men were the first enslaved Africans brought to New Amsterdam in 1625. The eleven former slaves, Paulo Angola, Big Manuel, Little Manuel, Manuel de Gerrit de Reus, Simon Congo, Anthony Portuguese, Garcia, Peter Santomee, Jan Francisco, Little Anthony, and Jan Fort Orange had served for eighteen to nineteen years as the labor force in New Amsterdam. [44]

Under the terms of the grant of freedom, the men and their wives were freed "to earn their livelihood by agriculture" on land to be granted them. There were, however, conditions. First, the men were required to serve the West India Company in New Netherland "on land or water, wherever their services were required, on condition of receiving fair wages from the Company". They were guaranteed that they would not be required to work in any of the Company's other colonies. They were not free from company service, but they would be paid.

It was the opinion of the Company that these men would be unable to support their wives and numerous children if they remained in the service of the company. Each man received between one to twenty acres of land [45] and they were freed on the condition that they pay back to the company annually "22 ½ bushels of maize, wheat, or corn and one fat hog valued at thirty guilders to the company or be re-enslaved."[46] A caveat was attached that specified that their children "already in existence or hereafter born, shall be slaves."[47]

These African parents were deeply concerned about the welfare of their children. Their dreams for their baptized sons and daughters had rested on the indeterminacy of heir status, and they could not reconcile themselves to a principle they regarded as illegitimate.[48] The company slaves who petitioned for their freedom in 1644 gave the necessity of supporting their many children as one of the main reasons for requesting manumission. The African descendant children of New Amsterdam were cared for not only by their natural parents but by a wide circle of relatives and friends who willingly assumed responsibility for providing for the youngsters when circumstances warranted it. In other words, African surrogate parents quickly filled the void when natural parents died or were sold. The overriding concern of these adults of New Amsterdam was to smooth the path for the younger generation.[49]

Not all of those emancipated people of African descent were male. Three females of African descent also petitioned the company for their freedom in 1663. On April 19, 1663 one of those petitioners, Mayken, received her liberty, "she having served as a slave since the year 1628."[50] Additionally, Ascento Angola, Christopher Santone, Peter Petersen Criole, Anthony Criole, Lewis Guinea, Jan Guinea, Solomon Petersen, and Basije Petersen had successfully petitioned the court for full freedom, citing the fact that half-freedom was unacceptable to them.

It should also be noted that gaining freedom was nearly impossible for African descendants enslaved by individual colonialists and difficult even for those belonging to the Dutch West India Company. The company valued its enslaved work force and was willing to liberate only the elderly, perhaps understanding that such aged survivors would soon, if they had not already, become a liability.[51] These examples of conditional freedom and the lengthy terms of service performed by emancipated African descendants clearly indicate that any freedom from Dutch enslavement would be hard earned and only after many years of service. These "conditionally freed" Africans represented the first gradual emancipations in New York .

LAND PARCELED TO FREED AFRICANS

Between the years of 1635 and 1665, the Company gave approximately 150 to 200 acres of land to those recently freed, "… these land grants ran from Hudson Street along the south and east side almost to Astor Place (Sand Hill Road) in New Amsterdam."[52] Most of the families received grants to lands they had been farming before becoming "free", fig. 17. At the time of these land grants, the area involved was generally undesirable swampland that was frequently referred to as the "black ooze." [53] Today, most of the area of the initial farm plots is in Greenwich Village, New York City. It is also believed that these grants were an action, on the part of the Company, to free themselves of the responsibility of these aging slaves.[54] It is also believed that these plots of land given to these "freed" Africans on the outskirts of New Amsterdam was of a conscious design on the part of the company to provide a buffer between New Amsterdam proper and the surrounding hostile Native American peoples.

Henry Lanier in *Greenwich Village* suggests that this generosity on the part of acknowledged slave holders and property rights advocates was wholly out of character. He surmises that the Dutch had thousands of acres of land on Manhattan alone, based on West India Company annals and that this distribution of land was based on a scheme to keep all of the profits recovered from raids by privateers upon other nation's ships in the Atlantic. His contention is that several of the African descendants who received land grants in New

Amsterdam were members of the crews of these privateer ships and were entitled to a full share of any potential "booty" captured by these ships. The standard practice of the Company provided that everyone on board a ship including enslaved Africans were entitled to share in the profits.

Lanier conjectures that, "it seems that the Company realized that it could make a substantial profit and keep all of the proceeds by offering the enslaved sailors freedom and some land considered worthless."[55]

In 1659 and 1660, Director General Stuyvesant granted a series of house-and-garden lots along the wagon road (now Fourth Avenue) near his plantation. The recipients included a number of familiar names- Antony Antonyz, Manuel de Reus, Lucas and Salomon Peters. Domingo Angola, Big Manuel, and Pieter Tambour (alias van Campen) - and the heirs of some other familiar persons: Christoffel Santome (husband of Gtatia Angola's widow), and William Antonys Portuguese (apparently the son of Anthony Portuguese). Other freedmen in the same new neighborhood included Francisco Cartagena, Assento, Class de Neger, Assento Angola and Anthony, the blind Negro.[56]

Since several of these African descendants had already received larger patents at some distance from their new house-and-garden plots, it seems likely that they were following a custom still common in much of Europe, living together in a community along the highway rather than in widely separated farmhouses. This offered the advantages of social cohesiveness and mutual defense, but required an extensive trip each day to the fields.[57] It should also be noted that the British later confiscated the land given to these African descendants by the Dutch West India Company after their takeover of New Amsterdam.[58]

Nevertheless, the transformation of New Netherland from a string of trading posts to a settlement wedded to agricultural production placed a larger proportion of the African descendant population in the hands of individual planters. These slave holders had little interest in allowing them the benefits of freedom that once accrued to Africans enslaved by the company. Manumission, thereby became less frequent and "the place of those who had earlier obtained their freedom became increasingly marginal."[59]

Considering the motivations attributed to these grants of "conditional freedom;" it and other Dutch policies were later summarily decimated by the British and substituted with legalized oppression. Under British rule, additions to New York City's free African descendant population were very few. In fact, "between 1664 and 1712, when a restrictive manumission law was enacted, probably not more than a dozen slaves were freed, either in wills or through instruments of manumission."[60]

Figure 17
Free African American Farm Plots – NYC [61]

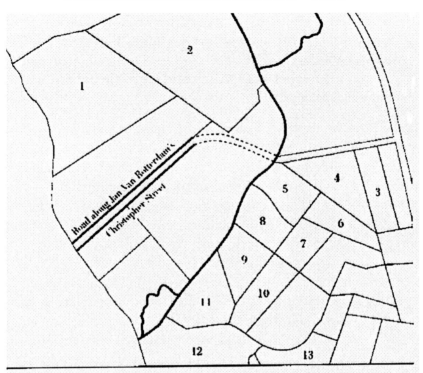

1. Cloff Stevensen (Mar. 12, 1647)
2. Cosyn Gerritsen (Mar. 13, 1647)
3. Manuel Gerrit of Reus (Dec. 12, 1643)
4. Manuel Trompeter (Dec. 12, 1643)
5. Anthony Potugese (before 1644)
6. Groot Manuel (Dec. 1644)
7. Cleyn Manuel (before 1644)
8. Paulo Dangola (Dec. 30, 1644)
9. Pieter Santone (Dec. 15, 1644)
10. Cleyn Antonio (Dec. 30, 1644)
11. Symon Congo (Dec. 15, 1644)
12. Tonis Nyssen (Apr. 3, 1647)
13. Jan Francisco (Dec. 1644)

Farms of free blacks near the Bowery in the 1640s. (Based on information from the Museum of the City of New York)

ECONOMIC AND POLITICAL SHIFTS LEAD NEW YORK TO GRADUAL ABOLITION

No one ever seriously proposed immediate abolition in New York. It was not politically viable. There were too many counties in New York where enslaved men and women made up a sizeable percentage of the labor force and general population.

In the early 1790s, the influence of the Dutch farmers in New York State began to decline both economically and politically. This shift in the economic and political landscape of New York State was essentially due to a relocation of its' chief agricultural center from the Dutch dominated southern regions of the state to upstate New York. The bulk of farm commodities were now sent to Manhattan for export came from the upstate communities settled by New Englanders, old opponents of enslavement. A reapportionment of the legislature in 1796 gave them greater political clout.[62] It should be noted however, that New Englanders' opposition to enslavement was not based on the wholesale rejection of enslavement on purely moral grounds. New Englanders bought few slaves, in large measure because New Englanders did not have the capital to purchase slaves, in part due to the topography of the land and the limited growing season in New England did not return major investments sufficient enough for them to invest in chattel bondsmen and women.[63]

New York begins Shift to Capitalist Economy

The financial well being and continued privilege that enslavement had afforded slave holders in New York was now at risk. "Progressive" forces - seeing enslavement and the economic advantages and political influence that it guaranteed to a specialized faction of the citizenry as "unfair competition" - were challenging the existence of enslavement all over the North. This unprecedented shift in the body politic of New York State proved to be the impetus for New York's re-examination of the issue of abolition.

In discussing the movement towards abolition, we must be ever cognizant of the geopolitical reality of New York's economy during this period. New York and the northern states were beginning to develop a more industrial economy in order to more successfully compete in the New World markets. A nascent manufacturing industry was developing. While agriculture was still important in this era of New York, it was beginning to be exploited as capitalist farming to create commodities for sale, rather than for barter or other forms of exchange.

Additionally during this period, a mass migration of Europeans was descending on their shores through the Port of New York. Steady immigration to New York in the opening decades of the nineteenth century played a large role in the declining density of African descendants in the overall population. At the time of the ratification of the Constitution in 1777, New York's population was 340,000. By 1820, the population of the state rose to 1.3 million - a fourfold increase; yet, the African descendant population growth was minimal in proportion. [64]

Employment, for their immigrant brethren and the thousands who were unemployed already in New York State due to the "advantages" of enslaved labor, was a compelling motivation to structure a change in the 'complexion' of the state's skilled and unskilled workforce to meet these new economic demands.

"During the early nineteenth century developing capitalism moulded an army of wage workers in North America, not out of thin air or solely from a declining artisanate, but by impressing immigrants, redundant agricultural labour", slaves, free blacks, women and children. Theirs was a history of movement from the land into the lower reaches of wage work, propelled by forces beyond their control..."[65]

This economic shift from enslavement towards capitalism and the exploitation of wage workers provided little redress with respect to the actual treatment of enslaved African descendants in New York. Enslaved African descendants were now "placed in a situation where their labor was viewed more explicitly as a commodity to be exploited as fully as possible as the social responsibilities of ownership were subjugated to the demands of commercial production."[66]

Additionally, the growing availability of white immigrant and unemployed workers served to contribute to an undermining of the slave economy in New York. Slave costs were relatively high, both from the standpoint of capital investment and the expense of maintaining slaves during periods of unemployment. As the supply of free workers increased and the wage rate fell, enslavement became more and more obsolete as a system of labor with which to base the economic survival of an entire region of a young and inexperienced democratic nation. "These changes gave impetus to the anti-enslavement movement. The ideal of freedom was a powerful motivating force, but the steady erosion of slave profits was an important factor in its widespread acceptance."[67]

THE NEW YORK MANUMISSION SOCIETY

With the failure of the New York State Legislature to enact any type of emancipation law in 1785, calls to abolish this "peculiar institution" once and for all in the Empire State, reached a feverish pitch. During the same period, several editorial pages of New York newspapers attacked enslavement. The *New York Gazetteer* described it as "the deprivation of all the rights which nature has given to man."[68]

In 1785, the Society for Promoting the Manumission of Slaves (New York Manumission Society) was founded in New York City with John Jay and Alexander Hamilton[69] at its head. Members also included Albanian Philip Schuyler[70] and future governor Lewis Morris, who had advocated passage of a state emancipation bill.

The Abolitionist Movement itself, in New York State took a very moderate and oftentimes contradictory approach to the concept of emancipation. Slave ownership by key members of the New York Manumission Society was a sharp contrast from the society's alleged "liberalism."[71]

"In fact, the New York Manumission Society was so conservative that after an extended period of debate

it could not agree to exclude slave holders from its membership."[72]

Its leadership of Alexander Hamilton and other Federalist made up the liberal wing of the merchant class, which by now owned the majority of slaves in New York City."[73]

John Jay

John Jay, one of the leading proponents of the Colonization Movement and the eventual signer into law of the 1799 Gradual Abolition Act, as Governor of New York, became identified as a leading anti-enslavement proponent. It is interesting to note that this leader of the first organized abolition movement in the state, even after election to the office of president of the Manumission Society, continued to own slaves. The New York Manumission Society minutes give a curious accounting of the sincerity of his abolitionist feelings. In 1798, John Jay listed slaves in an account of his taxable property, noting:

"I purchase slaves and manumit them at proper ages, and when their faithful services shall have afforded a reasonable restitution."[74]

In other words, Jay's position was that once a slave had produced for him through his/her forced labor an equivalent amount of profit essentially equal to their actual purchase price, maintenance and other expenses plus a respectable profit, the prospect of manumission was possible.[75] On March 21, 1784, Jay did however manumit one of his enslaved men, Benoit, whom he had purchased just five years prior in Martinique. In doing so, he wrote that "whereas the Children of Men are by Nature equally free, and cannot without Injustice be either reduced to, or held in Enslavement, And whereas it is therefore right... [Benoit] should be manumitted."[76]

It was Jay who was inspired by fellow Federalists Hamilton and Erastus Root to author the Preamble of the Society's Constitution, which stated plainly:

"It is our duty...to endeavor, by lawful ways and means, to enable [Africans and their descendants] to share equally with us in...civil and religious liberty...to which our brethren are, by nature, as much entitled as to ourselves."[77]

Society Struggles to Enlist Support

The Society had trouble enlisting a greater number of New York citizens for the support of its cause, primarily due to the fact that Quakers like John Murray, Jr., a prominent merchant and director of the Bank of New York, constituted a good portion of the initial membership. Abolitionist Societies in the east were constantly rebuked because of the Quakers' unwillingness to serve in the American Revolutionary War for religious reasons. It is likely that the future Governor Jay was chosen for his leadership in the Society in an effort to circumvent the animosity surrounding the Quakers and their unwillingness to participate in the War of Independence. His campaign for governor in 1792 became a focal point of debate between anti and pro-enslavement forces. Pro-enslavement representatives campaigned against his election by charging that he and his abolitionist cohorts were attempting "to rob every Dutchman of the property he holds most dear to his heart, his slaves."[78]

Similarly, Benjamin Franklin's election as president of the Philadelphia Society may have been an attempt to counter anti-Quaker sentiments and establish a more "Americanized" persona for the Society's leadership. Interestingly enough, pro-enslavement forces dismissed Franklin's participation in the Philadelphia Society as merely a manifestation of his senility.

The cause for emancipation in New York State was further hindered by the fact that, "the Society, which had confined its activities largely to the city of New York, was the only antienslavement society in the state."[79]

The New York Manumission Society did however attempt to thwart the illegal importation and exportation of slaves for sale. They also assisted free persons of African descent who were illegally held in bondage, such as Austin Steward who sued for his freedom in

1813 with the aid of the Society. In addition, the Society promoted boycotts of merchants who profited from the slave trade. According to Graham Russell Hodges in *"Root & Branch"*,

> **"The society's significance lies less in its members' halting, neocolonial liberalism than in its support for African Americans' legal actions for freedom, its hot-minded vigilance against dangerous slave catchers, its lobbying of recalcitrant slave masters, and its registry for freedom papers."**[80]

Progress towards Gradual Abolition

In 1785, the Society planned a gradual abolition of enslavement bill that could take twenty or more years before any slaves were actually freed. As mentioned earlier, prior to the 1830s, most antienslavement activists in the North and particularly in New York State focused their attentions on gradual emancipation. Most of these activists thought that the institution of enslavement would gradually whither away. This assumption on the part of northern abolitionists would later lead to the first major conflict in the anti-enslavement movement. No emancipation act in the north provided for immediate abolition. This gradualist approach derived partly from prevailing assumptions about social change. These men were confident of progress but saw no reason to suppose that social evils were amenable to radical actions of social engineering. Gradualism also represented a realistic assessment of certain practical difficulties, not the least being the necessity of winning support from the public so that some action could be taken.

> **Certainly the gradual abolition laws and tracts strongly suggest that the principal reality being faced was the immediate welfare of masters rather than the future benefit of manumitted slaves. Gradual emancipation may (or may not) have benefited African descendants, they were not intended as the primary beneficiaries.**[81]

The early abolitionists also gave constant and positive assurance to southerners that they had no intentions of interfering with the rights of property. Hence, slave emancipation was not to be achieved without compensation to the slave holders. In part, this attitude stemmed from the elite composition of its membership. The founders of the New York Manumission Society, for example, included such distinguished individuals as Phillip Schuyler, James Duane, and Chancellor Livingston. Such men of wealth or high station were highly sensitive to the sanctity of capital investments, however deplorable its form. Not through the purse strings would they strike.[82]

The New York Manumission Society, encouraged by the election of John Jay to the Governorship of New York in 1792, made another attempt to pass a gradual abolition bill through the legislature in 1796. Three years of extensive discussions and negotiations ensued. Primary to these deliberations was the means by which slave holders could preserve their "property rights" while at the same time developing a schedule for the eventual abolition of enslavement itself. It is significant that, "The respect due 'property' was the slogan with which every proposal for abolition was attacked."[83]

The possible ramifications of abolition caused slave holders in New York tremendous concern and anxiety. Graham Russell Hodges in *"Slavery and Freedom"* expresses the concerns of these slave holders succinctly when he articulates the questions that were on the minds of most New Yorkers:

> **"If parents are properties, who should be responsible for the cost of raising their freeborn offspring? If the state, in violation of every prior law and precedent, appropriates slaveholders' valuable properties, who should reimburse them? If slaveholders choose to impregnate chattel they have purchased – possibly fed and housed since childhood – and if this results in the birth of a property both made and claimed by the slaveholder, what right has any state to intervene in the disposition of that property?"[84]**

Opposition to gradual abolition had been well evident in previous debates in the state legislature. For example, in 1796, a committee of the legislature that had reported on an earlier version of the Gradual

Abolition bill to the floor had observed, "that it would be unjust and unconstitutional to deprive any citizen or citizens…of their property …without making them a reasonable compensation."[85]

The New York newspapers of the day were of no support to the bill either. Although as gradual abolition approached, some papers began to relax their critical editorials. The *Albany Argus* of 23 January 1796 asserted that the idea of abolition without compensation would be "an outrage of justice and liberty."[86] The *American Minerva* stated that even though enslavement was "one of the degrading badges of our colonial situation, its removal required great caution."[87]

Notwithstanding this opposition, in both the Assembly and Senate, delegates from New York City joined forces with their newly elected upstate counterparts to overcome opposition by Dutch legislators from southern New York and Long Island. As Senator Erastus Root recalled,

> *"the Dutchmen raved and swore by dunder and blixen that we were robbing them of their property. We told them that they had none and could hold none in human flesh."*[88]

Notwithstanding the waffling of political positions, the issue of compensation for the loss of the future services of the children of their slaves remained the primary stumbling block to the bill's passage. This political backdrop set the stage for New York State's "Great Compromise," which by all accounts would be better described as New York State's "Great Concession." After several unsuccessful attempts at modifying the face of enslavement in New York by way of legislation that was inspired and motivated ostensibly from the position of ensuring the continuation of profit first, the New York State Legislature passed the Gradual Abolition Act in 1799. Predictably, "the resulting law sidestepped all questions of legal and civil rights, thus avoiding the objections that had blocked earlier bills."[89]

ENDNOTES

1   By the late 18th and early 19th centuries, several northern states began to abolish slavery altogether or by degrees. Vermont (1777) banned slavery in its constitution; Massachusetts by judicial decision (1783); New Hampshire by constitutional interpretation. Legislation providing for gradual abolition was passed in Pennsylvania (1780), Rhode Island (1784), and Connecticut (1784 and 1797).

2   White, 19-21; Berlin, 55

3   Berlin, 15; White, 19-21; Also see: Nash, Forging Freedom, ch. 1; Salinger, "To Serve Well and Faithfully," chs. 2-4

4   William Strickland, Journal of a Tour of the United States of America 1794-1795, ed. J.E. Strickland, 1971, New York Historical Society, pg. 163-164

5   James Clyde Sellman, Abolition (Africana.com)

6   Arthur Zilversmit, The First Emancipation: The Abolition of Slavery in the North (Chicago and London: University of Chicago Press, 1967) 227

7   Henry P. Johnson (ed.), The Correspondence and Public Papers of John Jay (4 vols; New York, 1890-95), III,.342

8   Emancipation in New York State, www.slavenorth.com/nyemancip.htm

9   **NOTE**: Manumit or manumission refers to the formal act of freeing from slavery. It is usually undertaken by individuals or private entities through wills or formal certifications; as opposed to emancipation which speaks more to a legislative or governmental policy mandate.

10 "Letter To John Jay," March 14, 1779, *The Papers of Alexander Hamilton* (New York: Columbia University Press, 1961), vol. 2, 17-8.

11 Ibid

12 Ibid., p.18

13 New York State Constitution of 1777

[14] Mary White Ovington, *Half A Man: The Status of the Negro in New York* (New York: The New American Library, Inc., 1970), 8

[15] Henry P. Johnston, 407

[16] *New York Journal*, April 15th, 1784

[17] Strickland, 148

[18] Journal of the Assembly of New York State, 1785, 53

[19] Blackburn, 273

[20] Journal of the Assembly of the State of New York, February 25, 1785

[21] Edgar McManus, *A History of Negro Slavery in New York* (Syracuse: Syracuse Press, 1966),162.

[22] *Journal of the Senate*, March 9 and 12, 1785

[23] *Ibid.*, March 12, 1785

[24] The Council of Revision was established in 1777, it was created to insure that laws inconsistent with the Constitution did not become law. The Council was composed of the Governor, any two of the following: the Chancellor and Judges of the State Supreme Court. Their charge was to review all of the bills that passed the State Senate and Assembly before the bills became law. If they considered a bill to be improper, it was sent back to its House of origination and reconsidered. The negative actions of the Council constituted a veto of the legislation and required two-thirds of both Houses to become law. The veto powers of the Council of Revision are now vested in the Governor, alone, after the Council's abolishment in 1821. See Alfred B. Street, *The Council of Revision of the State of New York....*, 1859, Wm. Gould, Publisher, pg. 5-6

[25] Street, 268-269

[26] *Ibid,.*238.

[27] *Journal of the Senate,* March 21, 1785

[28] *Journal of the Assembly*, March 26, 1785

[29] Street, 269; Liwack, 8; Zilversmit, 147-150; McManus, Journal of Negro History, 209-210;

30 Chapter 68 of the Laws of 1785 of New York State

31 Chapter 40 of the Laws of 1788 of New York State

32 Ibid

33 Ibid

34 Winthrop Jordan, *White over Black*, , Chapel Hill: University of North Carolina Press, 1968) 108

35 Chamberlain's Records, *City of Albany Records,* 1783-1815, Box 1, item 74

36 Chamberlain's Records, *City of Albany Records,* 1783-1815, Box 1, item 74

37 Ibid

38 Arthur Zilversmit, *The First Emancipation: The Abolition of Slavery in the North,* (Chicago: The University of Chicago Press, 1967) 182; White, 20-23, 54-55

39 O'Callaghan, *Laws of New Netherland,* 36-37

40 Ibid

41 Ibid

42 James Fennimore Cooper, *Satanstoe or the Littlepage Manuscripts,* (W. A. Townsend and Company, NY, 1890) 8-81

43 **Half-freedom**: Sherrill D. Wilson, New York City's African Slaveholders: A Social and Material Culture History, (Garland Publishing, 1994) 37, Graham Russell Hodges, Root & Branch, 12; Williams-Myers, 15. **For Duty paid by Freed Slave**s: Henry Wysham Lanier, Greenwich Village: Today and Yesterday (New York: Harper and Brothers, 1949) 24. Also see Edward Abdy, Journal of a Residence and Tour in the United States of North America, from April, 1833 to Oct., 1834 (London: J. Murray, 1835); Wilson, 39; Williams-Myers, 15; McManus; Roi Ottley and William J. Weatherby, eds. The Negro in New York: An Informal Social History (Oceana Publications1967). **For status of children:** Graham Russell Hodges, Slavery and Freedom in the Rural North, 13

[44] Sherrill D. Wilson, 37, Graham Russell Hodges, Root & Branch, 12; Williams, 15

[45] Hodges, 13; Kruger, 52-53

NOTE: For an extensive accounting of the land in New Amsterdam/ Manhattan owned by Africans and their descendants and the communities that they established there see Hodges, Chapter I, 6-18

[46] Lanier, pg. 24, also see Edward Abdy, Journal of a Residence and Tour in the United States of North America, from April, 1833 to Oct., 1834,(London: J. Murray, 1835); Wilson, 39; Williams, 15; Condon; McManus; Ottley; also see Ashbury, 1977; Blackmar, 1989; and Stokes, 1915-1928

[47] Hodges, 13

Note: This caveat with respect to the children of these "free" Africans will be discussed latter in this work.

[48] Joyce D. Goodfriend, The Souls of African Children: New Amsterdam, www.common-place.org, vol. 3 no. 4 , July 2003

[49] Joyce D. Goodfriend, Black Families in New Netherland, Selected Rensselaerwijck Seminar Papers, 147

[50] Ibid

[51] Berlin, 52

[52] Lanier, 83

[53] Lanier, 43; also see: *African Burial Grounds*

[54] Hodges, 12

[55] Lanier, 84

[56] New York Colonial Manuscripts", X/3:329-32; "Land Patents", II: 102-07.

[57] Peter R. Christoph, The Freedmen of New Amsterdam, Selected Rensselaerwijck Seminar Papers, 158

[58] This issue of the confiscation of legitimately own property by African descendants will provide an interesting question as to the true

ownership of this land, once the issues of reparations from the state of New York are considered..

59 Berlin, 3

60 Goodfriend, 116

61 Hodges, 14

62 Burrows, Ewing and Mike Wallace, *Gotham:: A History of New York City to 1898* (Oxford Press, 1999) 349

63 Hoffer, 124

64 Kass, *Politics in New York State, 1800-1830*, p.18

65 Peter Way, *Common Labor: Workers and the Digging of North American Canals, 1780-1860*, 1997, (The John Hopkins University Press, 1997) 6

66 Ibid, 87

67 Edgar J. McManus, *Black Bondage in the North,* (Syracuse University Press, 1973) 176-177

68 *New York Gazetteer*, February 4, 1785

69 "Hamilton's ambitions to join the top ranks of urban society mandated his holdership of slaves", according to Bob Weston as quoted in Hodges, pg. 167

70 Who will be discussed in a later section of this work.

71 Graham Russell Hodges, *Root & Branch:* pg. 166

72 Arthur Zilversmit, pg. 166

73 Hodges, pg. 167

74 William Jay, *The Life of John Jay*, 1833, vol. I, pg.335

75 On March 21, 1784, Jay manumitted one of his two slaves, Benoit, whom he had purchased just five years prior in Martinique. In doing so he wrote that "whereas the Children of Men are by Nature equally free, and cannot without Injustice be either reduced to, or held in Slavery, And whereas it is therefore right… [Benoit] should be manumitted."

-- John Jay: *The Winning of the Peace, Unpublished Papers 1780-1784*, edited by Richard Morris (New York: Harper Row, 1980), p.705

76 John Jay: *The Winning of the Peace, Unpublished Papers 1780-1784*, edited by Richard Morris (New York: Harper Row, 1980),705.

77 Preamble, Constitution of the New York State Society for Promoting the Manumission of Slaves

78 Zilversmit, 165

79 Ibid, 173

80 Ibid

81 Winthrop, White over Black, 354

82 Quarles, 11

83 Zilversmit, 177

84 Graham Russell Hodges, Slavery and Freedom, 135

85 Zilversmit, 176

86 *The Argus*, 23 January 1796

87 *American Minerva* , 6& 8 February 1796

88 Burrows, Edwing and Wallace, 349

89 *Slavery in the Mid-Atlantic*, www.geocities.com

CHAPTER III

THE GRADUAL ABOLITION ACT

THE GRADUAL ABOLITION ACT

The last generation of children born to slave women in New York State between 1799 and 1827 were largely freed by the Gradual Abolition Act rather than by voluntary manumission. Children of African descent would, now, be controlled by a series of new laws designed to govern their lives until adulthood, leaving them as little control over their circumstances as earlier generations of slaves had experienced.

New York State's slave legacy has been documented in earlier Chapters of this work, and yet, the story of human bondage and the resulting "crimes against humanity" committed by the State of New York are only partly explained by this historical record.[1] The gradual abolition of enslavement in New York State was finally passed on 29 March 1799. Its enactment provides a tale just as horrific and destructive as the institution of enslavement itself.

THE POLITICS OF GRADUAL ABOLITION

The New York State mandate for gradual abolition was a well wired and orchestrated compromise reached between the abolitionist and slave holder factions of the state and their respective representatives in the state legislature over the issue of compensating slave holders for the loss of their future "property" to abolition. It occurred at a time when Federalist "needed to prove that they were genuine friends of liberty. In this climate the passage of an emancipation law could significantly assist Federalist leaders to re-establish their concern for civic freedom. On the other hand, The New York Argus, a leading Republican newspaper, had published articles … which supported emancipation and warned that votes would be withheld from Republicans who failed to do so."[2]

A majority of both houses were clearly prepared to end enslavement in New York. Opposition to gradual abolition however, continued. Opponents argued that gradual abolition would become a burden on the community. They urged that gradual abolition would promote the notion that there should be a community of goods and an equal sharing of property.[3] It was also argued that the poor man was more dependent on his slave domestic than the rich, 'wallowing in luxury' and with armies of servants. And it was also said that emancipation would rob widows and orphans of slaves that were their only means of support.[4] Lastly, they argued that slave holders would see little benefit in raising slave children who would become free upon adulthood.

Interestingly enough, this compromise occurred during a period in time when Federalists and Republicans loved to oppose one another. And yet, gradual abolition attracted almost equal support from representatives of the two groupings. The extent of Republican support was remarkable since New York abolitionism had heretofore been a Federalist cause."[5] This concept, which had already been legislated in other northern states, met little opposition in legislative debates, as the bill was passed by a vote of 68 Federalists to 23 Republicans in the Assembly and 22 to 10 in the Senate.[6] After years of considerable debate over the last half of the 18th century, it was finally agreed by all factions that:

1- **African descendants already in bondage would remain so for the remainder of their natural lives, so that no investment would be lost;**

2- **Slave holders would have the option of manumitting any of their slaves without having to pay any bond requirements;**

3- **Slave holders were given permission to abandon any and all infirmed, dependent, or aging slaves without any financial obligation.**

As one-sided as these results might seem, the major concession that was made to the slave holders of New York State was centered squarely on *the fate of the Children*.

THE PROVISIONS OF THE GRADUAL ABOLITION ACT

The Gradual Abolition Law had stipulated that:

1- any child born of a slave within the State after July 4, 1799, should "be deemed and adjudged to be born free";

2- these same children shall be the servant of the legal "owner" of his or her mother until such child, if a male, reaches the age of twenty eight years and, if a female, the age of twenty five;

3- the slave owner of the mother and master or mistress of the slaves' child(ren) were required to register each child with the town clerk under the penalty of a fine;

4- should the slave owner of the mother choose to abandon his/her rights to the child's service, he/she was required to notify the town clerk;

5- town clerks would declare an abandoned child a pauper thus allowing the Overseers of the Poor (the predecessor of the Social Services and Corrections Departments) in that town to bound out the child to any interested parties;

6- the Overseers of the Poor were to be compensated or reimbursed by this law at a rate of $3.50 per month per child for maintenance and support by the Comptroller and Treasurer of New York State until the child was contracted or bonded out to a new "employer;" and

7- until the children were bound out to an "employer" by the Overseers of the Poor, these children were allowed to remain in the care of their mother's owner and these owners, not the Overseers of the Poor, were entitled to receive the full state allocated maintenance payment..[7]

The fundamental aspect of this new law revolved around the concept of "abandonment of responsibility" and its concomitant subsidy provision. This abandonment and subsidy option was a major concession to New York's slave holders to garner their support for the passage of the bill. In reality, it represented a thinly veiled scheme to provide for a state sponsored compensated abolition program. The abandonment program, as it has been referred to,

> **"had been inserted into the 1799 act to gain the cooperation of pro-enslavement forces in the passage of the bill. This disguised compensated abolition scheme permitted slaveholders to abandon children and then receive them back into their homes as boarders until (and if) they were bound out to service – for which they would receive monthly payments from local poor authorities.[8]**

The abandonment program of the Gradual Abolition Act of 1799 was amended in 1802 when the amount of monthly maintenance was reduced to $2.00 per child per month. The duration of eligibility for this subsidy was also reduced to four years by this amendment. Now, abandoned children (abandoned at the age of one-year old) were to be bonded out by the Overseers of the Poor by the age of four (4) years old. After this period of time, the state would not be required to continue its subsidy for maintenance and support. The entire provision was later abolished in 1804 after five years of implementation and expense to the state.[9] Slaveholders were now required to either abandon the young children of slaves without compensation or assume the cost of their upkeep through the ages of twenty-five for females or twenty-eight for males.

> **"In one important respect the New York law did reflect a radical democratic approach: it conferred full civic rights on freedmen, allowing them to vote and bear arms. In this respect New York showed greater respect for republican equality than Massachusetts or Rhode Island where Blacks suffered legal discrimination."[10]**

Manumission Provisions

The 1799 Law had provided, that "… it shall be lawful for the owner of any slave immediately after the passing of this act to manumit such slave by a certificate for that purpose under his own hand and seal."[11] This action on the part of the slave holders, however, required certification by the Overseer of the Poor that these adults could support themselves independently of local expense. An amendment to the 1799 Law, in 1804, stipulated that this process of manumission could occur once these young adults reached the age of twenty-one for males and females, the age of eighteen years.[12]

The 1799 law had also placed a moratorium on the posting of a bond of $250 by the slave holder to ensure that no financial burden was placed on towns for their support of manumitted slaves. This bond had been an aspect of previous manumission requirements under various state laws. In its place, the statute provided that it was lawful for the owner of any slave immediately after the passing of this law, to manumit a slave by certification and the seal of the owner. It would be interesting to research just how many of the more than 21,000 "slaves", who lived in New York during this period, were actually freed under Gradual Abolition.

Some research does exist with respect to this manumission issue. Harry P. Yoshpe, in the Journal of Negro History, documents the manumission of only twenty-three (23) slaves during the period 1796-1800 in the County of New York and seventy-six (76) total manumitted in the State between 1783 and 1800.[13] It is more likely that the slave holders saw this provision as an opportunity to relieve themselves of the expenses inherent in the upkeep of older and sickly slaves. In fact, in counties throughout New York State manumission was a very rare occurrence. For instance, in Ulster County of the 207 wills of slaveholders probated from 1696 to 1816, only five provided for the manumission of their slaves.[14]

Other Provisions of the Act

Several other provisions were added in later years including an Act that was passed on 30 March 1810. This law stipulated that, "every person entitled to the services of a child born of a slave after July 4, 1799 shall cause the child to be taught reading so as to be able to read the Holy Scriptures, previous to becoming 21 years of age. Failure to cause the child to be so taught shall release the child from service at the age of 21 years."[15] Again, the slave holders resisted. Why should they have to pay for the education of their slaves when their own children remained illiterate? Again, research is limited with respect to compliance with this requirement of the law. There are, however, a few records that illustrate that New York slave holders did attempt to educate their slaves. **Document 4** represents a bill from March 1800 to Caldwell Watson from James Bleecker for "teaching your Black man Dick". The price for such instruction is described as "One Quarter and % and half load of Wood (?)."[16]

Document 4
Bill for Teaching Black man Dick

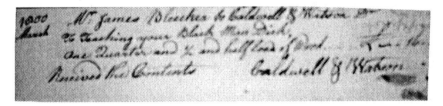

This transaction was undertaken some ten (10) years prior to the passage of the 1810 law. It represents more of a commitment on the part of Caldwell Watson than an obligation required by law.

In 1817, the State Legislature passed "An Act relative to slaves and servants" which constituted a major revision to the amended Gradual Abolition Act and represented the state's Final Abolition Law. The length of service for children born after July 4, 1799 had been reduced several times by previous amendments to the Gradual Abolition Law, first, to eighteen years for females and to twenty-one years for males and by way of the 1817 Law age requirements were "rolled back" to the original provisions of the 1799Law in an effort to guarantee slave holders the maximum term of 25 years for a female child and 28 years for a male child prior to the passage of Final Abolition.[17]

This new law stipulated that children born to slave women between July 4, 1799 and March 31, 1817 were still required to be servants to their mother's owner until the ages of twenty-five years for females and twenty-eight years for males, respectively. To confuse the issue even further, children of either sex born after the passage of this Act in 1817 through July 4, 1827, when this law became effective, owed service for only twenty-one years and were then to be freed.[18]

IMPLEMENTATION OF THE ACT

"Whites made no manifest effort to distinguish statutory slaves from slaves, because there was no effective difference in their treatment or employment. In fact, there is some evidence that some slaves' children born after passage of the gradual emancipation statutes considered themselves slaves."[19]

STATUS OF AFRICAN DESCENDANT CHILDREN

Although these children born after July 4th 1799 were not legally "slaves", they were *given* to the "owner" of their mothers as "servants" for a period of 25 or 28 years. This state sponsored program of *"de jure"* enslavement is a far cry from the freedom promised in the law. Moreover, this form of "servitude" was considerably different from the European system of "indentured servitude", which required between 3-7 years of service depending on the circumstance under which the individual was bound. The European system also made some provisions for the servant to purchase his or her freedom.

Much debate has ensued among historians with respect to the exact status of these African descendant children during Gradual Abolition. Historian Joanne Melish suggests using the term "statutory slave" for those born to slaves after the gradual emancipation statutes were passed. She points out that, unlike white indentured servants, such African descendant "statutory slaves" received nothing in return for their indenture. She recommends the use of the term "Slave" for a person considered a permanent piece of property and "Statutory slave" for one born immediately into a bondage that expires at a certain age. She further suggests that "Indentured servants" more accurately describes those African descendants and whites who contractually indenture themselves to a master.[20]

Ira Berlin in *"Many Thousand Gone"* offers an observation on gradual abolition as well, wherein he surmises that gradual abolition actually blurred any differences between enslavement and the "indentured servitude" created by the law.

> **"Although servitude, unlike slavery, was not hereditary, servants lived under the control of a master or mistress, and their rights to their labor could be sold or traded like other property. The more closely that indentured servitude became identified with black labor, the smaller the difference between the treatment of slave and servant ... The line between servitude and slavery was fine indeed for black indentured servants, particularly since white servants rarely served more than 7 years and rarely after the age of twenty-one."[21]**

PARTICIPATION OF ENSLAVERS

> **"Because the Overseer of the Poor would be inclined to bind out the child to the owner of the child's mother, masters could expect to derive a lucrative income from abandonment." "... this abandonment clause was, therefore, a disguised scheme for compensated abolition and it undoubtedly served to make gradual abolition more acceptable to slave holders conscious of their property rights."[22]**

As is usually the case when government attempts to protect the interests of certain entrepreneurial endeavors, this abandonment system was corrupted. In many instances, the original slave holders, after "abandoning" their rights to these children, were the recipients of the services (bondage) of the children (servants) and the compensation from the State for their maintenance and support. **Enslavers were <u>now</u> registered and subsidized by the State of New York.**

An example of this manipulated process is the case of Betty born on March 13, 1800, and Jeffery, born the following year, to a slave named Suke. Daniel Whitehead Kissam, a resident of North

Hempstead, owned Suke. These children were obviously abandoned by Kissam but placed back with Mr. Kissam by the Overseers of the Poor of North Hempstead. The following is an account from Aug. 28, 1804, of a state payment to Kissam for the support of Suke's children:

> *"To board and maintenance of Betty a female black child (free born) the daughter of Suke a female slave of the said Dan'l Whitehead Kissam (she being four years old the 13th day of March last) . . . being 12 months at $2 per month. . . . {$24} . . . To board and maintenance of Jeffery a male black child (free born) the son of the said Suke . . . born 3rd May 1801 {$24}."[23]*

This Warrant also includes an addition payment request of $48 for a child of Sarah another slave of Kissam's.

> *"To board and maintain of a female Black child named Jan(free born)[according to the Gradual Abolition Act of 1799] the Daughter of Sarah the slave of the said Dan'l Whitehead Kissam being 3 years old the 27th July last from the 27th July 1802 to the 27th July 1804 being 2 years old ... 2dollars per month .... Born 27th July 1801."[24]*

Note that this is an example of the state directly paying the slave owner or Master, Kissam, to board and maintain three children of two of his *own* slaves. Kissam was taking advantage of the abandonment provisions of the 1799 Law. Document 5 is a record of submission by Town of North Hempstead to the State of New York for Payment to Daniel Whitehead Kissam.

Document 5
Record of submission by Town of North Hempstead to the
State of New York for Payment to Daniel Whitehead Kissam [25]

28 August 1804

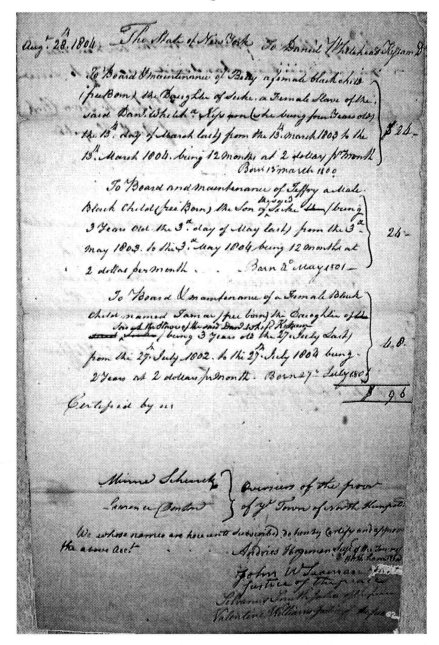

This provision made these abandoned children paupers, subject to being bound out by the Overseers of the Poor, who could use state monies in the amount of $3.50 a month per child to subsidize their support and maintenance. The law did not prohibit the Overseers of the Poor from binding children out to the same slave master who had abandoned them in the first instance; neither did it prohibit the Overseers from boarding these abandoned children with their mother's owner until such time as they were bound out to another. Slave holders could be paid $3.50 a month for the maintenance of every child born to one of their slaves. In the example above, Kissam was paid only $2 a month due to an amendment to the law passed in 1802 that lowered the rate of subsidy to $2.00 a month per child.

The infant abandonment program was very popular in New York State and large numbers of African descendant children were given up to local Overseers of the Poor under its provisions. The eagerness with which slave holders participated in the program was reflected in the universally high rate of compliance with the statute, which required slave holders to register their intention to abandon an infant within one year after their birth. This high degree of compliance with the provisions of the 1799 Law provides intimation into the nature of the slave holder's mentality and the economic importance of slaves to the overall economy and continued well being of those in positions of power in New York State. Slave holders had been successful in preserving their "rights to property" over and above the protestations and lobbying efforts of the abolitionist forces of the state. The Gradual Abolition Law's abandonment provisions proved to be so advantageous to the state's slave holders, that cities and towns far removed from the Dutch dominated southern counties of New York State complied vigorously.

WASHINGTON COUNTY

Cities, towns and villages in counties throughout New York State judiciously followed the reporting and registration requirements of the Gradual Abolition Law. The small rural towns of upstate New York and Washington County provide a very clear example of this participation. In the Town of Salem, "The Minutes of the Town of Salem" list the various reporting categories that were required by the 1799 Law. [26] Included in these official minutes outlined in Table 1 are the dispositions of various slave categories submitted by Salem slave holders that required certification or approval of the Town Clerk or Overseers of the Poor, as required by the Gradual Abolition Act of 1799.

Table 1

SALEM, NY TOWN MINUTES (1790-1826)

SUBJECT	YEAR	MONTH/DAY
Slaves (certificate by Poor master that slave, Lottee, is manumitted, by Edward Savage)	1818	7-Jan
Slaves (certificate of birth of Cato to slave, Amy, Owner Anthony Blanchard)	1818	5-Sep
Slaves (certificate of birth of male, Dick, to slave Violet, owner Margaret Warford)	1807	1-Oct
Slaves (certificate of birth of Sylvia, mother-Rose, owner Ebenezer Proudfit)	1805	11-Jul
Slaves (certificate of mulatto birth, male named Cuff, owner James Harvey)	1808	24-Mar
Slaves (certificate of ownership of child slave, Moses to Ebenezer Russell)	1803	17-Aug
Slaves (certification of Peter, born to slave, Beck; owner Anthony Blanchard)	1810	27-Apr
Slaves (certification that manumitted slave, Amy is capable of supporting herself)	1820	29-Nov
Slaves (certification that slave Jack Becker or John Dean can support himself)	1825	8-Mar
Slaves (certificate claiming slave child, Charles Woods, owner Nathan Wilson)	1821	11-May
Slaves (John Williams abandons right to slave child, London, born of slave Dina	1803	17-Oct
Slaves (Poor master certification that former slave, Flora can provide for herself)	1818	9-Mar
Slaves (slave Charles of owner Nathan Wilson, Esq. is set free)	1826	11-Jan

The initial category, the registration or certification of the birth of a slave child, is highlighted as "certified by the Town Clerk or Poor Master" in six instances between the years 1803-1818. One such registration is recorded as such:

> **Sir, my Negro woman Rose had a child on the third of April last whom she named Sylvia and who you will plan to record in the Town Book agreeable to Law.   Ebinezer Proudfit   Salem July 1ˢᵗ 1805**

Another record states:

> **I certify that a certain male Child born of a Negro wrench a slave belonging to me was born on the 24ᵗʰ day of September 1807 in my family and that said Child is a Molato to which I have given the name of Cuff.**
> **Salem County of Washington, March 24ᵗʰ 1808**
> **   James Garvey[27]**

It would seem that Mr. James Garvey was attempting not only to meet the requirements of the Gradual Abolition Law but at the same time, it can be argued that he was also making a statement with respect to the parentage of this young boy, Cuff.

Town officials were also required to certify the official abandonment of the children of slaves. Table 1 identifies one instance of abandonment when John Williams abandons his rights to a slave child named London, born to one of his female slaves named Dina Williams. Williams makes the following statement with respect to this abandonment:

> **Pursuant to the Law of this State [posted] sp. this 8ᵗʰ of April 1801 I do hereby abandon my right of a Negro male child named London about ten months old which said Negro male child of a Female Slave purchased by me from one McGeorge Ashley of Whitehall named Dina.**
> **Salem Oct. 7ᵗʰ 1805   John Williams[28]**

In addition, these official records identify the instances of slave holders, Ebinezer Rupill and Nathan Wilson - registering slave children Moses and Charles Woods, respectively. These two records provide another interesting insight into the provisions of the 1799 Law. Unlike John Williams, who abandons his rights to the slave child London, these two slave holders are asserting and receiving certification of their rights to ownership. Mr. Rupill's certification assumes the following form:

> *I Ebenezer Rupill of Salem in the County of Washington and State of New York do hereby certify in compliance to an Act of the Legislature of the State in such cases made and provided that I am the owner of a certain Male Negro Child named Moses aged eight months.*
> *Salem 17th August 1803*   *Ebenezer Rupill*

This statement of ownership reflects the newly acquired status of "slave ownership" sanctioned by the State of New York under the provisions of the Gradual Abolition Act of 1799. The 1799 Law also provided guidelines for the manumission of slaves. The Law had placed a moratorium on previous requirements of the posting of a bond of $250 by the slave owner to ensure that no financial burden was placed on towns for their support of manumitted slaves. These Salem Town minutes record five (5) instances of manumissions on the part of the town's slave holders.

Recorded manumissions of Amy (1820), Jack Becker/John Dean (1825), and Flora (1818) address specifically the requirement of certification by the Poor Master [Overseer of the Poor] that they are capable of supporting themselves. In two other recorded manumissions, Lotte (1818) manumitted by Edward Savage is certified by the Poor Master while Charles (1826), owned by Nathan Wilson is just "set free". It would seem that in Lotte's case, the requirement of certification had been met, even though it doesn't specifically speak to the issue of being able to support herself. Charles, on the other hand, probably qualified under an amendment of the law that set manumission eligibility at twenty-one years of age for males instead of the original law's twenty-eight year requirement.

Likewise in other Washington County towns like Hebron, town minutes record similar actions of the town slave holders and the

Overseers of the Poor with respect to the required reporting and certification of African descendants and their "statutory slave" children under the Gradual Abolition Act of 1799. [29] One such record lists the birth of an African descendant child as follows:

> **"Born on the twentieth second day of last year (1800) a black Negro male child his mothers name is Bett. Childs name is Anthony said Bett is a slave to me**
> **Hebron Feb. 7th 1801   William McCracken**
> **Entered on the record May 1801   signed: Wm. McClellan, T.Clerk"[30]**

DUTCHESS COUNTY

In Dutchess County, towns like Beekman contain records that provide us with similar information in their endeavors to comply with the requirements of the 1799 Law. [31] Town Records for 10 August 1800, record the fact that:

> **On this date,** *was born Dinah, a black girl, daughter of Susan now in possession of ZACHARIAH FLAGLER.*

In the town of Lloyd, Dutchess County; The Slave Book of the Town of Lloyd, New York[32] records the registration of the births of "statutory slaves" to the following town slave holders:

3-31-1801	*Josaphat Hasbrouck reported birth of Lucy;*
4-7-1801	*Daniel Woolsey reported birth of Rachel;*
3-6-1802	***Josiah R. Eltinge reported birth of Trine;***
10-4-1802	*Ketcham, late reports of Bob & Fillis;*
2-18-1803	*Josaphat Hasbrouck reported Abraham;*
8-8-1803	***Josiah R. Eltinge reported Nan;***
3-6-1805	*Griffin Ransom reported Jane;*
11-5-1805	*Wm. Kctcham reported Susannah;*
3-9-1808	***Josiah R. Eltinge reported boy Degaun;***
3-10-1809	*Titus Ketcham reported Frank;*
3-10-1810	*Zacharias Hasbrouck reported Isabel b. 1804, Jane b. 1805, Sara b. 1807;*

11-9-1809	*Joseph Ransom reported Caesar Primes;*
4-9-1810	***Josiah R. Eltinge reported Peg;***
5-15-1813	*Titus Ketcham reported Ann;*
5-23-1813	***Josiah R. Eltinge reported Anthony;***
12-22-1815	*Abram J. Eltinge reported Caesar b. 1809, Peter b. 1811, Mire (Myra) b. 1814;*
1-2-1816	*Titus Ketcham reported Susan;*
4-3-1816	*Zacharias Hasbrouck reported Dinah;*
2-8-1817	***Josiah R. Eltinge, reported Betty;***
4-12-1818	***Josiah R. Eltinge reported Susan;***
3-10-1808	***Nathaniel Potter & Josiah R. Eltinge, two of the overseers of the poor, declared free, Abram, former slave of Alexander Coe;***
11-16-1813	*John I. LeFevre reported he had Hannah.*

"The book was closed 1825 and in 1827 all slaves were free."

It is interesting to note that in many cases the Overseers of the Poor in these New York State cities and towns, the individuals charged with the responsibility of managing (if you will) these abandoned African descendant children, were either slave holders themselves or relatives of slave holders. (**See highlighted entries above.**)

Also in Dutchess County, the small Town of Northeast documents the following records required by the 1799 Law:

> *Record of Katy Jones, who was born May 27th, 1801, at the house of Martu Lawrence, in the town of Northeast. Her mother was a slave to said Lawrence, named Dinah.*
>
> *Recorded December 30th, 1812   ISRAEL HARRIS, Clerk.*

Also:

> *We, the subscribers, Overseers of the Poor of the Town of Northeast, in the County Duchess, do certify that Driss, a slave of Nicholas Row, of said Town of Northeast, appears*

to be under the age of fifty years, and of sufficient ability to'
provide for himself.

Northeast Town, Oct. 26,1813   Jeptha Wilbur, Philo M.
Winchell, Overseers of Poor [33]

In another small town in Dutchess County, Amenia, their Town
Record Book of 1800 lists the following slave manumission records
required by the 1799 Law:

Date	Remarks
7.28.1808	*Dinah. A black woman, slave to estate of Conrad Winegar of Amenia, is not over 40 years; sufficient ability to provide for herself. Signed 7. 2.1808, James P. Smith & John Garnsey, overseers of poor*
11.9.1808	*Charles – a black man, slave to George Wheeler of Amenia; is under age of 50 and of, sufficient ability to provide for himself; do admit as one of the inhabitants said town.*
4.3.1809	*Nan – a negro woman; slave to Cyrus Crosby; is under age 50 and sufficient ability to provide for herself.*
4.3.1809	*Bett – a negro woman; slave to John Guernsey; is under age 50 and of sufficient ability to provide for herself.*
3.6.1811	*Titus Frankinson – male slave of Henry Delavergne; desireous to manumit the slave; under age of 50 and sufficient to maintain himself.*[34]

Also included in this Amenia Town Record Book is a listing of
'children born of slaves":

Record of children born of slaves in Town of Amenia.

2.14.1801:   *Skies – son of Clara, a slave property of Cap!. Jacob Backed 4.13.1800: Clara - dau. of Jude, a slave of Maj. Nathan Conklin*

4.13.1800:   *Clara - dau. of Jude, a slave of Maj. Nathan Conklin*

1.16.1802:   *Prime – son of Jude, a slave of Maj. Nathan Conklin*

5.14.1803:   *Nestor – son of Leah, female slave of Ebenezer Mott*

10.1.1803:   *Leonard Cockswain – son of female slave of Jacob Backee*

5. 2.1800:   *Genny – dau. of Nancy, slave of Martin De Lamatter*

5. 7.1802:   *Fenda – dau. of Nancy, slave of Martin De Lamatter*

8.17.1804:   *Phoebe – dau. of Nancy, slave of Martin De Lamauer*

8.18.1806:   *Hannah Cockswain - dau. of female slave of Jacob Backee 10.16.1807: Sally – dau. of female slave of Isaac Smith*

3.16.1812:   *Vici – dau. of Clara, a female slave of Jacob Backee*

3.27. 1814:   *Dolly – dau. to Lucy, a female slave of William Nase*

5. 7.1815:   *Philip – son of Dinah, a slave of Benj. B. Adams*

end of slave manumission records"[35]

In large, Dutchess County cities, local officials and slave holders alike were willing participants in this registration and subsidized abandonment process. The City of Poughkeepsie kept extremely detailed records with respect to the requirement of this 1799 Law, the Town Record Book, a record of all city related transactions, lists entries from 1769 to 1833.[36] "Town Minutes of Poughkeepsie" detail the disposition of forty-five (45) instances, between the years 1799 and 1807, of enslaved children registrations, manumissions and child abandonments, (See Table 2 below.)

Table 2
Town Minutes Poughkeepsie from 1769 to 1833

TOWN MINUTES - POUGHKEEPSIE
DUTCHESS COUNTY, N.Y.
TOWN RECORD BOOK (1799 - 1807)

SUBJECT	YEAR	MONTH/ DAY	
Slaves (certificate by Overseers of the Poor that slave Hannibal, owned by John Wellsey, can support self)	1799	July	27
Slaves (slave, Bet, of owner William Reade is certified by him as liberated, recorded Town Clerk	1799	October	19
Slaves (slaves manumitted and set free by Thomas Casey: Prince, 37 years; Connie (sp) 33 years; Hannah, 16 years; Ginny, 14 years; Jacob, 12 years; Lucy, 10 years. Miranda, 8 years; Mary, 5 years and Prince, 2 yrs)	1800	April	21
Slaves (certify manumission of Bet by John Reade, recorded by Town Clerk)	1800	Feb.	12
Slaves (manumission of Joe Whome by John Van Denburgh, who bought slave the same day at vendue)	1800	March	25
Slaves (certificate of birth Bill; 8 months, mother not named, owner Smith Thompson, recorded T. Clerk).	1800	June	5
Slaves (certificate of birth Tom, 6 months, mother not named, owner Charles Hoffman, recorded by T. Clerk)	1800	June	3
Slaves (certificate of birth Harry, 5 months, mother Mary, owner Gilbert Livingston, recorded by T. Clerk)	1800	May	20
Slaves (certificate of manumission of Peggy owned by Francis Pitts, recorded by T. Clerk)	1800	June	30
Slaves (certificate of birth Jean, mother not named, owner James Westervedt, recorded T.Clerk)	1800	Sept.	26
Slaves (certificate of birth Cloi, mother Mary, owner Henry Dodge, recorded T.Clerk)	1800	June	24
Slaves (certificate of manumission of Susannah, owned by Myndert Van Wilick estate, recorded T.Clerk)	1800	Nov.	27
Slaves (certificate of manumission of Harry, owned by Jacob Duryee, recorded T.Clerk)	1800	August	11

Slaves (certificate of birth of Henry born 26 June 1801 of Charrity, owned by Robert Noxen, recorded T.Clerk)	1801	Nov.	17
Slaves (certificate of birth Mable, 27 April1801, mother Rose, owned by Thomas Mitchel, recorded T.Clerk)	1801	Nov.	17
Slaves (cerrtificate of birth Nancy, 11 Feb.1802, mother Aime, owned by Gideon Boyce,recorded T.Clerk)	1802	April	7
Slaves (certificate of birth Samuel, 15June1800, mother Bett, owned by Richard Davis, recorded T.Clerk)	1801	Jan.	8
Slaves (certificate of birth Romeo, 2 Aug.1800, mother Jude, owned by James Branble, recorded T.Clerk)	1801	Feb.	25
Slaves (certification of manumission Jack, owned by Theodorus Bailey, recordedT.Clerk)	1801	Feb.	27
Slaves (certification of birth Bet, 5Dec.1801, mother Eave, owned by John Wilsey, recorded T.Clerk)	1802	June	27
Slaves (cert.of birth Esther,last of Nov.1802, mother Grace, owned by Smith Thompson-disposed of to John Jacob Bush,recorded T.Clerk)	1802	Dec.	25
Slaves (certificate of birth Jane, 12Aug.1802, mother Sall, owned by Samuel Dinchney, recorded T.Clerk)	1803	Feb.	20
Slaves (certificate of birthDomp(sp.), 8Sept.1803, mother Flora, owned by James Westervedt,recorded T.Clerk)	1803	Sept	19
Slaves (certificate of birth Ab, mother Bitt, owned by Rich Davis)	1803	May	8
Slaves (certificate of birth Gilbert, 25April1803, mother Peg, owned by William Mory, recoeded T.Clerk)	1803	Sept	5
Slaves (manumission Sall, owned by John Bailey, recorde T.Clerk)	1803	March	20
Slaves (certificate of birth Susan, 14 Aug.1803, mother Rose, owned by Thomas Mitchel, recorded T.Clerk)	1803	Sept.	22
Slaves (certificate of manumission of Abraham , 21 years, recorded T. Clerk)	1803	Oct.	6
Slaves (certificate of manumission for Sall a.k.a.Mary James, owned by John Bailey, recored T.Clerk)	1804	March	20
Slaves (certificate of birth Tunes,June1802 and Loretta,Nov.1802, mother Nancy owned by John Cooke, provides for manumission of Tunes at age 28, recorded T.Clerk)	1804	March	31

Slaves (certificate of manumission of Debby Morris, owned by Samuel Luckey, recorded T.Clerk & cert.Overseers of Poor) — 1804 — May — 13

Slaves (certificate of birth no name, mother Flora, owned by John Read, recorded T.Clerk) — 1804 — July — 19

Slaves (certificate of birth Phebe 20Nov.1803, mother Jane, owned by Dearin, recorded T.Clerk) — 1804 — April — 13

Slaves (certificate for manumission of Margaret Fox by husband Tony Fox, recorded T Clerk & cert. Overseers of Poor) — 1804 — Oct. — 29

Slaves (certificate of manumission for Nanny Dearing, owned by James Devine, recorded T.Clerk & cert. Overseers) — 1804 — Aug. — 27

Slaves (certificate of birth Cloi, 24June1804, mother Manda, owned by Elizabeth Rogers, recorded T. Clerk) — 1805 — June — 1

Slaves (certificate of birth Boyson(sp.), 2Sept.1805, mother Sylvia owner by Rob(sp.) Gill, recorded T.Clerk) — 1805 — June — 28

Slaves (certification of manumission for Adam Luckey owned by Thomas W. Jaycocks, recorded T.Clerk & cert. Overseers) — 1805 — July — 3

Slave (certificate of birth Silver(sp.), 10July1805, mother Mary owner by Henry & Sarah Dodge, recorded T.Clerk) — 1806 — Feb. — 17

Slave (cert. of birth George, March 1805, mother Dido(sp.) owned by Caleb/Joseph Reade, recorded T.Clerk) — 1806 — May — 16

Slave (abandonment of Silver, daughter of Mary, owned by Henry and Sarah Dodge, recorded T.Clerk) — 1806 — May — 22

Slave (ecrtificate of manumission of Ishmael Fasher(sp.) owned by Henry Dodge, recorded T.Clerk) — 1806 — May — 26

Slave (certificate of birth Liz, 1April1806, (?)sp.), owned by Simon Trear, recorded T.Clerk) — 1807 — March — 4

Slave (certificate of birth Peter, 4June1807, mother Bett owned by Dorick and Catherine Wistervelt, recorded T.Clerk) — 1807 — July — 18

Slave (certificate of manumission of Benjamin James, 26 years, owned by James Dearin, cert. overseers of Poor) — 1807 — June — 4

Compiled from Poughkeepsie (Dutchess County), NY "Town Record Book" 1769-1833, Adriance Memorial Library, Poughkeepsie, NY 6/11/75

These records chronicle the certification and registration of twenty-five (25) births to enslaved women in Poughkeepsie. By registering themselves and the births of children to their female slaves with the town clerk, slave holders are following the mandates set out in the Gradual Abolition Act of 1799. All of these cases follow the same pattern for the certification of these children by the owner of their mothers and the Overseers of the Poor or Town Clerk. However, there is one specific instance where this simple registration provision is significantly different from the others. It speaks to the abandonment provision of the 1799 Law.

This example of abandonment, in fact a typical representation of the provisions of the 1799 Law, involves the registration and certification of the birth of a female named Silver (sp.) on the 10th of July 1805. Henry and Sarah Dodge of Poughkeepsie are the owners of Silver's mother, Mary. Their certification is recorded with the Town Clerk on the 17th of February 1806 and falls within the requirements for registration "within the first year of birth" under this Law. However, on the 22nd of May 1806, the Dodges abandon their rights to Silver and she is transferred to the Overseers of the Poor at age one year and one month. This example of the abandonment provisions gives us a clearer idea of the position of helplessness and insecurity that pervaded the lives of mothers of African descent and their children. In this case as in so many others, Mary loses her year old child to the Overseers of the Poor through no decision of her own.

Poughkeepsie Town Records also record sixteen (16) instances of enslaved manumissions between the years of 1799 and 1807. The certifications of manumission by slave holders in Poughkeepsie are recorded by the Town Clerk and are entered into the official record of the city. In most instances, these records indicate that the manumitted slave was under fifty years of age and able to provide for themselves. These requirements were stipulations of the laws that were passed after 1799. Three of these records are of particular interest and provide a view of the varying methods under which slaves were manumitted in New York State under the Act of 1799 and succeeding laws. One such record details the manumission of nine (9) slaves at one time by one Thomas Casey of Poughkeepsie.

I Thomas Casey of the town of Poughkeepsie in the County of Dutchess do hereby certify and make knowing that by virtue of an act of the Legislature of the State of New York entitled an act for the gradual abolition of Enslavement passed 29th March 1799. I have and by those present do manumit and set free the following from being the slaves of me the said Thomas Casey. To wit.. Prince a Negro man aged thirty seven years. Connie (sp.) a Negro woman of the age of thirty three years. Hannah a Negro girl of the age of sixteen years Ginny a Negro girl of the age of fourteen years Jacob a Negro boy of the age of twelve years Lucy a Negro girl of the age of ten years Miranda a Negro girl of the age of eight years Mary a Negro girl of the age of five years and Prince a Negro boy of the age of two years. In testimony whereas I have herewith set my hand and seal this Twenty first day of April in the year one thousand eight hundred.

Thomas Casey

Witness
Smith Thompson
Gilbert Livingston
Presented this 25th Day of April One thousand eight hundred

Richard Everitt, Town Clerk

It is not clear whether these individuals are a family unit. However, it would seem likely that if you were going to manumit your individual slaves, that you wouldn't manumit two and five-year olds but you would, rather, under the provisions of the 1799 Law, abandon your rights and obligations to them by transferring them to the Overseers of the Poor. Furthermore, because there is no certification by the slave owner or the Overseers of the Poor that these individuals were capable of providing for themselves, it could be argued that they were in fact a family unit. The manumission of nine (9) slaves at one time would seem to be an expensive proposition on the part of Mr. Casey. Perhaps Mr. Casey had Quaker or abolitionist motivations?

Another unusual case involves the manumission of Joe Whome (sp.) who is manumitted by Peter Van DenBurgh on the same day that he is purchased by him at a vendue of the heirs of John Van Denburgh, deceased. No indication is given as to whether there is any relationship between the purchaser and the deceased, however, the immediate manumission of Joe Whome would seem to indicate that there was some prior relationship between him and the purchaser. Why else would someone immediately free a slave that they had just purchased?

The third manumission entry is of great interest. It is the manumission of Margaret Fox by her husband, Tony Fox. This entry is recorded in this manner:

Whereas Tony Fox a free black man of the town of Poughkeepsie in the County of Dutchess and State of New York Labourer (sp.) has made application to us William Emott and Thomas Nelson Overseers of the Poor of the Town of Poughkeepsie in the County and State aforesaid In order to obtain a certificate immediately before the manumission of his wife and Slave Margaret Fox said to be under fifty years of age. Agreeable to an act of the Legislature of the State of New York entitled an Act concerning Slaves and Servants passed on 8th of April 1801 We the said Overseers having examined the before named Slave Margaret do on mature deliberation hereby certify that she appears to be under the age of fifty years and of sufficient ability to provide for her self giving under our hands the eighteenth day of June in the year one thousand eight hundred and four.

Witnesses Present}   Wm. Emott}   Overseers of
John Van Rluetz (sp.)   Thomas Nelson}   The Poor
Recorded the 29th Day of October 1804
Richard Everitt, Town Clerk

This is truly an historic example. The history of African descendants in New York State chronicles the practice of "free" African descendants willing in numerous cases to take on family members and spouses as "slaves" in order to prevent them from being sold to white slave holders and possibly taken to other parts of the state or country. They were also concerned about self determination with respect to the future and well being of their family members.

159

Further, this act of self preservation was also about attempting to keep their families under one roof, particularly if one spouse was free and the other labeled a "slave." In this instance, Tony and Margaret Fox found a way to manipulate the existing system of enslavement and continue their lives together as "free" people under the provisions of the 1799 Gradual Abolition Law.

ULSTER COUNTY

The practice of holding slaves was also quite common in the city of New Paltz. It was so universal, that most if not all persons of consequence were in possession of a number of slaves. Due to the Act of 1799 and its provisions, it became necessary to record the birth of slave children in the "Records of the Town of New Paltz"[37]. Some of these records include the following entries:

> *"Sept. 19, 1799: General Joseph Hasbrouck delivered to me a certificate that he had a Female Negro Child born, and Call'd her name Jane.*
>
> *Recorded by Josiah Hasbrouck, Town Clerk."*

> *"One Thousand Eight Hundred & One, October the twenty-second Coll. Jos. Hasbrouck, Farmer of the Town of New Paltz, Did Deliver to me a note in writing; the purport of it was that he had on the ninth Day of last July a black female Child born of my wench Kingo and named (Dian). Recorded by me, Josiah Hasbrouck, Town Clerk."*

> *"Sir, - agreeable to the Laws of this state I hereby, Request you to Inter in the Records of the town the Birth of a female negro Child which is born of my Negro Woman Slave on 27th of February, 1806, which said Child is named Jin. I am yours, Josiah Eltinge. New Paltz, Sept. 5th, 1806. "To Jacob Hasbrouck, Town Clerk of the Town of New Paltz."[38]*

Among those who had African descendant children "born to them" between 1799 and 1806, and of which a record is made in this Town Book", are the following:

Gen. Joseph Hasbrouck, Elizabeth Vandemerken, Nathaniel Deyo, Mary, widow of Charles Broadhead, Benjamin Hasbrouck, Solomon Eltinge Jr., Charles Broadhead Jr., Abraham J. Hardenbergh, Josiah Hasbrouck, Jacob LeFever, John Van Gordon, Daniel Johnson, Abraham D. Deyo, Josiah R. Eltinge, Roeliff Eltinge, Jacob Hardenbergh, Ester Wurts, David Deyo, John A. LeFever, Wilhelmus Hasbrouck, Daniel DuBois, Tunis van Vliet, Nathaniel LeFcver, Henry Eltinge, Daniel Requa, Benjamin Freer, Philip Deyo, Griffin Ransom, Cornelius DuBois, Zacharias Hasbrouck, Daniel Hasbrouck, Simon L. Deyo, John C. Low, David Lockwood, Daniel Deyo, Peter Freer, William Kitchim, William Ketchim, Solomon Eltinge, Johannes LeFever, Josiah R. Eltinge, Daniel Woolsey, Daniel Jansen, Jonathan Deyo, Mathusalem DuBois, Petrus Freer, Titus Ketchum, Jacob LeFever, Jacob Wurts, Samuel Hasbrouck, and Matthew LeFever..[39]

WESTCHESTER COUNTY

Town Records for the Town of Yorktown in Westchester County give us a fuller story of the fate of African descendants and their children just prior to and after the passage of the Gradual Abolition Act of 1799. York town (as it was spelled in early town documents) was what could be described as a "Quaker Town" for obvious reasons because of its large population of Quaker residents. It is well documented that the Quakers had taken a stand against enslavement by the mid-1700s. It was their practice to purchase slaves from their owners and set them free.

Table 3 details the "Records of Negro Children Born to Slaves in the Town of Yorktown after the 4th Day of July in the Year of 1799,"[40] the year that the law was enacted, to the year 1810. Fourteen (14) such records are compiled for the period 1799-1810 of these records four (4) entries for the "certification of the birth" of children born to "slave" women, as well an additional eight (8) entries that record the manumission of slaves by Yorktown resident slave holders.

Table 3
"Yorktown Record of Negro Children Born to Slaves"

RECORD OF NEGRO CHILDREN BORN OF SLAVES IN
YORKTOWN, NY AFTER THE 4TH DAY OF JULY, 1799

SUBJECT	YEAR	MONTH/ DAY	
Slaves (certificate of manumission of Dianah, 22 years, owned by Isaac Forster, recorded T. Clerk& Overseers)	1799	Dec.	20
Slaves (certificate of manumission of Dick, owned by Ebenezer White, cert. Overseers of the Poor) and Justices of the Peace, recorded T. Clerk)	1800	Nov.	27
Slaves (certificate of manumission for Eve,42 years, owned by Richard Davenport, recorded T. Clerk)	1800	Dec.	26
Slaves (certificate of manumission of James, 60 years, owned by Richard Davenport, recorded T. Clerk)	1800	Dec.	26
Slaves (certificate of manumission of Solomon, 27 years, owned by John Hyatt, recorded T. Clerk)	1801	May	23
Slaves (certificate of birth of Peggy, 25 July 1802, owned by George Sittar, recorded T. Clerk)	1803	Jan.	10
Slaves (certificate of birth of Harriet, 28 Oct. 1803, mother Hannah, owned by Susan Delancy, recorded T. Clerk)	1804	June	15
Slaves (certificate of birth of Nance, 24 June 1803, owned by Gabriel Knopp, recorded T. Clerk)	1804	Dec.	10
Slaves (certificate of birth of Brister, 22 Dec. 1804, owned by Caleb Morgan, recorded T. Clerk)	1805	Feb.	23
Slaves (certificate of manumission for Primas, owned by Ebenezer White, recorded T. Clerk, cert. Overseers & Justices of Peace)	1806	Jan.	(?)
Slaves (certificate for manumission for Dianah, certified by Overseers of the Poor & Justices of Peace, recrd T. Clerk)	1806	Sept.	26
Slaves (certificate of manumission for Mingo, owned by Amos Whitney, cert. Overseers & recorded T. Clerk)	1806	Oct.	25
Slaves (certificate of birth of Ben Dater, 23 July 1806, mother Hannah, owned by Elijah Lee, recorded T. Clerk)	1807	Jan.	9
Slaves (certificate of birth of Erine Dater, 25June1809, mother Bet, owned by Ebenezer White, recorded T.Clerk)	1809	July	28

This small increase in births over an eleven-year period seems to contradict the fact that the Town Census records for 1799-1810 include sixty-five (65) African descendants. In fact, the number of manumissions recorded during this same period offsets the number of births. It is clear that the residents of Yorktown remained very active in the institution of enslavement even after the enactment of the 1799 Law and with the knowledge of impending "total abolition". Yet, the number of free residents of African descent rose from 17 to 127 individuals, living in 63 households, with 14 of these households of African descent.

It would seem that the two competing forces of pro-enslavement Dutch and abolitionist Quakers staged an all out battle over enslavement and abolition in this small but significant New York town. The increase in free African descendants may be attributed to a number of factors:

1- The Quaker practice of buying slaves and freeing them may have accounted for some of this number;

2- The 1799 Law, which provided for the gradual abolition of enslavement, no doubt gave incentive to others; and,

3- Free African descendants from other areas may have also traveled to Yorktown to work on the large farms that were typical of the area.

ONTARIO COUNTY

In the upstate County of Ontario similar records are found in the Ontario County Archives and Records Center. However, these records are more often than not included in the Highway books as opposed to town clerk records or specific records designated as slave related.

In 1797, Moses Atwater of Canandaigua (Ontario County), who is described as a respected local judge and physician, records his purchase of Esther, an "indentured servant for life (slave)", from Martin Dudley. He carefully points out that Esther's two-month old child would remain the property of Capt. Dudley, doc. 6.[41] Here we have another example of the separation of mother and child during Gradual Abolition, a subject that will be discussed in greater detail later in this work.

Document 6
Purchase Of Ester And 2 Mo. Old Child

I hereby certify this day I have purchased of Capt.
Martin Dudley of this Town a Negro woman named
Ester an Indented Servant for life — And that the said
Negro girl had a male child at the time of two months
old, which child the said Dudley retains as his prop-
= erty.
Canandaigua March 6th 1797   Moses Atwater.

Another Canandaigua entry from 1 October 1815, well into the legislated period of Gradual Abolition, documents John C. Spencer a local attorney, state official and later presidential cabinet member, enforcing his legal claim to the life and services of Harriet, born 29 January 1815, the ten-month old daughter of his slave named Phoebe. This process of registration is required by the Gradual Abolition Act and indicated Mr. Spencer's intention not to abandon his rights to the services of this "statutory slave" Harriet, but rather plans to retain her services for his own needs. In this instance, Phoebe and her child are not separated by their slave holder/master; however Harriet, a "statutory slave" can expect her treatment to be no different than her enslaved mother. Harriet's birth is recorded by the Town Clerk on 18 November 1815.[42]

The record states that Harriet and her mother Phoebe are eventually freed by state law in 1827. This statement is relevant to Phoebe's enslavement however it assumes that Harriet is freed as well. The fact of the matter is that Harriet under the provisions of the Gradual

Abolition Act could have legally been held as a "statutory slave" by Mr. Spencer until 1840. This would have indicated that she had the status of "statutory slave" for the full twenty-five (25) years allowed by this law, (doc. 7). [43]

Document 7
Birth Of Harriet To Phoebe

9 January 1815

A BRIEF HISTORY OF THE LIFE OF LLOYD COLBERT

The story of Lloyd Colbert is an interesting account of a family of African descent and their survival during enslavement and gradual abolition in New York State. In Canandaigua, Ontario County on 18 October 1814, the Overseers of the Poor, Phineas Bates and Ambrose Phillips certify "that a negro slave named Lloyd Colbert ...owned by Judge Nathanial Howell appears to be under the age of forty-five years and of sufficient ability to provide for himself." This document is witnessed by Walter Hubbelle. Essentially, this document supports the manumission of Lloyd Colbert by Judge Howell, as required by "the third section of the act named "An Act concerning slaves and servants", which stated that the Overseers of the Poor were required to personally certify all manumissions. Lloyd Colbert is certified as capable of supporting himself and doesn't require any assistance from the Town of Canandaigua, (doc. 8). [44]

Document 8
Overseers Of The Poor Manumission Of Lloyd Colbert [45]

18 October 1814

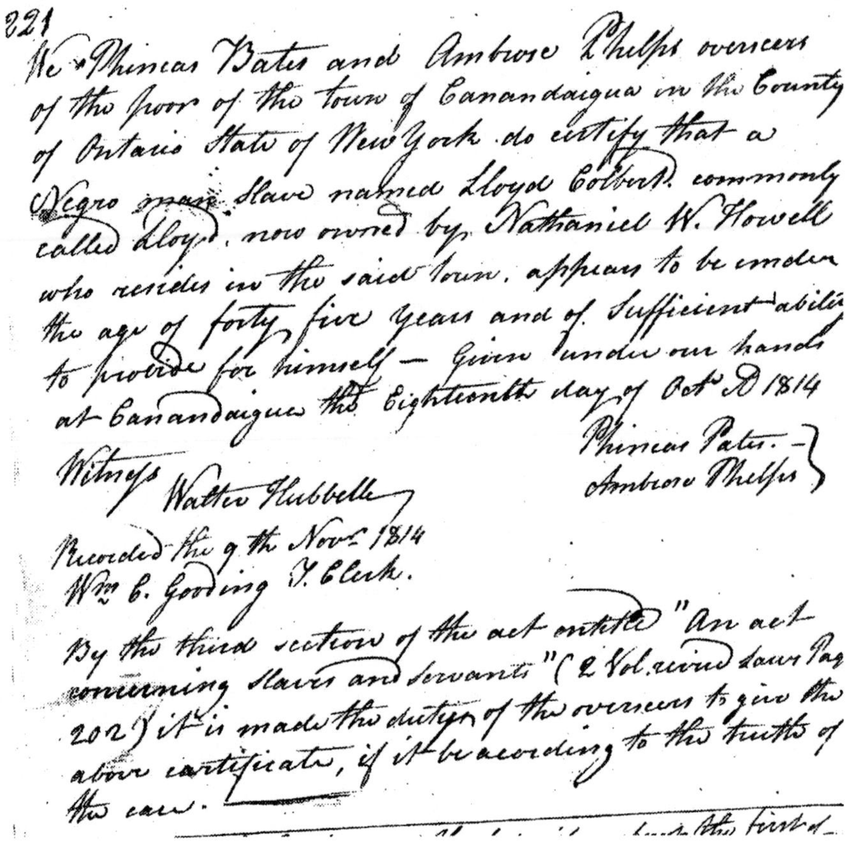
221
We Phineas Bates and Ambrose Phelps overseers of the poor of the town of Canandaigua in the County of Ontario State of New York do certify that a Negro man slave named Lloyd Colbert commonly called Lloyd now owned by Nathaniel W. Howell who resides in the said town appears to be under the age of forty five years and of sufficient ability to provide for himself — Given under our hands at Canandaigua the Eighteenth day of Octr AD 1814

Phineas Bates
Ambrose Phelps

Witness Walter Hubbell

Recorded the 9th Novr 1814
Wm C. Gooding T. Clerk

By the third section of the act entitled "An act concerning slaves and servants" (2 Vol. revised laws Pag 202) it is made the duty of the overseers to give the above certificate, if it be according to the truth of the case.

The Colbert family was one of the oldest African-American families in Canandaigua. Daniel Dorsey, who settled around Lyons, brought the Colberts to Ontario County as slaves from Maryland. Among them was Lloyd Colbert, oldest son of Phoebe Holland and James Colbert. Judge Nathanial Howell purchased Lloyd Colbert from Daniel Dorsey in 1812.

After his manumission in 1814, Lloyd Colbert and his family purchased property in Canandaigua in 1843. Like his half-brother, Richard Valentine, and other former slaves and free Africans, Lloyd

Colbert became a productive and contributing member of the Canandaigua community. At the end of his life, Lloyd Colbert lived on Butcher (Granger) Street in the village with his sister, "Neckie" (Nancy). He eventually married a woman named Chloe, born in New Jersey.[46]

Figure 18
Lloyd Colbert [47]

(1784-1866)

A Former Slave in Canandaigua

Lastly, in the Town of Gorham (Ontario County), Robert Buchan, who was previously a slave holder in Maryland, frees his 70-year old slave, Bettee or Betsey in September 1821. This record indicates that this manumission was at the "request and solicitation" of the slave, "Bettee or Betsey", herself. It is witnessed by John Buchan, probably a relative of Robert Buchan, and recorded on September 30, 1821, (doc. 9). There is no indication as to whether "Bettee or Betsey" is capable of supporting herself as required by law. In 1827, all slaves born prior to 1799 were freed by law.

Document 9
Manumission of Bettee or Betsy [48]

29 September 1821

RENSSELAER COUNTY

In the City of Troy (Rensselaer County), African descendants were intimately involved in a sincere quest for emancipation from enslavement by any means possible. Thomas Adams a slave of Elias Lasell of Troy is manumitted on the 1st of April 1819 as outlined in Document 10 and witnessed by Daniel (last name illegible) and Lewis T. Tillman.[49] This manumission was well within the parameters of the Gradual Abolition Act and the final abolition legislation passed by the State of New York in 1817. In 1820, his freedom status was further certified by way of a document stipulating that on 1 April 1819, the undersigned witnessed the instrument used by Elias Lasell to manumit Thomas Adams, (doc. 11). Thomas is listed in this affidavit as being "five foot five inches in height, thick set stout built and [illegible] complexion. This document further states that he is fifty-five years of age and was born on [a] lot [on] Stephen Schuyler's farm in the city of Troy and that he became free on or about the first of April 1819. The affidavit is signed by David Briel, Jr. Judge of Rensselaer County.

Document 10
Manumission Certificate Of Thomas Adams [50]

1 April 1819

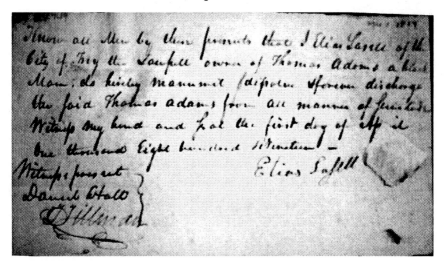

Document 11
Affidavit of witness to Freedom of Thomas Adams of Troy [51]

1 April 1819

This following story illustrates the process for determining an African descendant's slave status as free or slave. In the City of Troy the case of Prince Williams revolves around his status as a free man being brought into question in 1821. He is asked to submit an affidavit and witness to prove his contention that he is a free man and was born a free man, (doc. 12-1). In this affidavit Prince is described as being "twenty-five years & upward, about five foot nine inches high & that he was born a free man at Springfield, Massachusetts & never was a slave." Prince brings a witness with him to this court who proceeds to verify Prince's free status. Samuel Baltimore in his sworn statement explains that "he hath known personally said Prince for three years last past & he (Prince) hath been always considered a free man & this deponent has no doubts that he (Prince) is a freeman – has never been a slave." This affidavit is signed and sworn by Prince Williams with an X and by Samuel Baltimore on 25 April 1821.[52]

In **Document 12-2,** William L. Marcy the Recorder of Troy informs us that he is certifying the affidavit of Prince Williams. He states that he is, "satisfied that Prince Williams coloured man about twenty-five years and about five foot six inches in height was born free & is free according to the Laws of this State & entitled to all the privileges of a free man in this State." It is dated 25 April 1821 and signed by William L. Marcy, Recorder of Troy.[53]

Document 12-1
Affidavit Of Freedom Of Prince Williams [54]

25 April 1821

Document 12-2
Certificate Of Freedom Of Prince Williams [55]

25 April 1821

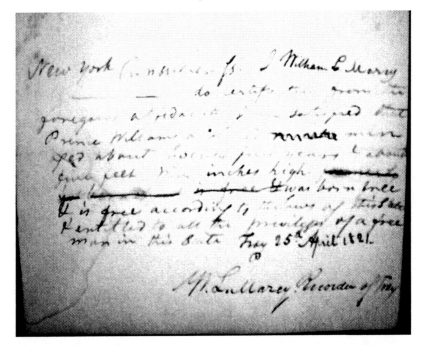

This procedure would lead one to wonder how often African descendants were challenged concerning their 'free' status. The prospect that freed African descendants could be challenged to provide proof of their 'freed status" was raised with the passage of the federal Fugitive Slave Law of 1793. Article 4 of this Law stipulated that:

For the better security of the peace and friendship now entered into by the contracting parties, against all infractions of the same, by the citizens of either party, to the prejudice of the other, neither party shall proceed to the infliction of punishments on the citizens of the other, otherwise than by securing the offender, or offenders, by imprisonment, or any other competent means, till a fair and impartial trial can be had by judges or juries of both parties, as near as can be, to the laws, customs, and usage's of the contracting parties, and natural justice: the mode of such trials to be hereafter fixed by the wise men of the United States, in congress assembled, with the assistance of such deputies of the Delaware nation, as may be appointed to act in concert with them in adjusting this matter to their mutual liking. And it is further agreed between the parties aforesaid, that neither shall entertain, or give countenance to, the enemies of the other, or protect, in their respective states, criminal fugitives, servants, or slaves, but the same to apprehend and secure, and deliver to the state or states, to which such enemies, criminals, servants, or slaves, respectively below.[56]

This law was reinforced by a statute passed in 1817 in New York State that essentially served as a New York State "Fugitive Slave Law. It stated that any African descendant in New York owing service or labor in any other state could be seized and returned. These laws in effect and practice put all freed Africans in New York State in jeopardy of being captured by malicious and unscrupulous slave catchers, who by way of clandestine and secretive measures, could force these freed citizens to be taken south and enslaved.[57]

Numerous examples of these nefarious practices occurred throughout the northern states. Austin Steward, who will be discussed in more detail in a later Chapter of this work, wrote in *Twenty-two Years a Slave, and Forty Years a Freeman*[58], about his experience of being captured in New York and enslaved in the south.

As mentioned earlier, Solomon Northrup from Saratoga Springs writes of his capture and enslavement in 1841 in his Narrative titled: *Twelve Years a Slave: Narrative of Solomon Northup, a Citizen of New-York, Kidnapped in Washington City in 1841, and Rescued in 1853*[59].

It is therefore of value to the premise of this work to explore the efforts undertaken by "free" African descendants to vigorously fight to have their "freed status" certified and acknowledged by some local or state court, or other administrative entity. Once again, in the City of Troy, we witness just such a proceeding. In fact this proceeding takes place on the same day, with the same official William l. Marcy, Recorder of Troy, and with the same witness as testified in the similar proceeding of Prince Williams cited above.

In this instance similar to that of Prince Williams, Frisbee Way of Troy provides a sworn affidavit that attests to the fact that he was born free in Limsbury, Connecticut and that he never was a slave. He further states that "he has lived in Troy for three years, is about thirty-three years old & about five feet six inches high, thick set. He provides a witness' statement on his affidavit. The witness that assists him in this effort is none other than Samuel Baltimore, the same witness from Prince Williams' proceeding. Baltimore swears that "he was from the same county in Connecticut that said Way came from & knows the mother of said Frisbee." He further swears "that said Frisbee was born free & is now a freeman & that this deponent hath known said Frisbee eighteen or nineteen years."

The affidavit, Document 13-1, is signed by both Frisbee Way and Samuel Baltimore and is swore before and signed by W. L. Marcy, Recorder of Troy.[60] Attached to this document is the ruling of William L. Marcy, Recorder of Troy. In this written ruling, Document 13-2, he certifies that he is "satisfied that Frisbee Way a coloured man aged about thirty-three years & about five feet six inches high, thick set was born in Limsbury, Connecticut a free man." He

Document 13-1
Affidavit Of Freedom Of Frisbee Way [61]

25 April 1821

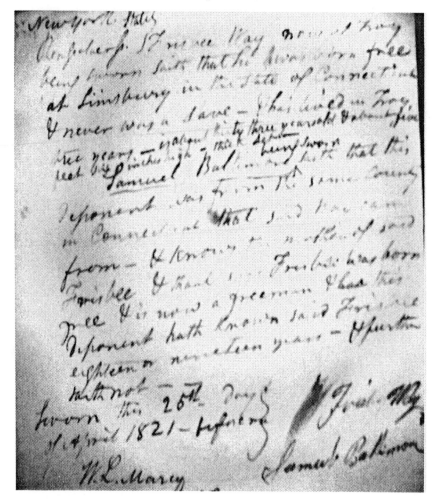

Document 13-2
Certificate Of Freedom Of Frisbee Way [62]

25 April 1821

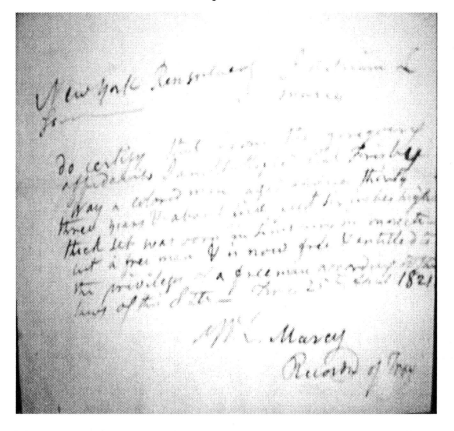

further states that "Frisbee is now free & entitled to the privileges of a free man according to the law of the State – this 25th April 1821." It is signed W. L. Marcy, Recorder of Troy.

Notice the fact that Samuel Baltimore is the witness in both of these "freedom" proceedings. What are we to make of their witness Samuel Baltimore? Samuel Baltimore is listed in the 1820 census for the City of Troy however the census provides very little information other than the fact that Samuel Baltimore's name is listed. No delineation is made with respect to ethnicity or the informational categories listed in the census, itself. It would seem logical to assume that given the fact that the condition and circumstances of enslavement was still rampant during these proceedings that Samuel Baltimore was in fact a white man. Consider the fact that these proceedings would have little validity if an African descendant's word was accepted by this city official without further verification, particularly, considering the fact that these proceedings were related to the freedom status of these two African descendants. However, there is strong evidence of generations of a family named Baltimore living in troy, NY. In fact, Garnet Baltimore a third generation resident of troy was the first African American to earn a degree from Rensselaer Polytechnic Institute (RPI), the prestigious engineering school in Troy, NY.

Again in Rensselaer County, an unusual case for the manumission of Amariah Paine of the Town of Schodack is recorded on the 27th of November 1816. The Gradual Abolition Act of 1799 allowed for the emancipation of slaves who had the ability to support themselves and were under fifty years of age. In this particular instance, it states "that Amariah Paine being sworn saith that he (her slave owner) applied according to the Statute in such case made I provided to the Overseer of the Poor of Schodack for a certificate of the ability of his Negro female slave to support herself on being manumitted which was confirmed & that he then said Amariah has given ten days notice to said Overseer of his intended application to the present general session."[63] This seems to be a case of Amariah Paine suing for her freedom based on eligibility information being communicated to her by her former slave holder. She prepares an affidavit outlining the process as her slave holder has explained to her and she is now requesting confirmation concerning her manumission based on her qualification with the requirements of the law, and she signs her full name, (doc. 15). There is no record as to whether or not Amariah Paine was freed and she is not listed in any census records after this date.

Document 14
Amariah Paine Vs. Overseer Of The Poor, Town Of Schodack [64]

27 November 1816

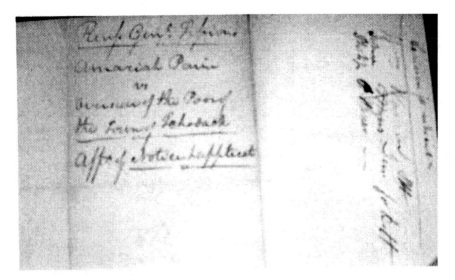

Document 15
Affidavit Of Mariah For Manumission[65]

27 NOV. 1816

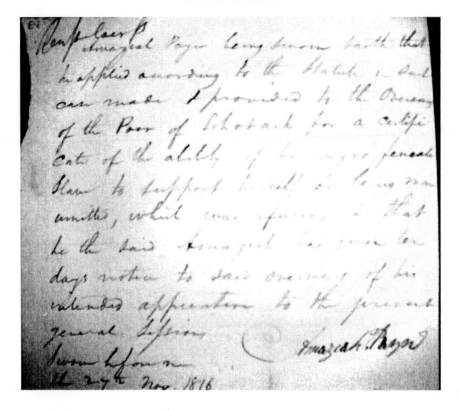

Finally, we have the case of Peggy Pruy (Van Vranken) who along with two other slaves Harry Pruy(sp) and "a negro girl Mary", are freed at the death of Dirck Y. Vanderhyden of Troy (Rensselaer County). The Executors stipulate in this document that it was the intention of Vanderhyden to free these three slaves immediately upon his death in order 'to free and discharge my heirs & Estate from being liable for their maintenance and support." The Executors in keeping with this request to manumit the three slaves, he "discharge[s] them [from] Enslavement." [66] The document is signed by the three Executors and an error is corrected by the recorder, (doc.16).[67] Manumission at death was a significant means by which African descendants were able to obtain their freedom. In this case it may be safe to assume that the three individuals freed by this document were a family or at the very least related to each other.

However, the Executors of this request by Vanderhyden had not taken into account that the Gradual Abolition Act stipulated that slaves may be free if they meet certain age requirements and are capable of supporting themselves. Consequently, Peggy Pruy(sp) now Van Vranken appears before the Overseers of the Poor to have her freedom certified. The Overseers of the Poor for the city of Troy, John London and Nathan Bouton, certify in Document 17 that Peggy "appears to be under the age of forty-five years and of sufficient ability to provide for herself." They sign and date this record on 9 April 1818.[68]

Document 16
Executors Manumit Three Slaves In Troy [69]

14 June 1818

Document 17
Overseers Of The Poor Grant Peggy Freedom[70]

9 April 1818

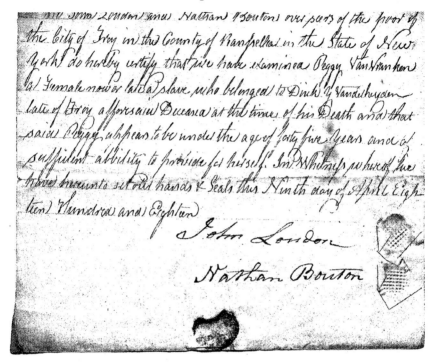

The above examples should not lull the reader into forming a positive opinion with respect to Rensselaer County's recorded history concerning the Gradual Abolition Act of 1799. Manumissions and emancipation were not the only transactions that occurred in this county. I have focused on theses examples to illustrate the extent to which African descendants were willing to go to obtain their freedom. To complete the record with respect to Rensselaer County, I have included the following extremely unusual documentation of one slave holder literally giving one of his "statutory slaves" to another slave holder.

Document 18 states that on twenty-three November 1804, Johannes Hardenburg gives to Joseph Duprey, Esq. a slave boy named Jack born of Hardenburg's 'wench' Gin.[71] He further states that he is conducting this transaction "under the Manumission Act of the

Legislature of the State of New York." In point of fact the Gradual Abolition Act of 1799 had no provisions that dealt with either the sale or gift of a "statutory slave" to another individual. It is probable that this transaction involved the actual purchase of Jack, however, it would seem that any such purchase and price would have been included in a document that is witnessed by two individuals including Hardenburg's brother John. [72]

Document 18
A slave boy named Jack born of Gin Given to Joseph Duprey
from Johannes Hardenburg[73]

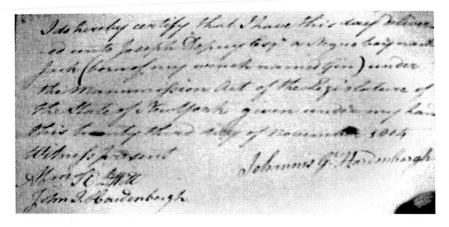

It should also be noted that a brief survey of Town Clerk Offices in upstate New York reveals that similar records like those above appear in the town minutes of a number of other smaller upstate towns such as: Willsboro (Essex County); Chilli and Penfield (Monroe County); Palatine (Montgomery County); Unadilla (Otsego County) Phillipstown (Putnam County); Brunswick (Rensselaer County); Owego (Tioga County); Barrington (Yates County); Argyle (Washington County); and, Berne, Bethlehem, Guilderland and Watervliet (Albany County).

These records provide an interesting insight into the day-to-day operation and implementation of the Gradual Abolition Act. The fact that the Overseer of the Poor (Poor Master) financial records are scarce for this period in these towns' archives prevents us from obtaining a complete picture of the implementation and inner workings of the period of Gradual Abolition in New York State.

ENDNOTES

[1] **Slavery in New York:** Ira Berlin, *Many Thousands Gone: The First two Centuries of Slavery in North America (Cambridge::* The Belknap Press of Harvard University Press; *1998*); Edgar J. McManus, *A History of Negro Slavery in New York* (Syracuse: Syracuse University Press, 1966); A. J. Williams-Myers, *Long Hammering* (Trenton: Black World Press,1994); Joyce Goodfriend, *Before the Melting Pot: Society and Culture* in Colonial New York City, 1664-1730 (Princeton: Princeton University Press,1992); Graham Russell Hodges, *Root & Branch African Americans in New York & East New Jersey, 1613-1863,* (Chapel Hill and London: University of North Carolina Press,1999) Ottley, Roi and William J. Weatherby, eds. *The Negro in New York: An Informal Social History (*Oceana Publications,1967); Graham Russell Hodges, *Slavery and Freedom in the Rural North*: *African Americans in Monmouth County, New Jersey, 1665-1865,* (Madison: Madison House,1997) ; Burrows, Ewing and Mike Wallace, *Gotham: A History of New York City to 1898 (London:* Oxford Press, 1999) ; Arthur Zilversmit, *The First Emancipation: The Abolition of Slavery in the North* (Chicago and London: University of Chicago Press, 1967*);* Vivienne L. Kruger, *Born to Run: The Slave Family in Early NY, 1623-1827*, PHD(Columbia University; 1985); Shane White, *Somewhat More Independent the end of slavery in New York City, 1770-1810* (Athens: Athens Press-University of Georgia).

[2] Blackburn, Robin, *The Overthrow of Colonial Slavery* , Verso(New Left Books, 1998) 273

[3] Ibid, 274

[4] Blackburn, 273

[5] Ibid

[6] *N.Y. State Senate Journal*, March 25, 27, 1799; *N.Y. State Assembly Journal*, March 28, 1799

[7] Chapter 62 of the Laws of 1799 of New York State

[8] Kruger, 822

[9] Chapter 40 of the Laws of the State of New York of 1804

[10] Zilversmith, 176-82, McManus, Black Bondage in the North, 171-8

NOTE: This seemingly positive act of civic rights, however, would be vehemently challenged and revoked by Republicans during the gradual abolition years.

[11] Chapter 62 of the Laws of the State of New York of 1799

[12] Chapter 40 of the Laws of New York State of 1804

[13] Harry P. Yoshpe "Records of Slave Manumission in New York During the Colonial and Early National Periods", *Journal of Negro History,* vol. XXVI, 1941

[14] Anjou, Gustave. *Ulster County, NY Probate Records.* New York: Published by the author, 1906

[15] Chapter 115 of the Laws of New York State of 1810

[16] Single folder, EV749/*Slave Documents - 1775-282*, Collections, Albany Institute of History and Art

[17] Chapter 188 of the Laws of 1817 of New York

[18] Ibid

[19] Joanne Pope Melish, *Disowning Slavery: Gradual Emancipation and 'Race' in New England, 1780-1860*, (Ithaca: Cornell University Press, 1998), 88-89

[20] Ibid

[21] Ira Berlin, *Many Thousand Gone,* (Harvard University Press,1998) 238

[22] Zilversmit, 182

[23] A0827-78, *Care of Children of Slaves,* F-3, New York Sate Archives

[24] Ibid

[25] A0827-78, *Care of Children of Slaves,* F-3, New York Sate Archives

[26] Town o Salem Minutes 1790-1826, Washington County Clerk's Office, 1992

[27] Ibid

[28] Ibid

NOTE: The fact that these declarations were handwritten leaves some translation to individual interpretation but the guest of these records is accurate with respect to this abandonment information.

[29] Hebron (Washington County) Town Record Book, 1784-1845, Office of Town Clerk, 11/28/75, NY State Archives

[30] Ibid, 206

[31] Debbie Axtman, trans. Early Beekman (NY) Records, 1999, 138-139, NY State Archives

[32] Warren Sherwood quotes the "Slave Book of the Town of Lloyd", as cited in *Black History of New Paltz* by William Heidgerd, 1989, Part 1, Haviland-Heidgerd Historical Collection, Elting Memorial Library, 3-4

[33] *http:/www.usgennet.org/usa/ny/town/pineplains/history.html*

[34] Town of Amenia Record Book 1800, *The Dutchess,* Winter 2000-2001, vol. 28 No.2,48

[35] Ibid, 49

[36] Poughkeepsie (Dutchess County) Town Record Book 1769-1833, Adriance Memorial Library, Poughkeepsie 6/11/75, NY State Archives

[37] Entire New Paltz record: William Heidgerd, Black History of New Paltz, 1989, Haviland-Heidgard Historical Collection, Elting Memorial Library

[39] Ibid, Part 2, 5-6

NOTE: The Josiah R. Eltinge listed in this record and the previous example of New Paltz records is the same as the Overseer of the Poor for the Town of Lloyd.

[40] Yorktown, NY Records, Series #A707, NY State Archives

[41] Town of Canandaigua Highway Minutes, 1791-1846. Also see Local Slave Records, The Evils of Slavery Duly Recorded, *http://raims. com/historian/NLTAUG04.htm, 1*

[42] Ibid

43   Ibid

44   Chapter 115 of the Laws of New York State of 1810

45   Town of Canandaigua Highway Minutes, 1791-1846. Also see Local Slave Records, The Evils of Slavery Duly Recorded, *http://raims. com/historian/NLTAUG04.htm*

46   Ibid

47   Photo courtesy of the Ontario Historical Society

48   Town of Canandaigua Highway Minutes, 1791-1846. Also see Local Slave Records, The Evils of Slavery Duly Recorded, *http://raims. com/historian/NLTAUG04.htm*

49   Single folder, EV749/*Slave Documents - 1775-282*, Collections, Albany Institute of History and Art

50   Ibid

51   Ibid

52   Single folder, EV749- Item #21/*Slave Documents - 1775-282*, Collections, Albany Institute of History and Art

53   Single folder, EV749/*Slave Documents - 1775-282*, Collections, Albany Institute of History and Art

54   Ibid

55   Ibid

56   A Chronology of US Historical Documents, University of Oklahoma, College of Law

     http://www.law.ou.edu/hist//fugslave.html

57   Chapter 135 of the Laws of 1817

58   Austin Steward, *Twenty-two Years a Slave, and Forty Years a Freeman*

59   Solomon Northrup, *Twelve Years a Slave: Narrative of Solomon Northup, a Citizen of New-York, Kidnapped in Washington City in 1841, and Rescued in 1853*

[60] Single folder, EV749-Item #22/*Slave Documents - 1775-282*, Collections, Albany Institute of History and Art

[61] Ibid

[62] Ibid

[63] Ibid

[64] Ibid

[65] Ibid

[66] Van Vranken Papers, Manuscript #16910, New York State Archives

[67] Ibid

[68] Ibid

[69] Ibid

[70] Ibid

[71] Single   folder, EV749-Item #14/*Slave Documents - 1775-282*, Collections, Albany Institute of History and Art

[72] Ibid

[73] Ibid

CHAPTER IV

ALBANY COUNTY AND
THE GRADUAL ABOLITION ACT

ALBANY COUNTY'S RESPONSE TO THE GRADUAL ABOLITION ACT

ALBANY SLAVE HOLDERS RESPONSE TO IMPENDING EMANCIPATION

Prior to the enactment of the Gradual Abolition Act of 1799, Albany County slave holders responded to impending abolition in ways that were very typical of other Dutch dominated counties outside of New York City. Deliberations concerning gradual abolition legislation in New York State began in 1776, and while this legislative maneuvering was taking place in the state legislature, it seemed to have very little bearing on the status and inner workings of the slave owning aristocracy in Albany and New York State.

One prominent example of this detached and dispassionate attitude towards the emancipation rumblings on the part of Albany slave holders is Phillip Schuyler. Schuyler was a former General in the Revolutionary War and a prominent Freeholder and citizen of Albany, the capital of New York State, where these legislative debates on abolition were taking place. Schuyler's prominence emanates from the fact that he had also served a number of terms in the state and U.S. Senate prior to the introduction of this new gradual abolition legislation. In fact, he had just served another term as a state senator before retaking his U.S. Senate seat from Aaron Burr in 1797, one year after new gradual abolition legislation was introduced in the New York State Legislature. Incidentally, Schuyler was one of many slave holding members of the New York State Manumission Society.

Notwithstanding his political record, Schuyler represents accurately both the attitude and the arrogance of the Dutch aristocracy with respect to the abolition of enslavement in New York State. His recorded response to the most recent introduction of abolition legislation in 1796 was his continuing effort to purchase more slaves to work on the grounds of his 80 acre 'Schuyler Mansion in the City of Albany. A receipt for the purchase of a male slave named Toby and a female slave named Sylvia and her two children in 1797 exemplifies the prevailing callous attitude of New York slave holders toward the inevitability of the abolition of enslavement - **Business as usual!**

> *"Received Albany July 21 1797 from Philip Schuyler the sum of eighty pounds for a Negro woman named Sylvia and two children this day sold him and also the sum of one hundred and fifteen pounds for a Negro man named Toby this day sold him."[1]*

This attitude towards the abolition of enslavement is also clearly illustrated in 1801, two years after the enactment of the 1799 Law, when Schuyler continued to purchase slaves for his Albany estate. This time he purchased a slave named Prince Anderson from Joseph Rufs with the condition that Prince be manumitted in seven years.[2]

Dutch slave holder practices in Albany are further illustrated by the actions of Gerrit Van Zandt, an Albany merchant whose family had lived in Albany since the 1600s. Although the following transactions were not undertaken during Gradual Abolition, they do give the reader a feel for what might be called the "normalcy" of the institution of enslavement in Albany during this period, (Docs. 19, 20 and 21). Around the period of the legislature's first attempt at gradual abolition in June 1785, and as witnessed by Mathew Vischer, Van Zandt sells a slave named Antoine to William Robbins. Just prior to the legislature's attempt at Gradual Abolition in 1785, Van Zandt made two purchases of slaves for his Albany estate. The first on 16 August 1784 involved the purchase of a male slave named Class from Jacob Schemerhorn for the price of sixty-seven pounds ten schillings (67:10:0).

Document 19
Sale to William Robbins by Gerrit Van Zandt

a Negro man named Antone
10 June 1785

I do hereby certify that I have this day sold to William Robbins a certain Negro man Antone of the aged about Sixteen years who as lost all his fingers & part his feet being frost bitten — and I do hereby release and for Ever quit Claim all my Right and Title to the sd William Robbins his heirs Executors and administrators, and assigns for Ever As Witness my hand & Seal. Dated his Tenth Day of June 1785 —

Gerrit Van Zandt

was Signed by Mathew Visher and James Bleecker

I do Certify the Above is a True Copy of the Original

Barent Johnnes Justice

Document 20
Affidavit by Matthew Vischer as witness to sale of slave Antone to William Robbins [3]

June 1785

Document 21
Sale of Slave named Class to Gerrit Van Zandt

16 August 1784 [4]

Notwithstanding these earlier transactions of Van Zandt, further investigation attests to his attitude with respect to the passage of the Gradual Abolition Act in 1799. On 19 April 1799, twenty-one days after the passage of the Act, Van Zandt purchases a second male slave named Frank from Francis Salisbury of Catskill, New York for one hundred and five pounds. A receipt for this transaction witnessed by Volkert Jackson and James Bleecker is issued on 24 December 1800, (doc. 22).

Document 22
Receipt of sale of slave, Frank, to Gerrit Van Zandt of Albany [5]

24 December 1800

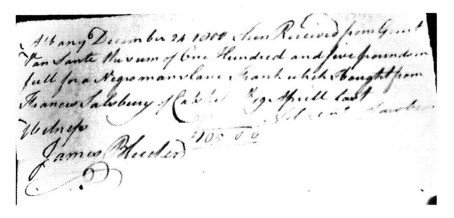

In keeping with this dispassionate "business as usual" attitude and lacking in any sentiment for the actions of abolition recently undertaken by the legislature; and the rise of abolitionists activities in the state, Van Zandt continues with his business of buying and selling slaves. He purchases an advertisement from Johannis Hodges Webster on 22 December 1804, for "the sale of a Negro wench". The receipt for this transaction is issued on 10 May 1806, (doc. 23), and puts the cost of running this advertisement "27 times" at two pounds three schillings (2:3:0).

Several concerns immediately arise with respect to this advertisement, not the least of which is, the fact that Mr. Van Zandt had to run the advertisement twenty-seven (27) times. Does this indicate anything significant? Does it in any way illustrate a change in the attitude of

New Yorkers with respect to enslavement and abolition? Does the year and a half period before the sale of this slave is consummated speak more to her physical condition or to a change in the climate of enslavement in the state? Or perhaps it speaks to a decline in overall slave sales in general?

Document 23
Bill for the advertisement of a Negro wench for sale by Garrit Van Zandt [6]

22 December 1804

Irrespective of these questions, one fact is eminently clear; Mr. Van Zandt was not discouraged in his business of buying and selling slaves during Gradual Abolition. Once again, Van Zandt makes a slave purchase. On 20 March 1806, seven years into Gradual Abolition, Van Zandt purchases a thirty-seven year old "Negro wench named Dine and her child" for one hundred and fifty dollars ($150). The receipt is signed by Hugh Boyd, (doc. 24).

What *is* obvious from these transactions undertaken by Gerrit Van Zandt is that he and other Albany slave holders were not concerned with the Gradual Abolition Act restricting the "status quo" operations of enslavement and its impact on the profitability of their individual business ventures. The reality is that the Gradual Abolition Act of 1799 did little to restrict the buying and selling of African descendants and their children. More importantly, no provisions of the Act provided any penalty or punishment for these transactions. Therefore, these occurrences would lead one to consider the fact that the true meaning of the "abolition" of enslavement -- that is the act of abolishing a system or practice or institution -- was never the designed purpose or the primary intention of the Gradual Abolition Act of 1799.

Document 24
Receipt for sale of Dine and her child to Gerrit Van Zandt [7]

20 March 1806

Another example of the Albany aristocracies' lack of interest in the concept of the emancipation of their human property is further illustrated by Volkert A. Down and Stephen Lush, "both gentlemen" and members of families of wealth and influence in the City of Albany. Mr. Lush is in fact the brother of the Albany Town Clerk, who was responsible for recording these transactions as they relate to the Act of 1799. Seven months prior to the passage of the Gradual Abolition Act, these two Albany "gentlemen" enter into an agreement for the sale of a slave named Jacob, (docs. 25-1 and 25-2).

> *"Know all men by there presents that I T. Volkert A. Douw*
> *___ in the City of Albany Gentleman in consideration of*
> *the sum of two hundred & fifty Dollars of lawful money*
> *of the State of New York to me in hand paid by Stephen*
> *Lush of the City of Albany examine(?) at and before the*
> *ensealing and delivery of this presents the receipt whereof*
> *I do hereby acknowledge have bargained sold release_*
> *granted and confirmed and by those presents do bargain*
> *sell release grant and confirm to the said Stephen Lush a*
> *certain Negro man Slave named Jacob aged about thirty-*
> *seven years old now in the possession of said Stephen*

together with his bedding and wearing apparel. (December 3, 1798)" [8]

Document 25-1
Sale of Slave Jacob to Volkert Douw [9]

3 December 1798

Document 25-2
Sale of Slave Jacob to Volkert Douw (con't)[10]

3 December 1798

GRADUAL ABOLITION IN ALBANY

The Albany County "Register of Manumitted Slaves; 1800-1828" provides us with the most comprehensive record of the responses to the requirements of the Gradual Abolition Act of 1799 by Albany slave holders, outside of New York City and southern New York State.[11] The most significant aspect of these records relates to the "abandonment" provisions of the 1799 law. Dr. Vivienne Kruger in her dissertation "*Born to Run*" has calculated the abandonment rate of children born to slaves during gradual abolition at thirty-seven percent

(37%) in the southern twenty-eight (28) towns in her study. [12] These towns represent a strong Dutch dominated population of slave holders.

One interesting aspect of Albany County's rate of abandonment included in Tables 4-1 and 4-2 is that between the years of 1800 and 1805, county records document the registration of fifty-two (52) births of slave children. Of this number, thirty-four (34) or sixty-five percent (65%) of these slave children were abandoned. [13] Astonishingly, this rate of abandonment is almost twice the rate of abandonment recorded in the Dr. Kruger study of southern towns.

According to the Gradual Abolition Act of 1799, the State of New York was responsible for the maintenance and support of any slave children abandoned under the provisions of this Act and placed with the Overseers of the Poor or as subsidized "statutory slaves" placed in the homes of local slave holders. It can be argued that this higher abandonment rate is due to the fact that residents of Albany, the capital of New York State, were more cognizant of the subsidy provisions of the 1799 law -- and all New York state laws for that matter -- than outlining areas of the state. Given their intimate access to first-hand information and legislative circulars, it would seem plausible that the subsidy aspect of the 1799 law would have had a more significant impact on the rate of abandonment in the city of Albany.

Table 4-1

ALBANY COUNTY
REGISTER OF MANUMITTED SLAVES
1800 - 1805

SUBJECT	YEAR	MONTH/ DAY	
Slaves (cert. of birth and abandonment of Nan 10 Aug.1799, owned by Jacob Bleecker, recorded T. Clerk)	1799	Dec.	9
Slaves (cert. of birth of Thomas 4July1799, owned by Stephen Lush, recorded T. Clerk)	1800	Jan.	28
Slaves (certificate of birth and adandonment Andrew10 sept.1799, born to Nell, owned by Richard Lush and wife,and Eloise Fonda, recorded by T. Clerk)	1800	Feb	5
Slaves (certificate of Nann 6 July 1799, owned by John Wendall, recorded by T.Clerk)	1800	April	24
Slaves (cert. of manumission Anthony 17 May 1800, owned by John McAlson, recorded T. Clerk)	1800	May	17
Slaves (cert. birth and adandonment of Charles 13 March 1799, mother Peggy, owned by William Bill, recorded T.Clerk)	1800	June	28
Slaves (cert. of birth Negro female, 8 mos. 27 days old, owned by Gerrit Bogart, recorded T. Clerk)	1800	July	3
Slaves (cert. birth and abandonment of Lan 2 Nov. 1799, mother Bett, owned by Peter Dox, recorded T. Clerk)	1800	July	22
Slaves (cert. birth and abandonment of May, 8mos. 7 days, mother Diane, owned by Jacob Pueryn, recorded T.Clerk).	1800	Aug	28
Slaves (cert.of manumission of Henry by Dudley Walsh, recorded T.Clerk)	1800	Oct.	27
Slaves (cert. birth and abandonment of Sarah by Jacob Bleeker, recorded T.Clerk)	1801	June	13
Slaves (cert. of manumission of Dick, owned by _____, recorded T.Clerk)	1799	March	27
Slaves (cert. birth and abandonment of Peepee 14 Jan.1801, mother Diane owned by Lybrant Dow, recorded T.Clerk)	1801	March	12
Slaves (cert. birth and abandonment of Flora 8Nov1800, mother Diana owned by Abraham Lansingh, recorded T.Clerk)	1801	March	12

Slaves (certr. Birth and abandonment of Hannah 4May1800, mother Ave owned by Abraham Lansing, recorded T.Clerk)	1801	March	12
Slaves (cert. of birth of Alpert 8July1800, owned by Rev. Thomas Ellison, Rector St Peter's Church, father Minck, owned by Chief Justice of NY-John Lansing, mother owned by John Lansing, recorded T.Clerk)	1801	April	3
Slaves (cert.of manumission of Sam, owned by John Winnie, recorded T.Clerk & Judge)	1801	April	11
Slaves (cert. of Manumission of Dinah owned by Eliphalet Nott, recorded by Judge)	1801	March	14
Slaves (cert. of manumission of Tony owned by E. Nott, recorded by Judge of Supreme Crt)	1801	March	14
Slaves (cert. of birth and abandonment of Prince 9Jan. 1801, mother Diana owned by John McLaux, recorded T.Clerk)	1801	April	20
Slaves (cert. manumission of Prince Anderson as condition of sale to Philip Schuyler after seven years of service (Johannes Rufs)recorded T.Clerk and Town Recorder)	1801	April	24
Slaves (cert. of Birth Hanover 4July1800, owned by Philip Schuyler, recorded T. Clerk)	1801	May	15
Slaves (cert.of birth and abandonment of Philip 4Jan.1801, mother Diane owned by _____, recorded T. Clerk)	**1801**	**Sept**	**16**
Slaves (cert.of birth of Ned 5Oct. 1800, mother Clare, owned by Abraham Van Vechten recorded T.Clerk)	1801	Sept	18
Slaves (cert. of birth and abandonment of Bena 10 Nov.1800, mother Pye, owned by Peter Elmendorf, recorded T. Clerk)	**1801**	**Oct.**	**7**
Slaves (cert.of birth of Jack 6Feb.1800, owned by Sanders Lansing, recorded by T.Clerk)	1801	Nov.	21
Slaves (cert.of birth and abandonment of Tom 30 Nov.1800, owned by Christopher Beekman, recorded T.Clerk) .	**1801**	**Nov**	**21**
Slaves (cert.of birth and abandonment of Kate 21 May1801, mother Joan, owned by Nettie Puryor, recorded by T.Clerk)	**1802**	**Jan**	**15**
Slaves (cert. of manumission of Samuel, owned by John Lansingh, recorded by T.Clerk)	1802	Jan	21
Slaves (cert. of birth and abandonment of Elisha 10 ___1801, mother Jean owned by Ryha Dow, recorded T.Clerk)	**1802**	**Feb**	**1**

Slaves (cert. of birth and abandonment of Susan 3March 1801, mother Diane owned by Isaac Bogert, recorded T.Clerk).	1801	Dec	7
Slaves (cert. of birth and abandonment of Titus 16Feb.1801, mother Nan owned by Peter Yates, recorded T.Clerk)	1802	Feb	14
Slaves (cert. of birth and abandonment of Dianna 14 Sept. 1801, mother Nan owned by John Maley, recorded T.Clerk)	**1802**	**April**	**17**
Slaves (cert. of birth and abandonment of Frank 20 may 1801, mother Hager owned by John Magoffin, recorded T.Clerk)	**1802**	**May**	**3**
Slaves (cert.of manumission of John/Jan owned by Sarah Ten Eyck, recorded T.Clerk and Judges)	1802	May	6
Slaves (cert.of birth and abandonment of Diana 20 Aug. 1800, mother Rose, owned by The Bloodgoods, recorded by T. Clerk)	1802	June	11
Slaves (cert.of birth and abandonment of Dianah 27April1802, mother Peg owned by John Wendell, recorded by T.Clerk)	**1802**	**July**	**10**
Slaves (cert.of birth and abandonment of Eliza 1 Jan. 1802, mother Bett, owned by George Merchant, recorded by T.Clerk)	**1802**	**Sept.**	**30**
Slaves (cert. of manumission for $225 of Anthony (Tone) owned by Cornelius Van Schelluyne recorded Judges & T.Clerk)	1802	Oct.	6
Slaves (cert. of abandonment by Alida Van Denkurgh, recorded T.Clerk)	1802	Nov.	25

Table 4-1a

ALBANY COUNTY
REGISTER OF MANUMITTED SLAVES
1800 - 1805

SUBJECT	YEAR	MONTH/ DAY	
Slaves (cert. of birth of Tom 6 Aug. 1802 owned by Charles Martin recorded T.Clerk	1803	Oct.	8
Slaves (cert. of manumiision of Sarah (Sars) for $100 by Cornelius Van Schelluyne recorded Judges & T.Clerk)	1803	Oct.	17
Slaves (cert. of manumission of Jude by Robert Mc-Clellan, for $250 ($100 paid, $100 secured) recorded by T.Clerk and Recorder)	1802	May	25
Slaves (cert. of birth and abandonment of twins (Prince &?) 6Nov.1801, mother Dinah,owned by Hoosick, recorded T.Clerk)	1802	June	5
Slaves (cert. of birth of Peter 5mos.21days owned by Paul Hochstruters(?), recorded T.Clerk)	1802	July	14
Slaves (cert.of birth and abandonment of Nicholas 15Dec.1801, owned by Abraham Lansing, recorded T.Clerk)	1802	Aug.	27
Slaves (cert. birth and abandonment of Jack 5Dec.1801, owned by Van Derhayden Family recorded T.Clerk)	1802	Sept.	25
Slaves (cert. of manumission of Flora owned by George Pearson, recorded T.Clerk)	1802	Dec.	3
Slaves (cert. of birth and abandonment of Levy 1June1802, mother Emme, owned by John Jauncey, recorded T. Clerk)	1803	June	9
Slaves (cert.of birth and abandonment of Peter 14July1802 by Hochstraser, recorded T.Clerk)	1803	March	9
Slaves (cert.birth and abandonment of Francis Nov. 1803, mother Molly, owned by John Dow, recorded T. Clerk)	1803	April	25
Slaves (cert. of birth and abandonment Jim(?) 1June 1802, owned by The Leonards, recorded by T.Clerk)	1803	May	11
Slaves (cert. of birth and abandonment of Sarah 1Jan.1803, mother Diana, owned by The Dows, recorded T.Clerk)	1803	May	17

Slaves (cert. sale for 21 years Iris, 4years old, for $30 from Mr.Hogan to James Sinacse recorded T.Clerk)	1803	Nov.	30
Slaves (cert. of birth of George 23 Aug. 1803, mother Sarah owned byS.Skinner recorded by T.Clerk)	1804	March	28
Slaves (cert. of birth of Anthony 3mos.11days owned by Stephen Lush recorded by T. Clerk)	1804	April	3
Slaves (cert. of birth of Anthony 7mos.14days owned by Srephen Lush, recorded by T. Clerk)	1804	July	30
Slaves (cert. of birth of Tom 6 Aug.1802 owned by Charles Martin, recorded by Tclerk)	1803	Oct.	8
Slaves (cert. of manumission of Catherine (Cate)wife owned by Joseph Sharpe,for $150. recorded by T. Clerk)	1803	Nov.	30
Slaves (cert. of manumission of Tom Buck owned by Abraham Schuyler, recorded by Mayor, Recorder and T. Clerk)	1804	May	3
Slaves (cert. of manumission of Dean for $1 owned by Robert W. Clallen, recorded by Mayor, Recorder and T.Clerk)	1804	May	24
Slaves (cert. of manumission of Thomas Hogner owned by Nicholas Bleecker, recorded Mayor, Recorder and T. Clerk)	1804	Sept.	1
Slaves (cert. of birth of Harry 11 June 1803 owned by John Wendell recorded by T. Clerk)	1804	Sept.	11
Slaves (cert. of birth of Robert 4July1803, mother Diana, owned by John Wendell, recorded by T. Clerk)	1804	Sept.	11
Slaves (cert. of birth of Dean 8mos.8days owned by Robert Hurst, recorded by T. Clerk)	1804	Dec.	8
Slaves (cert. of manumission of Anthony (Tone) 48, Stephen 30, Pheobe 30, Silva 30 and 3 children: Sallyho, Sam & Hanover, Owned by estate of Phillip Schuyler, deceased, recorded by Mayor, Recorder & T. Clerk)	1804	Dec.	18
Slaves (cert. of manumission of Bett owned by Jacob Bleecker, recorded T. Clerk)	1804	Dec.	25
Slaves (cert. of birth and abandonment of Nann 14 May1803, mother Bett owned by John Bleecker, Jr. recorded)	1804	Dec.	24
Slaves (cert. of manumission of Stephen recorded by Mayor and Recorder)	1804	Dec.	20
Slaves (cert. of manumission of Sam for $200 by Derek Schuyler, recorded Judge & T. Clerk)	1805	April	2
Slaves (cert. of manumission of Jack owned by Henry Stands, recorded by Judge & Tclerk)	1805	April	9

Slaves (cert. of manumission of Nann 45, owned by Jane & Ann Moore, recorded by Mayor, Recorder & T. Clerk)	1805	April	24
Slaves (cert. of manumission of Sarah 36, owned by Phillip S. Van Rensselaer, if she moves out of County forever within 8 days, recorded by Mayor, Recorder & T. Clerk)	1805	July	11
Slaves (cert. of manumission of Marina 38, owned by Phillip S. Van Rensselaer, if she moves out of County forever within 8 days, recorded by Mayor, Recorder & T. Clerk)	1805	July	10
Slaves (cert. of manumission of Betty for $1 owned by George Merchant, recorded by Mayor, Recorder & T. Clerk)	1805	July	8
Slaves (cert. of manumission of Peter owned byMatthew Trotter, recorded by Mayor, Recorder and T. Clerk)	1805	July	21
Slaves (cert. of birth of Mary 7 Aug. 1804, mother Dina owned by Mr. Fonda, recorded by T. Clerk)	1805	Feb.	5
Slaves (cert. of birth of Jim 9Sept.1804, mother Bitt owned by Mr. Graham recorded by T.C.)	1805	Sept.	9
Slaves (cert. of birth of Elize 1 Jan. 1804 owned by Joseph Palmer, recorded T.Clerk)	1805	Sept.	30
Slaves (cert. of birth and abandonment of William 24 July 1804, mother Jane owned by John Bleecker, recorded T. Clerk)	1805	Feb.	28
Slaves (cert. of birth of Mary 5 May 1804 owned by Sam Stringer, recorded T.Clerk)	1805	Sept.	30

Table 4-2

Albany Register 1800-1805 (cont'd)

SUBJECT	Year/Month/Day
Slaves (cert. of birth of Tom, 6 August 1802, owned by Charles Martin, recorded Town Clerk)	1803 October 8
Slaves (cert. of manumission of Sarah (Sans) for $100 by Cornelius van Schelluyne recorded Judges and Town Clerk)	1803 October 17
Slaves (cert. of manumission of Jude by Robert McClellan, for $250 ($100 paid; $100 secured) recorded by Town Clerk and Recorder)	1802 May 25
Slaves (cert. of birth and abandonment of twins (Prince & ?), 6 November 1801, mother Dinah, owned by Hoosick, recorded Town Clerk)	1802 June 5
Slaves (cert. of birth of Peter, 5 mos. 21 days, owned by Paul Hochstruters (?), recorded T. Clerk)	1802 July 14
Slaves (cert. of birth and abandonment of Nicholas, 15 December 1801, owned by Abraham Lansing, recorded Town Clerk)	1802 August 27
Slaves (cert. birth and abandonment of Jack, 5 December 1801, owned by van Derhayden Family, recorded Town Clerk)	1802 September 25
Slaves (cert. of manumission of Flora, owned by George Pearson, recorded Town Clerk)	1802 December 3
Slaves (cert. of birth and abandonment of Levy, 1 June 1802, mother Emme, owned by John Jauncey, recorded Town Clerk)	1803 June 9
Slaves (cert. of birth and abandonment of Peter, 14 July 1802, by Hochstraser, recorded Town Clerk)	1803 March 9
Slaves (cert. of birth and abandonment of Francis, November 1803, mother Molly, owned by John Dow, recorded Town Clerk)	1803 April 25
Slaves (cert. of birth and abondonment Jim (?), June 1802, owned by the Leondards, recorded by Town Clerk)	1803 May 11
Slaves (cert. of birth and abandonment of Sarah, 1 January 1803, mother Diana, owned by the Dows, recorded Town Clerk)	1803 May 17
Slaves (cert. sale for 21 years Iris, 4 years old, for $30 from Mr. Hogan to James Sanacse recorded Town Clerk)	1803 November 30

Slaves (cert. of birth of George, 23 August 1803, mother Sarah owned by S. Skinner recorded Town Clerk)	1804 March 28
Slaves (cert. of birth of Anthony, 3 mos 11 days, owned by Stephen Lush, recorded by T. Clerk	1804 April 3
Slaves (cert. of birth of Anthony, 7 mos 14 days, owned by Stephen Lush, recorded by T. Clerk	1804 July 30
Slaves (cert. of birth of Tom, 6 August 1802, owned by Charles Martin, recorded Town Clerk)	1803 October 8
Slaves (cert. of manumission of Catherine (Cate) wife owned by Joseph Sharpe, for $150 recorded by Town Clerk)	1803 November 30
Slaves (cert. of manumission of Tom Buck owned by Abraham Schuyler, recorded by Mayor, Recorder and Town Clerk)	1804 May 3
Slaves (cert. of manumission of Dean for $1 owned by Robert W. Clallel, recorde by Mayor, Recorder and Town Clerk)	1804 May 24
Slaves (cert of manumission of Thomas Hogner owned by Nicholas Bleeker, recorded by Mayor, Recorder and Town Clerk)	1804 September 1
Slaves (cert of birth of Harry, 11 June 1803 owned by Robert Hurst, recorded by Town Clerk	1804 September 11
Slaves (cert. of birth of Robert 4 July 1803, mother Diana, owned by John Wendell, recorded by Town Clerk)	1804 September 11
Slaves (cert. of birth of Dean 8 mos. 8 days owned by Robert Hurst, recorded by Town Clerk	1804 December 25
Slaves (cert. of manumission of Anthony (Tone) 48, Stephen 30, Pheobe 30, Silva 30 and 3 children Sallyho, Sam & Hanover, owned by estate of Philip Schuyler, deceased, recorded by Mayor, Recorder and Town Clerk)	1804 December 18
Slaves (cert. of manumission of Bett owned by Jacob Bleecker, recorded T. Clerk	1804 December 25
Slaves (cert. of birth and abandonment of Nann 14 May 1803, mother Bett owned by John Bleeker, Jr. recorded)	1804 December 24
Slaves (cert. of manumission of Stephen recorded by Mayor and Recorder)	1804 December 20
Slaves (cert. of manumission of Sam for $200 by Derek Schuyler, recorded Judge & T. Clerk)	1805 April 2
Slaves (cert. of manumission of Jack owned by Henry Stands, recorded byJudge & T. Clerk)	1805 April 9
Slaves (cert. of manumission of Nann 45, owned by Jane & Ann Moore, recorded by Mayor, Recorder and Town Clerk)	1805 April 24

Slaves (cert. of manumission of Sarah 36, owned by Philip S. Van Rensselaer, if she moves out of County forever within 8 days, recorded by Mayor, Recorder & T. Clerk)	1805 July 11
Slaves (cert. of manumission of Marina 38, owned by Philip S. Van Rensselaer, if she moves out of County forever within 8 days, recorded by Mayor, Recorder & T. Clerk)	1805 July 10
Slaves (cert. of manumission of Betty for $1 owned by George Merchant, recorded by Mayor, Recorder and Town Clerk)	1805 July 8
Slaves (cert.of manumission of Peter ownded by Matthew Trotter, recorded by Mayor, Recorder and Town Clerk)	1805 July 21
Slaves (cert. of birth of Mary 7 Aug. 1804, mother Dina owned by Mr. Fonda, recorded by Town Clerk)	1805 February 5
Slaves (cert. of birth of Jim, 9 September 1804, mother Bitt owned by Mr. Graham, recorded by Town Clerk)	1805 September 9
Slaves (cert. of birth of Elize 1 January 1804 owned by Joseph Palmer, recorded by T. Clerk	1805 September 30
Slaves (cert. of birth and abandonment of William 24 July 1804, mother Jane owned by John Bleecker, recorded Town Clerk)	1805 February 28
Slaves (cert. of birth of Mary 5 May 1804 owned by Sam Stringer, recorded Town Clerk)	1805 September 30

Another indicator that might have had an impact on this higher rate of abandonment in the City of Albany is the official position of some of the individuals who owned and/or abandoned the children of their slaves during this period. Responsible for certifying the registration of slave children, the Town Clerk of the City of Albany, Richard Lush and his family are cited a number of times as registering and abandoning the children of their slaves. One such example is the certification of the birth and the intention to abandon the rights to Andrew born 10 Sept. 1799 to his slave woman Nell. The notation is made that his wife and Eloise Fonda also owned Nell.[14]

This transaction involving Eloise Fonda was not her only excursion into the arena of "human property". On 10 March 1792 she and another individual purchased for the price of twenty-six pounds "a certain Negro woman slave named Dina" from V. A. Douw, (doc. 26).[15] It seems that Ms. Fonda was consistent in her peculiar pattern of jointly purchasing slaves with her friends, as if 'owning' slaves was some type of social activity.

Document 26
Deed of V. A. Douw to Elsie Fonda for a slave named Dina[16]

It appears that slave holding was an activity in which the entire Fonda family indulged. Eloise's husband, Major Fonda, was also an owner of human property. On 6 November 1785, he writes a letter to A. Van Campen (sp) of Montgomery County requesting that he assist in the return of one of his slaves, William (formally Leon), who has escaped, (doc. 27-1 and 27-2). He indicates that he believes that the description that Van Campen (sp) gave his wife fits this escaped slave, William (Leon). He requests that if Van Canpen (sp) should return to the place in search of his own escaped slaves that he would be willing to pay ten pounds and refund Van Campen (sp) for his expenses, if he could secure and detain William (Leon). He describes William (Leon) as being "a tall 'molatta', with long hair and pretty well marked with the small pox."[17] William (Leon) is also described as having very large hands and feet and is about forty years old". Major Fonda thanks Mr. Van Campen in advance for his effort.

Document 27-1
Letter from Major Fonda to A. Van Campen to assist in the return of a slave named William formally Leon [18]

6 November 1785

Document 27-2

Letter from Major Fonda to A. Van Campen (con't)[19]

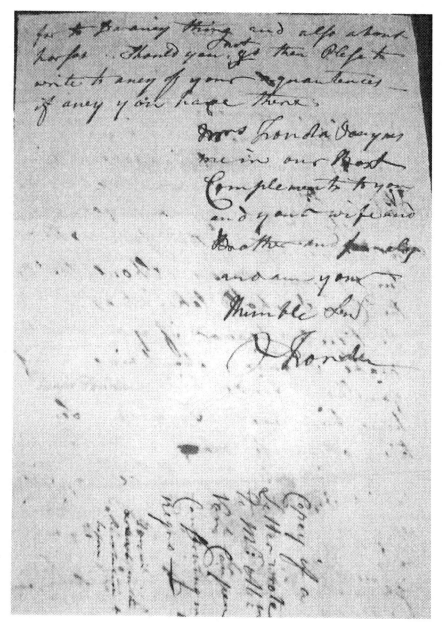

Other prominent Albanians listed in Tables 4-1 and 4-2 include the 'cream' of the Albany social set and government life. Richard Lush, the Town Clerk, and his brother, Stephen Lush, Mayor of Albany, Phillip S. Van Rensselaer and the City Recorder, Mr. Lansing are counted in this number. Other individuals of prominence who are listed in this 'Register' as owning slaves are Rev. Thomas Ellison, Rector of St. Peter's Church in Albany; Chief Justice of the New York Court, John Lansing, former General Phillip Schuyler, the Ten Eyck family; the Van Derheyden family; and the Bleecker family, to name just a few.[20]

The position held by these individuals and families within the governmental and the societal structure of Albany would seem to support the contention for a higher rate of abandonment of slave children based on their access to pertinent state information. This issue of abandonment and its accompanying subsidy payments would be a perfect opportunity to use your access to the legislative process to acquire important legislative information with respect to its implementation and its financial benefits. The fact that Albany's rate of abandonment was almost twice as high as the rate in Dr. Kruger's study may in fact, be due to this proximity to the State Capitol and the intimate relationships that existed between elected city and state officials and the citizenry of Albany.

Similar records exist for other cities and towns within Albany County, including: Watervliet, Guilderland and Bethlehem.

Town of Watervliet

The records for Watervliet record the registration of twenty (20) slave children born to the slaves of Watervliet slave holders between the years 1801-1807, of this number, these slave holders abandoned twelve (12) slave children, Table 5.[21] This represents a sixty per cent (60%) rate of abandonment which is consistent with the sixty-five percent (65%) rate for the city of Albany.[22] These records also highlight an extremely unorthodox certification relating to the manumission of Joan by Catherine Van Den Burgh. In this record, Catherine Van Den Burgh states:

"Know all men by these Present that I Catherine Van Den Burgh of the Burght (sp) in the county of Albany – By virtue and in pursuance of an act of the legislature of the State of New York entitled an Act for the gradual abolition of Enslavement passed the twenty ninth March 1799 have manumitted and set free and by these present do manumit & set free my Negro girl Slave, named Joan at present aged about Two Years – In witness whereof, I have hereunder set my hand and seal, the thirteenth day of February in the year one thousand eight hundred & one.

Her
Catherine   X   Van Denburgh
Mark

Sealed & delivered
In presence of}

Tunis Lansing
Cornelius Van Den Burgh" [23]

This certified record of manumission provides quite a dilemma with respect to the Gradual Abolition Act of 1799. The Law provided for the manumission of slaves by their slave owner upon its enactment, and it required no bond. It stipulated however, that the individuals to be manumitted must be under fifty years of age and capable of supporting themselves once freed. This case would not have met the requirements of the law. Nevertheless, it is curious that a slave owner would manumit a two (2) year old child instead of abandoning her to the Overseers of the Poor for maintenance and support.

Table 5

TOWN OF WATERVLIET MINUTES
1793 - 1844

SUBJECT	Day/Month/Year
Slaves (cert. of manumission of Joan, age 2 years, owned by Catherine Van Den Burgh, certified by Overseers of the Poor)	13 February 1801
Slaves (cert. of birth and abandonment of Jan, 26 June 1800, mother Maria, owned by Henry Apple, recorded)	21 May 1801
Slaves (cert. of birth of Will, 18 October 1800, mother Pegg, owned by Jacob Lansing, recorded)	3 July 1801
Slaves (cert. of birth and abandonment of Jude, 31 January 1800, mother Rose, owned by John van Rensselaer, recorded)	14 July 1801
Slaves (cert. of birth of William, 22 December 1800, mother Dina, owned by Nocholas Quackenbush, recorded)	7 September 1801
Slaves (cert. of birth of Sam, 4 June 1800, mother Dina owned by Volkert Veeder, recorded)	12 August 1801
Slaves (cert. of birth of Susan, 13 April 1800, mother Susan, owned by Peter Veeder, recorded)	12 August 1801
Slaves (cert. of birth and abandonment of Gin, 7 October 1801, mother Maria, owned by Henry Apple, recorded)	24 June 1802
Slaves (cert. of birth and abandonment of Ashmen, 15 January 1802, mother Susan owned by Eldert Timerse, recorded)	28 June 1802
Slaves (cert. of birth and abandonment of Dayan, 7 February 1801, mother Nan owned by Eldert Timerse, recorded)	19 June 1803
Slaves (cert of birth and abandonment of Gin, 20 June 1803, mother Jude owned by Mathias Bieavie (sp) recorded)	28 December 1804
Slaves (cert. of birth of Henry, 2 July 1803, parent Jack owned by L. Lansing recorded, Town Clerk)	18 November 1804
Slaves (cert. of birth and abandonment of Dayan, 29 April 1803, mother Dean owned by Volkert Rothand (sp) recorded)	13 December 1803
Slaves (cert. of birth and abandonment of Lar, 15 October 1802, mother Chris, owned by Michael Freligh, recorded	15 June 1803
Slaves (cert. of birth of Mary, 24 July 1804, owned by Enoch Leonard (sp) recorded)	15 February 1804

Slaves (cert. of birth of John, 2 June 1804, mother Dean, owned by Henry Cothoudt, rec'd)	11 April 1805
Slaves (cert. of birth of Tom, 30 May 1805, mother Dean owned by Volkert Cothoudt, rec'd)	18 October 1805
Slaves (cert. of birth and abandonment of Henry, 20 February 1805, mother Nan owned by Eldert Tymesen, recorded)	September 1805
Slaves (cert. of birth and abandonment of Jamime, 13 November 1804, mother Susan owned by Eldert Tymesen, recorded)	September 1805
Slaves (cert of the birth and abandonment of Jamime, 11 November 1804, mother Mary owned by J. Famy Van Vranken, recorded)	8 March 1805
Slaves (cert of birth and abandonment of Tom, 7 November 1805, mother Mary, owned by Levinus Lansing, recorded)	9 March 1807

Documents in the library of the Albany Institute of History and Art record another transaction that occurred in Watervliet during Gradual Abolition, Docs. 28-1, 28-2 and 28-3).[24] This transaction on the thirty-first (31) day of June 1802 recorded the sale of "a certain Negro man slave named Richard aged about twenty-four years" who is sold for "the sum of one hundred & twenty five dollars' by Dirck De Lametly of the City of Hudson to Abraham Ten Eyck of Watervliet.[25] Richard is sold to Ten Eyck "for the term of six years from the eleventh day of June last here." This would mean that Richard would work for Ten Eyck until June 1806 when he would be thirty years of age. This six year sale would allow De Lametly to retain 'ownership' of Richard after its expiration. At which time, Richard could be resold if De Lametly chose to do so.

Because the provisions of the Gradual Abolition Act did not apply to slaves born prior to 1799, Richard was not eligible for emancipation under the 1799 law. In addition, due to the fact that New York State's final abolition law wasn't passed until 1817 and wasn't made effective until 1827, Richard will be forty-eight years of age before he would be able to obtain his legal freedom.

Document 28-1
Sale of Slave to Abraham Ten Eyck [26]

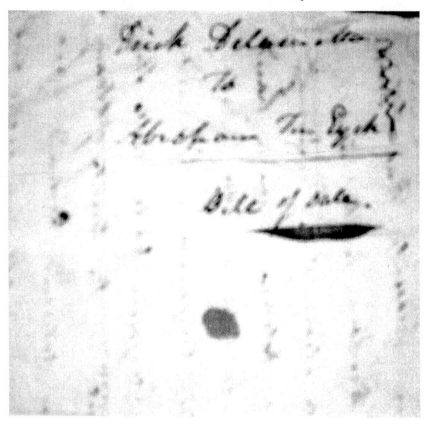

Document 28-2
Sale Of Richard For Six Year Period [27]

31 June 1802

Document 28-3
Sale Of Richard For Six Year Period[28]

31 JUNE 1802

Town of Guilderland

"Records of the Town Minutes of Guilderland, 1803 – 1834", Table 6, provide us with records for the birth and abandonment of slave children born within the town founded in 1803. [29] It should be noted that on 26 February 1803 the Town of Watervliet was divided to establish the separate town of Guilderland. It should be further noted that the State of New York included in the legislation that created Guilderland, a provision that allowed Guilderland to provide for its own poor:

> *"... to apportion the money and Poor belonging to the said Town of Watervliet previous to the division thereof agreeable to the State Tax list and that forever thereafter each of the said Towns shall support and maintain their own Poor."*[30]

Secretary, Office of the State of New York, April 12th 1803)

These Guilderland records list the birth of nine (9) slave children to Guilderland slave women, of which eight (8) were abandoned by the owners of their mothers. This would represent an abandonment rate of eighty-nine percent (89%), a thirty-seven percent (37%) increase over the city of Albany's abandonment rate of sixty-five percent (65%) and a forty-eight percent (48%) increase over its "sister-town" Watervliet. The fact that John Van Rensselaer, Peter Veeder, and Henry Apple are listed both as slave holders, Table 6, for Guilderland, as well as in Table 5 for Watervliet, may account for this increased rate of abandonment.

Other evidence as to why their rate of abandonment is so high might center on the fact that the initial meetings of the Town of Guilderland took place at Henry Apple's residence[31]. Mr. Apple, like the other two mentioned residents of Guilderland, was a former resident of Watervliet and is recorded as having previously abandoned two slave children born to his slaves while a resident of Watervliet. John Van Rensselaer and the Veeder family are also listed as having previously abandoned two slave children of their female slaves while residents of Watervliet. Therefore, this increased rate in abandonment for Guilderland would be consistent with a small population of slaves and the previous practices of these slave holders. Another element that impacted this abandonment rate to such a high degree was the fact that these three families owned four (4) of the eight (8) children abandoned.

Table 6

RECORDS OF THE TOWN OF GUILDERLAND
Records of the Birth of Slaves
February 1803 - 1807

SUBJECT	Day/Month/Year
Certification of birth and abandonment of Gin, 12 March 1803, mother Susan, owned by Peter Veeder	28 May 1803
Slaves [cert. of the birth and abandonment of Simon, 25 May 1802, mother Dianna, owned by Frederick Crouince (?)]	28 April 1803
Slaves [cert. of birth and abandonment of Jude, 31 January 1801, mother Rose, owned by John van Rensselaer, recorded by Benjamin Winne, Town Clerk]	14 July 1801
Slaves [cert. of birth and abandonment of Ian, 26 June 1800, mother Maria, owned by Henry Apple]	21 May 1801
Slaves [cert. of birth and abandonment of Gin, 7 October 1801, mother Maria, owned by Henry Apple]	24 June 1802
Slaves [cert. of birth and abandonment of No Name, 9 December 1802 mother Maria]	No date
Slaves [cert. of birth of Dianah, 21 March 1805, mother Gin, owned by John Howard]	31 December 1805
Slaves [cert. of the birth and abandonment of Tom, 15 May 1802, mother Pegg, owned by Mathias Frederick]	22 November 1804
Slaves [cert. of the birth and abandonment of Jack, 20 September 1803, mother Pegg, owned by Mathias Frederick]	22 November 1804

Town of Bethlehem

Data on the birth of slave children is represented in the Town of Bethlehem (Albany County), New York, Table 7 is recorded in a special document located in the Town Clerk's Office. This document entitled "Records of Bethlehem For the purpose of Intering Negro Children Born of Slaves from the First Day of July 1799"[32], although extensive, provides a condensed record of the birth of slave children born in Bethlehem, NY. An example of these records follows:

"John Slingerland
Being a Proprietor of a Negro woman Slave which said
Slave had a Child Born on the tenth Day of September
1799. Being a Boy named Jhack."[33]

Each record lists the name of the slave owner or "proprietor", the specific date of the child's birth to his/her slave (no names provided in these records); the sex of the child and his/her name. No records are given with respect to the mother of the child or whether or not the owner of the child's mother abandoned the child to the Overseers of the Poor. In addition, there is no specific acknowledgement that either the Town Clerk or Overseers of the Poor recorded these births officially, although a number of the individuals listed in these records did in fact hold those offices during the period reflected.

These records do, however, include the signatures and certifications required by state law with respect to the manumission of Bethlehem slaves. Several of these manumissions which occurred from 1809 to 1827 are also included in this document. Census records indicate that Bethlehem, NY did not have a large number of slaves from 1800 onward. In 1800, the census lists eighteen (18) non-whites as residents and, in 1810 those numbers are more defined as five (5) free African descendants and ten (10) slaves.

Table 7

RECORDS OF BETHLEHEM FOR THE PURPOSE OF INTERING NEGRO CHILDREN BORN OF SLAVES FROM THE FIRST DAY OF JULY 1799

CHILD'S NAME	SEX	MOTHER	SLAVE OWNER	DATE OF BIRTH	DATE RE-CORDED
Jhack	M		John Slingerland	10 Sept. 1799	
Deyan	F		John Nanariel (sp)	2 Sept. 1799	
Dine	F		Hendrick Vanier (sp)	10 Feb. 1800	
Ceasar	M		Francis Nicoll	18 March 1800	
Diana	F		Francis Nicoll	3 May 1800	
Dean	F		Mary Winne (widow)	17 Sept. 1799	12 May 1801
Dina	F		William Winne	12 June 1800	12 March 1801
Annah	F		John Hillenbrant	3 Feb. 1801	6 April 1801
	M		Peter Rosekrance	May 1800	April 1801
Nan	F		George Hurjick	15 April 1801	
Jake	M		John Dun	5 July 1805 (sp)	5 May 1807
Susanne	F		Anne Nicoll	25 Nov. 1801	3 Oct. 1803 (sp)
Jack	M		Wottie Becker	7 Dec. 1800	20 April 1802
Tom	M		John Burihans (sp)	15 ___ 1801	11 June 1802
Jon	M		Johnis Hillenbrant	29 March 1802	4 Sept. 1802
Nan	F		John Van Denhyden	8 Oct. 1802	25 July 1803

Name	Sex	Proprietor		
Sarah	F	John Legranger	17 Nov. 1802	17 Aug. 1803
Tobe	M	John Olliver	21 Dec. 1802	20 Sept. 1803
Dick	M	George Huyck	26 Aug. 1803	7 Dec. 1803
Hannah	F	Samuel Elmendorf	1 Nov. 1805	27 July 1806
Sam	M	Johanes Burhans	5 Oct. 1803	23 June 1804
Manner	M	Johanas Hilebrandt	12 Dec. 1803	19 July 1804
			Died: 1 June 1805	
Tom	M	Nicholas Smith	28 May 1804	6 March 1805
Bett	F	Jurian Hogan (sp)	23 Feb. 1806	19 April 1806
Will	M	John Hillebrant	29 Aug. 1805	3 June 1806

The use of the term "proprietor" in these records is an interesting synonym for "slave owner". It speaks to the description of habits and customs of wealthy Dutch Patroons and English "Lords of the Manor" titles conferred on their ancestors. These wealthy landholders or landed aristocracy were given or acquired large estates in New Netherland and/or Colonial New York. It also makes the distinct reference to their slaves as property owned by their "proprietor".

Two such individuals that provide some insight into Bethlehem's origin, development and history are Sylvester Salisbury and Killian Van Rensselaer. Towards the end of the 17th century Salisbury, a retired English army officer bought an estate of over thirty thousand acres on the west bank of the Hudson River near the Village of Catskill. Killiaen Van Rensselaer, mentioned earlier in this work, had been appointed Patroon and later Lord of the Manor of Rensselaerwick, an estate now called Bethlehem, consisting of thirteen hundred acres also located on the west bank of the Hudson about eight miles below the city of Albany.

CAESAR NICOLL, A BIOGRAPHY OF AN ENSLAVED AFRICAN

Included in the Archive Records in the Bethlehem, New York Town Clerk's office is a copy of a manuscript titled "Biography of a Slave" by Dunkin H. Sill, the Great-great-great-grandson of Rensselaer Nicoll. [34] Within this book we are introduced to an interesting aspect of both of these gentlemen's "holdings," a man of African descent by the name of Caesar Nicoll. A slave, Caesar Nicoll, was at one time owned by both of these aristocratic families. In a biography of his life entitled, "Biography of a Slave", we are provided with one version of the union of these two formidable families.

The manuscript begins by detailing the relationship of the Salisbury and Van Rensselaer families to the marriage of Elizabeth Salisbury, granddaughter of Sylvester Salisbury and Rensselaer Nicoll, the grandson of Killian Van Rensselaer and the inheritor of Killian Van Rensselaer's estate. This manuscript provides a synopsis of the life of Caesar Nicholl, a slave born in Bethlehem, NY, the former Rensselaerwick Manor in 1737. Caesar's life is unmistakably intertwined with that of the Nicoll family. The manuscript is an attempt to provide the reader with a view of the life of a slave in upstate New York during the 18th and 19th centuries. The account however, is very slanted with respect to the nature of enslavement in upstate New York during this period. However, I feel that it typifies the purpose of writing this work as outlined in the "Introduction".

Interestingly enough, the first references to slaves and enslavement in this account speaks clearly to the focus of this work. Sill recounts the marriage that serves as the union of these two influential families by stating:

> **"Among the many and varied wedding gifts were several Negro slaves, a gift from the bride's father [Francis Salisbury, son of Sylvester Salisbury].** [35]

Sill also makes several other comments with respect to enslavement that support the misspoken "benign nature' of northern enslavement. He recounts how,

"Slave owners, both Dutch and English, living along the Hudson valley in the early 18th Century, were extremely kind to their slaves; they were seldom worked in the fields, being kept more as household and personal servants."[36]

He further states:

"All slaves were members of the same church as their masters…the masters never separated a husband and wife. They were never whipped or severely punished and an adult slave was rarely sold….As a result of this treatment the slaves were devotedly attached to their masters and their families."[37]

And yet, he does qualify these statements with what seems to be acceptable custom and standards that totally negates this vision of supreme harmony and contentment, when he states rather matter of factly with respect to African descendant attendance at church, "… [a separate] gallery being set aside for them" and, with respect to whippings and other punishment not occurring in New York State, "…unless one became incorrigible, in which event the slave was shipped to Jamaica Island, in the West Indies, and there sold."[38]

Caesar who lived to be 115 years old is described as a "willing and delighted" companion to young master Francis during his early years in Rensselaerwick (Bethlehem). One of his assigned duties at about the age of thirty (was "… to put his [senile] master into his cradle and rock him to sleep." Due to the deaths of his former "masters", Caesar was 'inherited' or "passed by will with the [other] property" to surviving members of the Nicholl family. At the age of eighty years old (80) Caesar was "granted the privileges of age", which amounted to "… a room on the ground floor of the kitchen extension of the old house. This room had an outdoor entrance, and "stooep", also a large, open fire-place"[39]

Caesar is described in his later years as sitting on this "stooep" and either "… throwing chunks of wood or using his heavy staff on the heads of his great-grandchildren, who are described in this manuscript as "young niggers". It is unclear if this reference to Caesar's great-grandchildren is the author's or Caesar's, for it appears twice in quotations.[40]

Reference is also made in this manuscript to a New York State Law passed in 1808 that, *"… in keeping with the intent of the United States Constitution, all slaves under sixty-five years of age, in the State of New York, were freed."*[41] This of course is a misrepresentation of the history of abolition in New York, however, numerous attempts have been made to present the actual period of enslavement and abolition in New York State in a more humane light and it is not difficult to believe that New Yorkers and other Americans were totally confused with respect to the existence of enslavement in New York State, particularly, in 1924 when this manuscript was written. Still expresses this confusion when he states that,

> *"At the present time, 1924, it is difficult to realize that enslavement legally existed in the State of New York as late as 1852."*[42]

Caesar Nicoll died in 1852 at the age of 115 years of age. He is believed by Sill to be "… without a doubt the last person North of the Mason and Dixon line to die a slave".[43] Again, this misinformation occurs. It would seem that due to his family history, Mr. Sill was probably a well-educated man and a life-long resident of New York State and yet his knowledge of enslavement and abolition in the state is totally misguided. It is the position of this author that the knowledge of enslavement and abolition in New York State is still misguided and in the 21st century that borders on criminal.

The circulation or distribution of this manuscript is unclear however, its lack of factual information, makes its purpose very clear. The entire premise of this work, as a factual challenge to the misrepresentation of enslavement in New York State, is supported by the views of enslavement and life in New York State for African descendants chronicled in this book on Caesar Nicoll. The alterations of historical fact and its' attempt to "humanize" chattel enslavement are unfortunately still accepted as fact to this very day.

However, most significant for us to consider is the fact that Caesar Nicoll was not involved in this representation of his life, as other African descendants have been able to participate in the various Slave Narratives published in the United States and New York State.

Figure 19

Caesar Nicoll (1737-1852)

AGE 114

(Daguerreotype taken in 1851)[44]

ENDNOTES

[1] Albany County "Register of Manumitted Slaves, 1800-1829", Records Series, County Clerk's Hall of Records

[2] Ibid

[3] Ibid

[4] Gerrit Van Zandt Family, CJ541, Box 1&2, Item 319, Manuscript Collections, Albany Institute of History and Art

[5] Gerrit Van Zandt Family, CJ541, Box 1&2, Item 237, Manuscript Collections, Albany Institute of History and Art

[6] Gerrit Van Zandt Family, CJ541, Box 1&2, Item 257, Manuscript Collections, Albany Institute of History and Art

[7] Gerrit Van Zandt Family, CJ541, Box 1&2, Item 253, Manuscript Collections, Albany Institute of History and Art

[8] Chamberlain's records, City of Albany Records, 1783-1815, Box 1, item 99

[9] Ibid

[10] Ibid

[11] Albany County "Register of Manumitted Slaves, 1800-1829", Records Series, County Clerk's Hall of Records

[12] Kruger, 827

[13] **NOTE**: The "Register of Manumitted Slaves" lists over 99% of the residents in this Register as residents of the City of Albany.

[14] *Albany County "Register of Manumitted Slaves, 1800-1829"*, 1 ½

[15] Single folder, EV749/*Slave Documents - 1775-282*, Collections, Albany Institute of History and Art

[16] Ibid

[17] Single folder, EV749-Item #8/*Slave Documents - 1775-282*, Collections, Albany Institute of History and Art

[18] Ibid

[9] Ibid

[20] *Albany County "Register of Manumitted Slaves, 1800-1829"*

[21] Albany County Hall of Records, *"Town of Watervliet Minutes, 1793–1844"*, Vol. 1

[22] See Kruger study, Vivienne L. Kruger, *Born to Run: The Slave Family in Early NY, 1623-1827*, PHD, 1985, Columbia University, University Microfilms International

[23] Ibid, pg. 65

[24] Single folder, EV749- Item #17/*Slave Documents - 1775-282*, Collections, Albany Institute of History and Art

[25] Ibid

[26] Ibid

[27] Ibid

[28] Ibid

[29] "Records of the Town of Guilderland, 1803-1834", vol. 1, Guilderland Town Clerk's Office

[30] Ibid

[31] Ibid

[32] Bethlehem Town Records, *"Records of Bethlehem for the purpose of Intering Negro Children Born of Slaves from the First Day of July 1799"* Bethlehem Town Clerk's Office

[33] Ibid

[34] Dunkin H. Sill, "Biography of a Slave", 1924, Bethlehem Town Clerk's Office

[35] Ibid, 1

[36] Ibid

[37] Ibid, 1-2

38   Ibid, 2

39   Ibid, 5

40   Ibid, 5-6

41   Ibid, 5

42   Ibid, 6

43   Ibid

44   Dunkin H. Sill, "Biography of a Slave", 1924, Bethlehem Town Clerk's Office, 6

CHAPTER V

NEW YORK STATE'S
COMPENSATED ABOLITION PROGRAM

Document 29
New York State Gradual Abolition Of Slavery Act Accounts Of Payments

<u>CHILDREN OF SLAVES</u>

"To be maintained by the state at the rate of 3 dol.s per month until 26 March 1802. After that at the rate of 2 dol. s per month until 31st March 1804 when maintenance by the state ceases_____for such as were abandoned previous to that day Maintenance by the state to cease when the child arrives at the age of four years unless so to disease or infirm that it cannot be bound. To be maintained by the master until 1 year old. Abandonment to be within 1 year after birth of the child." [1]

SUBSIDY PAYMENTS MADE TO NEW YORK SLAVEHOLDERS

The above cover sheet identifies state payments made to New York slave holders by the State of New York. It records and categorizes the distribution of state-sponsored subsidies for abandoned African descendant children expended by the State of New York under the provisions of the Gradual Abolition Act of 1799. It also contains a listing of the participation of New York State slaveholders who qualified for this subsidy program and records the state subsidy payments made to them. These records are presently housed in the New York State Archives. However, these records were badly damaged in the 1911 fire at the State Capitol where they were previously held.

RECORDS OF THE CITY OF ALBANY

The records for the City of Albany, although not complete, give us an indication of the actual subsidized payments made to Albany slave holders for the maintenance and support of Albany's abandoned slave children. Table 8 is a partial record of subsidy payments made directly to Albany slaveholders according to the subsidy provisions outlined in the Gradual Abolition Law of 1799.[2] This table identifies approximately nineteen slaveholders who received subsidy payments from the State of New York for abandoned slave children within the city of Albany. (This information is partially recorded due to fire damage on the remaining data.)

The total number of abandoned children included in these documents is not clearly delineated in the records that remain however, the period listed for payment in Table 8 (1800-1803) would seem to indicate payments made for one slave child for each identified slaveholder with the exception of the two-bracketed entries and the payments made to Peter Lansing of $51.41.3 from the period 2/5/1802 to 2/5/1803. The Lansing record may represent payments for more than one abandoned child for this one-year period.

Table 8 would therefore, represent a minimum of twenty-four slave children in Albany who were abandoned by the owners of their slave mothers, thus making these slaveholders eligible for state subsidy payments for support and maintenance of these children by the State of New York.

If we review Table 8 and its approximate listing of twenty-four abandoned slave children in conjunction with the thirty-four slave children abandoned and recorded in Table 4-1 and Table 1-2 above, we can conclude that approximately seventy percent of the slave children abandoned in Albany during the period 1800 to 1803 were returned by the Albany Overseers of the Poor to their original "masters," the owners of these children's mothers. These actions allowed the original slaveholders the ability to receive subsidy payments from the State of New York. This compensation was designed by the legislature to compensate slave holders in New York State for the future loss of these children to emancipation. This documentation clearly illustrates the intentions of New York's "compensated abolition program."

The expenditures reflect the actual amount paid to these slaveholders for the support and maintenance of their abandoned slave children. This rate would have varied from $3.50 (March 29, 1799 to October 1, 1801) to $3.00 from Oct. 1, 1801 to March 26, 1802. Additionally, this rate of monthly subsidy payments would have then been finally reduced by the state to $2.00 from March 26, 1802 to March 31, 1804. On March 31, 1804, this subsidy program was eliminated by the state legislature. The total amount of subsidized payments allocated during the period (1800-1803) to these Albany slave holders by the State of New York totals $396.86.

Table 8

REGISTER OF PAYMENTS TO ALBANY, NY
SLAVE OWNERS 1800 - 1803

SLAVE OWNER	CITY	PERIOD	EXPENDITURE
Illegible	Albany	20 February 1802	$9.00
Illegible	Albany	2 November 1801	$10.00
John Beckman	Albany	5 March 1802	$9.00
Peter Lansing	Albany	4 February 1802	$40.00
Illegible	Albany	4 February 1802	$9.00
Bleecker	Albany	12/13/1801 - 6/13/1802	
Bleecker, Jr.	Albany	12/18/1801 - 6/18/1802	>>>>>>>>$58.70
Dow	Albany	2/2/1802 - 8/2/1802	
Alen	Albany	2/20/1802 - 8/20/1802	
Illegible	Albany	28 August 1803	
Illegible	Albany	14 October 1803	>>>>>>>>>>>>>$63.00
Illegible	Albany	1 September 1803	
Ten Eyck	Albany	1/4/1802 - 1/4/1803	$26.75
W. Griffin	Albany	5/28/1802 - 11/20/1802	$12.00
Puryor	Albany	5/21/1802 - 11/21/1802	$12.00
Bleecker	Albany	6/13/1802 - 12/13/1802	$12.00
Bleecker, Jr.	Albany	6/18/1802 - 12/18/1802	$12.00
Peter Lansing	Albany	2/5/1802 - 2/5/1803	$51.41
Illegible	Albany	8/3/1802 - 2/2/1803	$12.00
Illegible	Albany	8/20/1802 - 2/20/1803	$12.00
George Merchant	Albany	1/1/1803 - 7/1/1803	$12.00
John Maley	Albany	3/14/1803 - 9/14/1803	$12.00
Peter Lansing	Albany	3/28/1803 - 9/28/1803	$12.00
Dow	Albany	4/14/1803 - 10/14/1803	$12.00
TOTAL 23			$396.86

Table 9 – **"Abandoned Children Recorded for Albany, NY 1799-1806"** may in fact be a continuation of Table 8 - **"Register of Payments to Albany, NY SlaveHolders 1800 – 1803."** However, the records used to compile the data for Table 8 did not include the name and date of birth of the children who were subsequently abandoned. Table 9 listings appear to be a later action of the state Comptroller. Table 9 records were untitled and their content was significantly reduced by the aforementioned fire damage however, the information provided in this table was legible enough to recreate it in the resulting format. Due to the similarities in the data of Table 8 and Table 9, it is highly likely that they both reflect payments directly to Albany slaveholders. The inclusion of Table 9 in a later section of this Comptroller Report is probably due to the fact that these records reflect a later period (1804-1806) than the records included in Table 8 (1800-1803).

Table 9 records Albany slaveholders receiving subsidy payments from the State of New York for their abandoned slave children. The twenty-two abandoned slave children listed in Table 9 represent 65 percent of all the slave children abandoned in Albany during the period 1800 to 1805, as recorded in Table 4-1 and 4-2 above. The total amount provided by the State of New York to these Albany slaveholders for the support and maintenance of these abandoned children during the period (1804-1806) is $427.60.

The names of the slaveholders of the abandoned children recorded in Table 9 corresponding to the period 1804-1806 have been added in the instances where they did not exist in the initial data available to construct this table.[3] They have been added based on similar data included in Tables 4-1 and 4-2 for the same time period.

Notwithstanding the probability that Table 9 is a continuation of Table 8, what cannot be disputed is the fact that this data represents New York State subsidy payments made directly to Albany slaveholders for the children of slaves abandoned in Albany, New York. This is not to say that these records represent the only payments made to Albany slaveholders by the State of New York. There were probably additional payments and other records with respect to these subsidy payments prior to the aforementioned fire. What we do know is that during the period 1799-1806, Albany slaveholders received a total in subsidy payments from the State of New York for the support and maintenance of their abandoned slave children of $824.46 for approximately, twenty-two to twenty-four abandoned African descendant children. If we add the totals of payments made to slaveholders in Table 8 and in Table 9.

Table 9

ABANDONED CHILDREN RECORDED
FOR ALBANY, NY 1799 - 1806

CHILD'S NAME	DATE OF BIRTH	OWNER OF RECORD (a)	PERIOD	EXPENDITURE
Nann	14 May 1803	John Bleeker. Jr.	5/15/1804 - 1/15/1805	$16.00
Phillip	4 January 1801		1/4/1804 -1/4/1805	$24.00
Dianah	27 April 1802	John Wendell	4/27/1802 - 4/27/1804 - 1/15/1805	$17.50
			1/15/1806 - 7/15/1806	$6.80
Tom	30 November 1800	Christopher Beekman	9/1/1804 - 12/1/1806	$6.00
Prince	6 November 1801	The Hoosic Family	5/6/1804 - 1/15/1805	$33.20
			1/15/1805 - 7/15/1805	$12.00
Kate	21 May 1801	Nettie Puryor	5/21/1804 - 1/15/1805	$15.54
			1/15/1805 - 5/21/1805	$8.39
Nicholas	15 December 1801	Abraham Lansing	6/15/1804 - 1/15/1805	$14.00
			1/15/1805 - 7/15/1805	$12.00
Eliza	1 January 1802	George Merchant	7/1/1804 - 1/15/1805	$13.00
			1/15/1805 - 7/15/1805	$12.00

Bena	10 November 1800	Peter Elmendorf	6/25/1804 - 11/10/1804	$94.00
Frank	20 May 1801	John Magoffin	5/20/1804 - 1/15/1805	$15.61
			1/15/1805 - 5/20/1805	$8.31
No Name	28 March 1802		9/28/1804 - 1/15/1805	$7.09
Peepee	14 January 1801		10/14/1804 - 1/14/1805	$6.00
Sarah	1 January 1803	The Dows	7/1/1804 - 1/15/1805	$13.00
Dianna	14 September 1801	John Maley	9/14/1804 - 1/15/1805	$8.00
			1/15/1805 - 7/15/1805	$12.00
No Name	7 February 1802		1/15/1806 - 2/7/1806	$1.50
No Name	28 March 1802		1/15/1806 - 3/28/1806	$4.86
Dianah			1/15/1806 - 4/27/1806	$6.80
Francis	15 November 1802	John Dow	1/15/1806 - 7/15/1806	$12.00
Sarah	1 January 1803	The Dows	1/15/1806 - 7/15/1806	$12.00
Mary	7 April 1803		1/15/1806 - 7/15/1806	$12.00
Sam	1 October 1803		1/15/1806 - 7/15/1806	$12.00
Joe	7 February 1802		1/15/1805 - 7/15/1805	$12.00
TOTAL	**22**			$427.66

(a)   The column "Owner of Record" containing slave owners' names was added to Table 9 based on data provided in Table 4. (See highlighted entries) A relationship was made between the slave owners, name of slave child and date of birth listed in Table 4 with the data in Table 9. The Owner of Record (slave owner) column was then added to Table 9 and when the data in these two records matched, the corresponding name of the slave owner was added to this column adjacent to his/her appropriate abandoned slave child.

As mentioned earlier in this chapter, Albany records included in Tables 4-1 and 4-2 indicated that thirty-four children were abandoned between the years of 1800-1805. Of this number, approximately twenty-two to twenty-four of these abandoned children are accounted for in Tables 8 and 9. Records for the remaining ten to twelve abandoned children of Albany slave mothers were either destroyed in the fire of 1911 or payments were made directly to the Albany Overseers of the Poor and not directly to Albany slaveholders. It should be noted that Overseer of the Poor records for the period of Gradual Abolition (1799-1827) no longer exist in Albany within either the State Archives or the Albany County Hall of Records.

Given the documentation that we do have, we can confidently argue that the frequency with which New York slaveholders availed, themselves, of the abandonment and subsidy provision of the Gradual Abolition Act of 1799 was due to several issues that included but were not limited to:

1- **The availability of compensation for the loss of their African descendant children as perpetual slaves;**

2- **The availability of a return on their investment for the costs of childrearing;**

3- **The ability to reduce operating costs by the surplusing of slaves they didn't want through abandonment.**[4]

The information included in Tables 1 through 9 represents new data in the area of New York State's participation in the Gradual Abolition Act of 1799. This new data includes: a record of the births of children to enslaved African descendant women, the abandonment of slave children, manumissions of older enslaved African descendants and with respect to Tables 8 and 9, a record of state sanctioned subsidy payments made directly to individual slaveholders for the maintenance and support of their abandoned slave children after the enactment of the Gradual Abolition Act of 1799.

Additional Records exist within the New York State Archives which document the payments of state-sponsored subsidies to slaveholders in other cities and towns. An example of this documentation is the Town of New Utrecht in Kings County.

TOWN OF NEW UTRECHT

The town of New Utrecht (Kings County) provides us with a detailed example of a request for subsidy payments from the State of New York made by the Overseers of the Poor of that town in response to the Gradual Abolition Act of 1799. These requests for payment provide a record of New York State subsidy payments made to New Utrecht slaveholders for the support and maintenance of abandoned slave children in the year 1802.[5] These records of subsidy payments made to New Utrecht slaveholders by the State of New York are presented in Documents 30-1 and 30-2.

The following is a list of New Utrecht slaveholders who received subsidy payment from the state at the request of the Overseers of the Poor of New Utrecht. These slave holders' records are listed as follows:

1- To Thomas Hegaman(sp) for supporting a female Negro child named Pury(sp) from the 23rd of August 1800 to the first day of October 1801 at Dol. 3.50 cents per month and from the first October 1801 until the first day of February 1802 at Dol. 3 per month amounting to … Dol. 50.43

2- To Jaques Centilyon(sp) for supporting a male Child named Peter from the 13th August 1800 to the first day of October 1801 at Dol. 3.50 cents per month and from the first day of October 1801 until the first day of February 1802 at Dol. 3 per month amounting to … Dol. 59.60

3- To Catherine Van Dyke for supporting a female child named Sukefrom the 21st day of August 1800 to the first day of October 1801 at Dol. 3.50 cents per month and from the first day October 1801 until the first day of February 1802 at Dol. 3 per month … Dol. 50.66

4- To ____(sp) Van Brunt for supporting a male child named Peter from the 16th day September 1800 to the first day of October 1801 at Dol. 3.50 cents per month and from the first day of October 1801 until the first day of February 1802 at Dol. 3 per month … Dol. 55.75

5- To William Dempse(sp) for supporting a male child named Adam from the 12 day of July 1801 to the first day of October 1801 at Dol. 3.50cents per month and from the first day of October 1801 until the first day of February 1802at Dol. 3 per month ... Dol. 21.10

6- To Abraham Duryee(sp)for supporting a female child named Mary from the 22 day of July 1801 to the first day of October 1801 at Dol. 3.50 cents per month and from the first day of October 1801 to the first day of February 1802 at Dol. 3 per month ... 19.93

7- To Peter L. Castilyon(sp) for supporting a male child named Stephen from the 9th July 1801 to the first day of October 1801 at Dol. 3.50 cents per month and from the first day of October 1801 to the first day of February 1802 at Dol. 3 per month ... Dol. 21.45

8- To Albert Van Brunt for supporting a male child named Lons from the 11th day of December 1801 to the first day of February 1802 at Dol. 3 per month ... Dol. 4.90.

The total amount requested from the state for the support of these eight abandoned slave children is $299.82. This account is certified as a "just and true account of the Children abandoned agreeable to an Act of the Legislature passed the 29 of March 1799 for the Gradual Abolition of Enslavement. Witness our hands this 1st of February 1802." This document is signed by the town supervisor, the town clerk and two justices of the peace.

These records document subsidy payments made directly to slaveholders by the State of New York for the support and maintenance of slave children assigned to them by the New Utrecht Overseers of the Poor. It was a practice of the Overseers of the Poor of New York cities and towns to assign abandoned slave children to the slaveholders who had abandoned them in the first instance. This "compensation abolition program" was in fact an attempt on the part of New York State to compensate New York slaveholders for their future loss of the labor of their slave children to impending abolition.

Document 30-1
Payments Made To New Utrecht Slaveholders

1802

Document 30-2
Payments Made To New Utrecht Slaveholders

1802

SUBSIDY PAYMENTS MADE TO LOCAL GOVERNMENTS

CITY OF NEW ROCHELLE

The Town of New Rochelle (Westchester County) provides a variety of records to track the births, abandonment and subsidy payments made by the State of New York for abandoned African descendant children born of local slaves during Gradual Abolition. These records provide an accounting of transactions undertaken by the Overseers of the Poor of New Rochelle with respect to subsidy payments made to slave holders and directly to the town under the auspices of the Overseers of the Poor for the children of slaves born during this period in New York history.[6] A record of requests for payments to reimburse slaveholders for the maintenance and support of their abandoned children for the years 1804 to 1806 in the Town of New Rochelle is included in the this section. It provides information on the town's practices with respect to the registration, abandonment of slave children and the subsidy payments made by the state.

In Document 31, we are provided with a record of the registration of the birth of Tempe on 18 September 1801 to a slave woman owned by Peter Shute (sp). This document was required by the 1799 law to certify the abandonment of a slave child by the owner of the child's mothers. It further states that Shute(sp) "has legally abandoned all his rights of service" to Tempe. The document is certified by Elias Guion, Jr., Clerk of the Town of New Rochelle.

Document 31
Certification Of Birth And Abandonment Of Tempe[7]

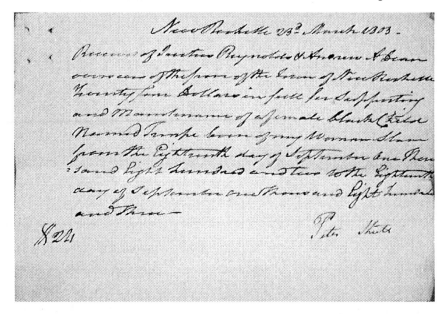

Additionally on 23 March 1804, a "slave Black child" by the name of Charles is born to the woman slave of a slaveholder named David Guion (possibly a relative of the Town Clerk) on the 20th day of August 1801. This document, (doc. 32), is used to register Charles' birth and also to record the fact that Guion intends to "legally abandons of all his rights of service" to Charles. Again, the document and its requirements are certified by the Town Clerk of New Rochelle, Elias Guion, Jr.

Document 32
Certification Of Birth And Abandonment Of Charles[8]

Subsequent to the abandonment of Tempe and Charles, we have two records that represent the costs for the support and maintenance of these two children that were submitted to the State of New York for reimbursement to the Town of New Rochelle's Overseers of the Poor. The first record, Document 33, is for the support and maintenance of Tempe from the period 18 September 1802 to 18 September 1803 "being the term of twelve months". The charge to the State for this twelve-month period is $24 at a rate of $2 per month as prescribed by the "An Act concerning Slaves and Servants". This request for payment from the State is signed by the Overseers of the Poor of New Rochelle and certified by three justices of the Peace, as required by law. It is dated 23rd day of March 1804 and submitted to the State.

Document 33
Request For Payment For Tempe[9]

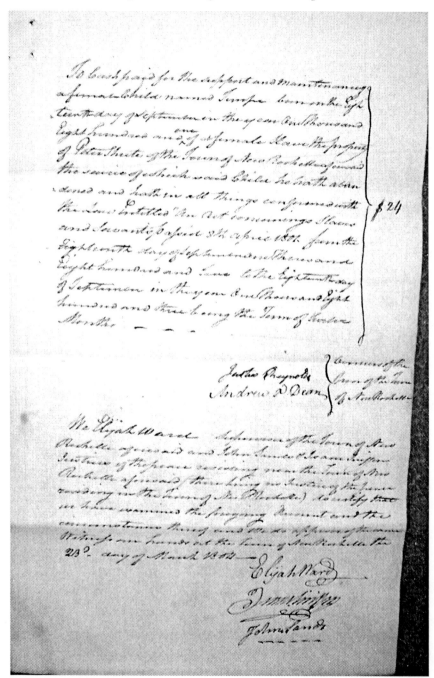

Similarly, Document 34 is a request for reimbursement for the support and maintenance of Charles "born of a slave the property of David Guion from the period, the 20th day of August 1802 to the 20th day of November 1803, being the term of fifteen months". The charge to the state for this fifteen-month period is $30. This request for payment from the state is also signed by the Overseers of the Poor of New Rochelle and certified by three justices of the peace as required by law. It is then dated 23rd day of March 1804 and submitted to the State.

Document 34
Request For Payment For Charles[10]

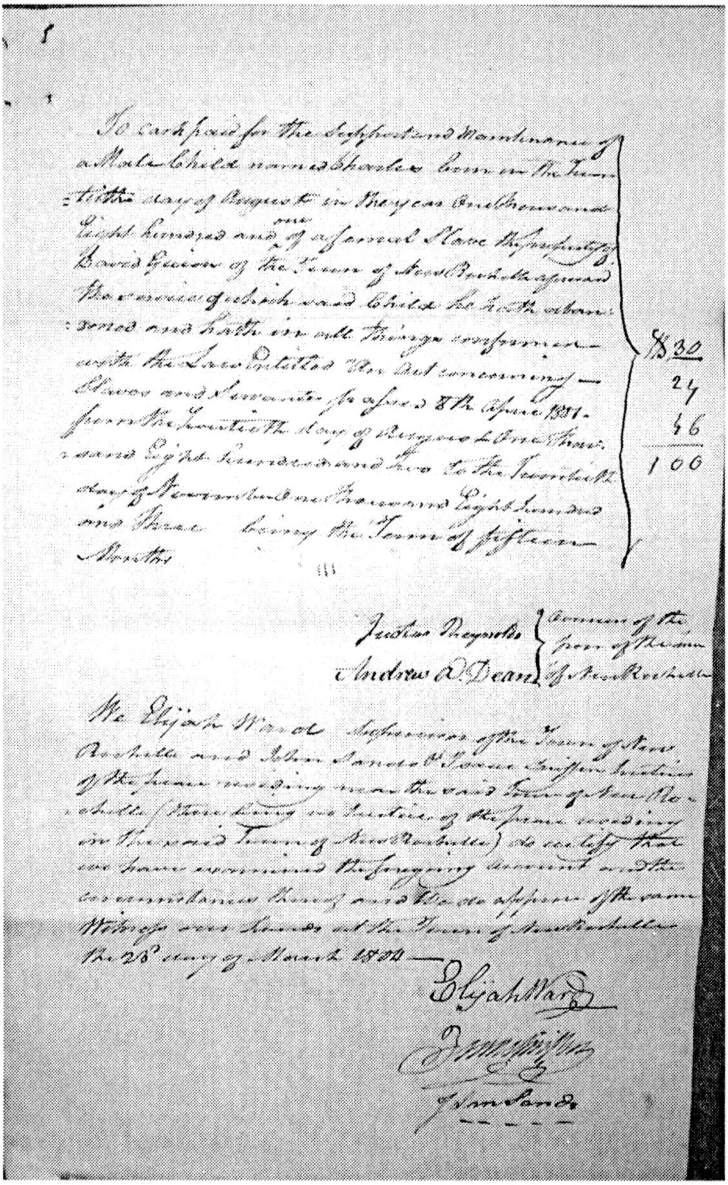

To cash paid for the support and maintenance of a Male Child named Charles born on the twentieth day of August in the year One thousand Eight hundred and one of a female Slave the property of David Guion of the Town of New Rochelle aforesaid the owner of which said Child he hath abandoned and hath in all things conformed with the Law Entitled the Act concerning Slaves and Servants passed 8th April 1801 — from the twentieth day of August One thousand Eight hundred and two to the twentieth day of November One thousand Eight hundred and three being the Term of fifteen Months

$30
24
46
100

Justus Reynolds } Overseers of the
Andrew D. Dean } poor of the Town of New Rochelle

We Elijah Ward Supervisor of the Town of New Rochelle and John Sands & James Griffen Justices of the peace residing near the said Town of New Rochelle (there being no Justice of the peace residing in the said Town of New Rochelle) do certify that we have examined the foregoing account and the circumstances thereof and the same appears ... Witness our hands at the Town of New Rochelle the 28 day of March 1804 —

Elijah Ward
James Griffen
John Sands

Interestingly enough, the Overseers of the Poor would often re-place these abandoned children with their original owners, thus qualifying these owners for the daily subsidy for support and maintenance from the State. The Overseers of the Poor of New Rochelle, unlike the case of Tempe who is under the direct auspices of the Overseers of the Poor, placed Charles with the owner of his mother and his original master, David Guion. This action made it possible for Mr. Guion to qualify for and receive any subsidy payments for the support and maintenance of Charles. Document 35 is a receipt written to the Overseers of the Poor from David Guion, dated 23 March 1804. This receipt details the fact that Mr. Guion received the sum of thirty dollars (as recorded in Document 34) from the Overseers of the Poor of New Rochelle "…in full for the support and maintenance of a Negro Male Child named Charles born of my woman slave from the Twentieth of August 1802 to the Twentieth of November 1803." The receipt is signed by David Guion and dated 23 March 1804 and then submitted to the State by the Overseers of the Poor with their initial request for reimbursement.[11]

Document 35
Receipt Of Payment From Overseers For Charles

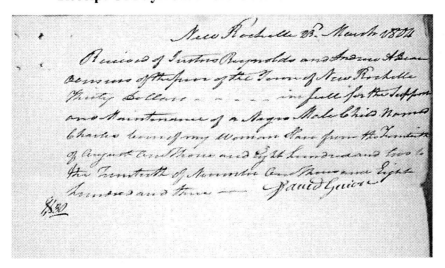

Various records show that payments to slaveholders were practiced throughout the State of New York and it further establishes the culpability of the State of New York in this "compensation abolition" scheme which was designed to provide slave holders with compensation for the future loss of the labor of their slave children to abolition.[12]

In another example of this practice, the Town of New Rochelle submitted Warrant #113, Documemt 36, to the state comptroller requesting payment in the amount of $121.44 for the support and maintenance from the State of New York for four children who were born to slave women in the town. George, Harriet, Jane and Ester were children born to slave mothers in New Rochelle and were totally unaware of these recorded transactions of individuals, municipalities and the State of New York that would dictate their future living conditions and in effect and practice make them orphans of the town and state. The mothers of these children were totally limited in their ability to alter these proceedings in any way due to their status as "human property."

Included in Warrant #113 is a list of certifications made by the town clerk of New Rochelle, (doc. 37). He is certifying that each of these four children was abandoned by their respective masters in the following manner:

1- "Theodorius Barton abandons George who was born on the 7th day of April 1801. It is witnessed by Elias Guion, Jr., Town Clerk of New Rochelle on the 12th of March 1805,

2- Samuel Purdy abandons Harriet who was born on 1st day of August 1802. "Witnessed my hand the 12th of March 1805, Elias Guion, Jr. Town Clerk of New Rochelle,"

3- Theodorius Barton abandons Jane who was born the 15th day of October 1802. "Witnessed my hand the 12th of March 1805, Elias Guion, Jr. Town Clerk of New Rochelle,"

4- Upon the death of John T. Harrison, his Executor abandons Ester who was born on the 2nd day of January 1803. "Witnessed my hand the 12th of March 1805, Elias Guion, Jr. Town Clerk of New Rochelle."

Document 36
Coversheet For Payment Submission To New York State[13]

21 March 1805

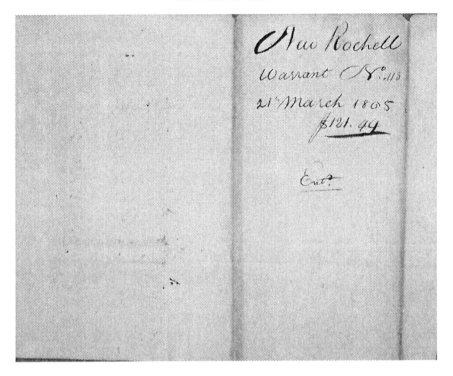

Document 37
Certification Of Abandonment For 4 Children[14]

12 March 1805

Three other documents are included in this Warrant #113 submission to the State of New York for reimbursement for the support and maintenance of George, Harriet, Jane and Grace. The first two of these documents represent a continuous accounting of the amount that the town is requesting from the State for the support and maintenance of these four abandoned children.

The first document, Document 38, identifies George and Harriet as children of slaves abandoned by the owners of their mothers and placed with the Overseers of the Poor. The Overseers are requesting reimbursement for the support and maintenance of these two children:

1- "For George "from the 23 March1804 to the 1st day of March 1805, being 11 months 7 days at $2 per month _____ Born 7 April 1801." They calculate the cost to be $22.50.

2- For Harriet "from the 1st day of August 1803 to the first day of March 1805, 1 year 7 months at 2 dollars per month_ _ _ _ Born 1st August 1802." They calculate the cost to be $38."

The total that they are requesting from the State for the support and maintenance of George and Harriet is $60.30.

Document 38
Request For Payment For George And Harriet [15]

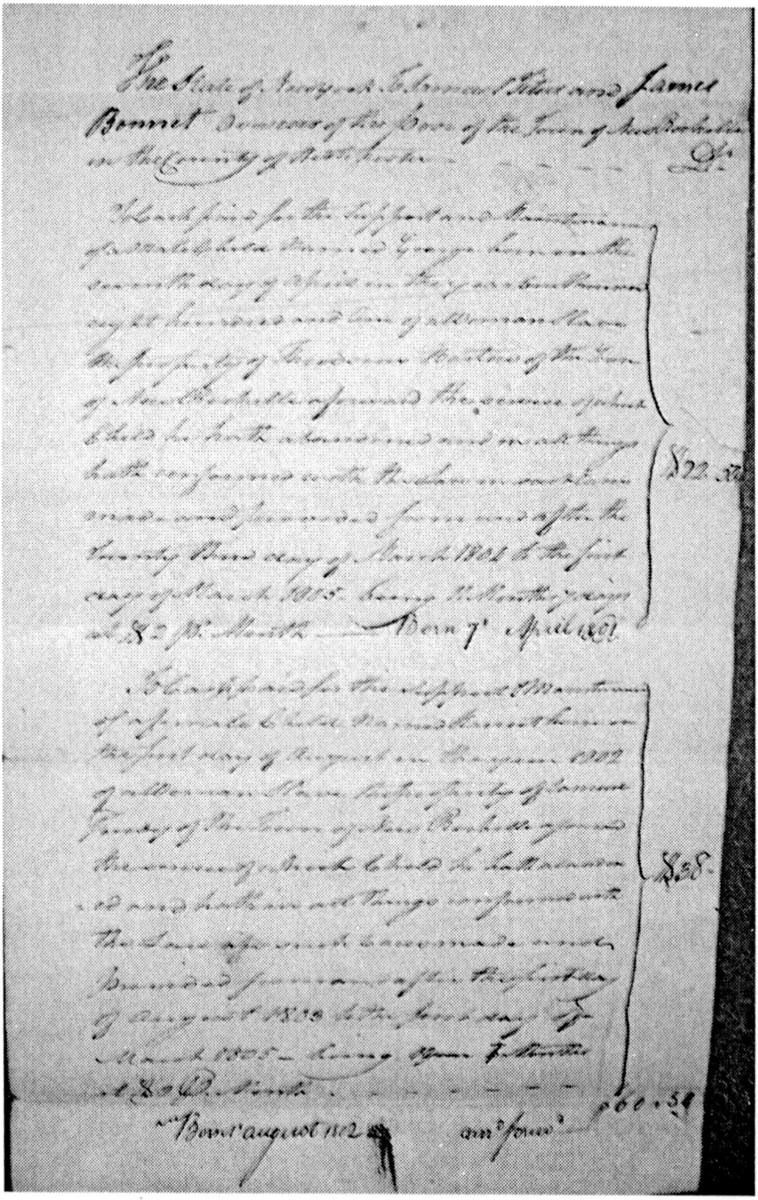

The State of New York To [illegible] and James Bonnet Overseers of the Poor of the Town of New Rochelle in the County of Westchester — — — Dr.

To Cash paid for the support and Maintenance of a Male Child named George born on the seventh day of April in the year one thousand eight hundred and one of a Woman Slave the property of [illegible] of the Town of New Rochelle aforesaid the owner of which Child he hath abandoned and in all things hath conformed with the law in such case made and provided from and after the twenty third day of March 1802 to the first day of March 1805 being [illegible] Months [illegible] at $2 per Month — Born 7th April 1801 — $22.50

To Cash paid for the support & Maintenance of a female Child named Harriet born on the first day of August in the year 1802 of a Woman Slave the property of [illegible] of the Town of New Rochelle aforesaid the owner of which Child he hath abandoned and hath in all things conformed with the Law in such case made and provided from and after the first day of August 1803 to the first day of March 1805 — being [illegible] at $2 per Month — — — — $38

$60.50

Born August 1802 — am^t forw^d

Document 39 is a continuation of the previous "request for payment for George and Harriet. It identifies Jane and Esther as abandoned children of slaves who were placed by the owners of their mothers with the Overseers of the Poor. The Overseers are requesting reimbursement for the support and maintenance of these two children:

1- "For Jane "from and after the 15th day of October 1803 to the 1st day of March 1805, being the Term of 16 1/2 Months at $2 dollars per month.' They calculate the cost to be $33.

2- For Esther, who was abandoned upon the death of her mother's slave holder, "from and after the 7th day of January 1804 to the 1st day of March 1805, being 14 months one week wanting at $2 dollars per month." They calculate the cost to be $27.94."

The total for this submission to the State of New York including the amount of $60.50 brought forward from Document 38 is $121.44. This document is signed by Sam Titus, Overseer of the Poor of New Rochelle and is executed on the 21st March 1805.

Document 39
Request For Payment For Jane And Esther[16]

21 March 1805

The final document included in Warrant #113 submission of 1805 to the State of New York is Document 40. It is represented as the final approval page and is signed by the superintendent of the Town of New Rochelle, Elijah Ward and two justices of the peace. A notation is made that the Town of New Rochelle had no justices of the peace so nearby justices were used in this case.

Document 40
Final Approval Page [17]

12 March 1805

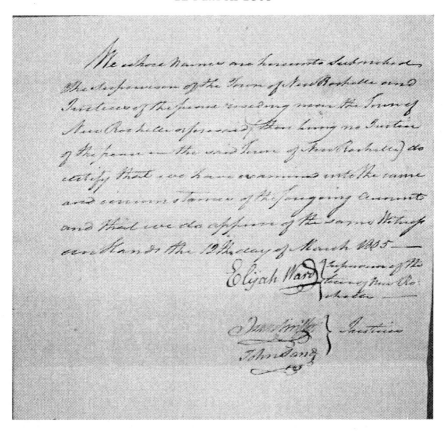

The next year on the 10th of March 1806, New Rochelle submitted Warrant #105 to the State of New York for payment in the amount of $65.50 for the support and maintenance of these same four children: George, Jane, Esther and Harriet.[18] The coversheet outlines the requirements of this charge for payment, (doc. 41).[19]

Document 41
Coversheet For Payment Submission To New York State

10 March 1806

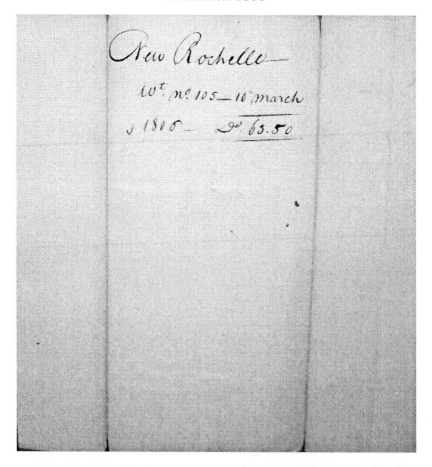

Included in this submission is a document addressed to the State of New York dated 17th January 1806. Document 42 lists the respective charges incurred for the support and maintenance of these four children of slaves:

1- "To the support and maintenance of a Male child named George from the 1st of March 1805 to the 7th of April 1805, being 1 month and 7 days abandoned by Theo Barton at $2 dolls per month. B[born]: 7 April 1801. They calculate the total at _ _ _ _ $ 2.50.

2- To the support and maintenance of a female Child named Jane from the 1st of March 1805 to the 15th of January 1806, being 10 months and 15 days abandoned by Theo Barton at $2 per month. [Born]: 15 October 1805. They calculate the total to be $21.00

3- To the support and maintenance of a female Child named Ester (sp) from the 1st March 1805 to 15th January 1806 being 10 months and 15 days abandoned by *illegible* Davenport ____ @ $2 per month. Born: 20 Jan 1803. They calculate the total to be ____ $21.00.

4- To the support and maintenance of a Female Child named Harriet from the 1st March 1805 to the 15 Jan 1806 being 10 months and 15 days, Abandoned by Sam Purdy. Born 1st Aug. 1802 at _ _ _ _ _ _ $2 dolls per Month _ _ _ $21.00."

The total of this submission is calculated at $65.50. This submission is certified and approved on 17 Jan. 1806 by the town supervisor and a justice of the peace.

Document 42
Request For Payment From NY State

17 Jan 1806

Oddly, also included in this submission is a note, Document 43, addressed to "Caleb Tompkins, Esq., New York State's Comptroller. It states: Sir; we are under the necessity to trouble you with the case (sp) of collecting the within Acct. if you will be so Oblying [obliging] as to take charge of the same you will very much oblige yours."

Signed: William Anderrigant (sp)   New Rochelle
           James Bonnet   March 3rd 1806

Document 43
Request For Assistance From Comptroller[20]

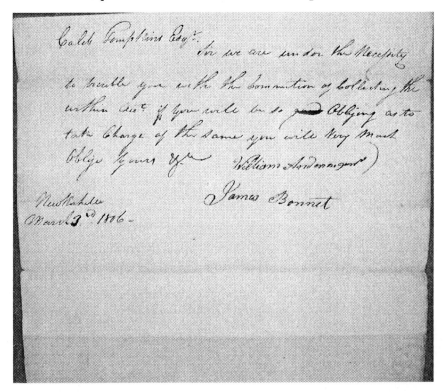

Several questions come to mind when this last section of this 1806 New Rochelle submission is analyzed. Why would the Town of New Rochelle need to contact the Comptroller of New York State to help expedite a warrant for $65.50? Could the financial situation in New Rochelle be so troubling that they would require an infusion of $65.50 to resolve it?

ADDITIONAL DOCUMENTATION

These Comptroller's *"Accounts for Payment"* also list the participation in this abandonment/subsidy program for the following upstate counties and towns: - Albany County: Bethlehem, Watervliet, Guilderland; - Columbia County: Clermont, Chatham, Hudson, Livingston, Kinderhook and Claverack; - Chautauqua County: Westfield; - Dutchess County: Rhinebeck; - Greene County: Catskill; - Madison County: Rochester; - Montgomery County: Amsterdam, Canajoharie and Palatine; - Orange County: Germantown, Newburgh and Montgomery; - Rensselaer County: Schodack; - Schenectady County: Schenectady; - Schoharie County: Cobleskill, Middleburgh and Schoharie; - Ulster County: Hurley, Kingston, Shawangunk; - Warren County: Queensbury; and Washington County: Cambridge. However, these records are badly damaged and only partially legible due to the aforementioned fire of 1911. This information would have proven invaluable in an extended study of subsidy payments made to municipalities and slave holders within New York State as provided for by the Gradual Abolition Law of 1799.

When we included the downstate cities and towns listed in Appendix I "Additional Documentation – Payments to New York State SlaveHolders" of this work, we now have a broader insight into the wide-spread nature of this effort on the part of the State of New York to undertake a comprehensive "compensated abolition program."

ENDNOTES

1   Register of Children of Slaves Abandoned 1800-1806 -"*Series A0827 –audited Accounts of Payments - State Comptroller and Treasurer*", NY State Archives. Note: The records for the cities, towns and villages in New York State that accompany this "Account of Payment" have been seriously damaged by fire. The listing of these municipalities is however extensive and includes various regions of the State of New York. The ability to include these records would have proven invaluable with respect to documenting the practice of "Abandoned Children" throughout New York State during this period.

2   Ibid

3   **NOTE**: Based on a correlation of the birth dates, children's names and slaveholders data from Figure 4, this additional data was inserted in Table 9. See highlighted entries in Table 4.

4   Also see Kruger, 832 – 833

    NOTE: This figure of 1,243 does not include slave children abandoned in New York State after the repeal of the abandonment subsidy in 1804.

5   *Care of Children of Slaves,* #A0827-78, Folder F-2, NY State Archives

6   Ibid

7   Ibid

8   Ibid

9   Ibid

10 Ibid

11 Ibid

12 **NOTE:** The fact that David Guion was related to the Town Clerk of New Rochelle probably helped to expedite this particular case.

13 *Care of Children of Slaves,* #A0827-78, Folder F-2, NY State Archives

[14] Ibid

[15] Ibid

[16] Ibid

[17] Ibid

[18] Ibid

[19] Ibid

[20] Ibid

CHAPTER VI

GRADUAL ABOLITION AND ITS FISCAL IMPACT ON NEW YORK STATE

THE STATEWIDE FISCAL IMPLICATIONS AND IMPACT

The "Gradual Abolition Act" and its provision for a financial subsidy to slave holders for abandoned slave children proved an inviting opportunity. Estimates are that slaveholders in New York used this program at a rate approaching forty percent (40%). This would mean that in ten (10) instances of slave mothers giving birth - four (4) slave children were forcibly given to the Overseer of the Poor in the town in which they were born by the "owners" of their mothers. This rate of abandonment further represents the mindset of the slave holders of New York in their depiction of "statutory slaves" created by the Gradual Abolition Act of 1799, as personal property to be sold, traded or abandoned, at will, even to local governments. In other words, these slave holders could dispose of these children easily, if they perceived the expenses for their upkeep too costly.

The fact that the State of New York sanctioned this practice through legislation and supported its implementation with a financial subsidy from tax-payer dollars further highlights its complicity in the commission of these "crimes against humanity," ultimately directed towards these innocent African descendant children and their families. The separation of families of African descendant had now been elevated to a higher level of criminality.

The breakup of African descendant families was a constant feature of the southern United States' version of enslavement, yet, we have been lead to believe that in the North the fate of the African descendant family and particularly its children were in more "humane" hands. Astonishingly, we find that public policy and taxpayer dollars were used to support these immoral crimes against African descendants that encouraged and supported the breakup of African descendant families, and the abandonment of their children at the whims of local officials and New York slave holders.

Neither these officials nor the slave holders had any interests in the welfare of these babies and children, other than financial. These practices could not have transpired without the unequivocal support of the State of New York, for its culpability in these actions served to reinforce and sanctioned a status of "non-citizen" in New York State developed and implemented purely along racial lines.

Since Overseers of the Poor were inclined to bond out these children to their former "owners", these slave holders were destined to receive both monthly subsidy payments *and* the daily services of these children. The following provides an example of just such a scenario which occurred in Flatlands, NY in 1801. Nicholas Schenck, a large slaveholder in Flatlands:

> *"abandons Peter born to his slave Margaret on January 27, 1801. On May 15, 1811, an indenture was made between the overseers of the poor of Flatlands and Nicholas Schenck. They place a poor black child named Peter, born January 27, 1801 with Schenck as a servant until age twenty-one. Schenck had abandoned Peter at age one, but accepted him back at age ten, when he considered his labor to have value."*[1]

STATE MODIFIES SUBSIDY PROGRAM

Subsidy Payment Schedule Modifications

1- **March 29, 1799 - Oct. 1, 1801 subsidy rate per child per month= \$3.50;**

2- **Oct. 1, 1801 – March 26, 1802 subsidy rate per child per month = \$3.00;**

3- **March 26, 1802 – March 31, 1804 subsidy rate per child per month=\$2.00 (subsidy eliminated after child reached the age of 4 years old); and,**

4- **Subsidy payments repealed March 31, 1804**

The state amended the subsidy provisions on several occasions in an attempt to rectify this collusion between local Overseers of the Poor and New York State slave holders. The State Legislature in 1802 passed a law that stipulated that the state would support (subsidize) abandoned children only until they reached the age of four years old. [2]

However, even this new law was slanted towards the interests of slave holders in its application and design for it only applied to children abandoned after March 1802.

Therefore, this modification meant that those children abandoned prior to this date and after the 4th of July 1799 were still entitled to carry with them the original subsidy of $3.50 until they reached the ages of twenty-five years for females and twenty-eight years for males. This elaborate compensation scheme, for all intents and purposes, can best be described as purely criminal in its intent and practice, since it served to further deteriorate the already deplorable conditions of these children and the unstable sociological environment surrounding them and their families.

The result was a whole generation of African descendant children effectively orphaned and separated from any knowledge of home or their families at the behest of the New York State Legislature. They were now forced to provide forced labor to parties' chosen by a foreign entity, the Overseer of the Poor, under the worst of conditions and circumstances that almost criminally lacked any standardized local or state guidelines and/or regulations for the Overseers' practices. The reality is that local governments, under the auspices of the Overseer of the Poor, and with the unprecedented support of New York State, became the "New Age Slave-Traders" of the 19th century.

Now, cities, towns, and villages in New York State, faced with the prospect of incurring skyrocketing financial shortfalls and added expenditures for the support of these abandoned African descendant children were placed in the business of bonding these abandoned children to slave holders and non-slave holders, alike. Let's be clear, this decision to abandon these children was not made by their parents, but by individuals who had their *own* best interests at heart. The era of enslavement in New York State had now taken a new turn of inhumanity. Not only is the ability to own a statutory slave now offered to any citizen at *no* initial cost of purchase, but these African descendant children have now become the prizes, literally, in a state sponsored 'free" labor give-away program. **NO PURCHASE NECESSARY!**

BUDGETARY IMPLICATIONS

> *"[abandoned slave children shall] be supported and maintained till bound out by the overseers of the poor... at the expense of the State – Provided however that the said support does not exceed three dollars and fifty cents per month for each child. And the comptroller is hereby authorized and directed to draw his warrant on the treasurer of this State for the amount of such account not exceeding the allowance above prescribed, and the accounts of the respective towns or cities being first signed by the supervisor of the town or the mayor of the city as the case may be where such child may be maintained."[3]*

The passage of the Gradual Abolition Act presented an unprecedented statement on the nature of "man's inhumanity to man" in New York State. It firmly established New York State's role financially and administratively in the "enslavement" of African descendant children. Essentially this law mandated that after the age of one year, a slave owner could abandon these slave children to the Overseers of the Poor in their respective towns and villages. The state would then reimburse the towns for the support and maintenance of these abandoned children at a monthly rate of up to $3.50 per month.

This state sponsored scheme for a compensated abolition program was now fully operational and backed by and enforced by the State of New York. However, the framers and supporters of this scheme did not take into account the vigorous participation of New York's slave holders, as documented earlier, nor did they foresee the tremendous financial burden that this effort to compensate and appease New York's slave holders would eventually have on their state treasury.

The following is an example of this administrative process. Document 44 represents the Town of Oyster Bay's (Queens County) request for payment from the state for the maintenance and support of an abandoned slave girl by the name of Rachel. The request is prepared by the Town Supervisor and certified by four (4) Justices of the Peace. In addition, approval for payment by a state official based in Albany is included in the lower right hand corner of the document. This document is but one of thousands of similar payment vouchers that were submitted by various cities, towns and villages to the State of New York for the support and maintenance of "abandoned" slave children provided for under the 1799 Gradual Abolition Act.

Several accountings have been made with respect to the expenditures associated with this 1799 Law.[4] It should be noted that the initial expenditures by the state for this law were minimal when singular submissions from localities were the rule. However, it became the practice of the local Overseers of the Poor to initially submit their vouchers to the state after the accumulation of a number of years of expenses therefore, there were very few vouchers individually submitted for the years 1799 to 1801.

Document 44
Town of Oyster Bay's (Queens County) Request for Payment [5]

Beginning in 1802, towns began to finally submit their first vouchers representing the period of the 4th of July 1799, the first year that the law was in effect, through January 1802, as in the Oyster Bay case and the following example from Mamaroneck, NY, (doc. 45).

This Mamaroneck document is an actual New York State Comptroller's Warrant that was submitted to the state treasurer for payment after review and approval by the NY State Comptroller. It is one of the few actual copies of these warrants that still exist in the State's Archives.

Document 45
Mamaroneck, NY's Authorization for Payment [6]

The total expenditures for the beginning phase of the Gradual Abolition Act of 1799 totaled $1,359.06.[7] That year, Elisha Jenkins, the State Comptroller, in his Comptroller's Report to the Legislature gives the legislature its first indication that this figure although manageable initially, would double to some $2,500 in the year 1802.[8] This estimate seemed to get the attention of the Governor of the State. In January of 1802, Governor De Witt Clinton warned the Legislature of the "growing expense" of this [subsidy] program if it were not altered.[9] The Assembly concurred, their feeling being that "the services performed by the children "freed" by this law would "make ample satisfaction" for the expenses involved in the rearing of these children, and passed a law repealing the "subsidy" aspect of the existing "Gradual Abolition Act". The Senate rejected this logic.

However, the Senate did acquiesce to the fiscal argument on 26 March 1802 by reducing the per month amount per abandoned child from $3.50 to $2.00 and eliminating payments for maintenance and support once these children reached the age of four years old.[10] The original law of 1799 provided for state subsidized support for these abandoned children until they were bound out to service by the towns' Overseers of the Poor. The fact that this subsidy from the state could last until these children reached adulthood was a major factor in persuading slave holders and their special interests groups to support the initial passage of this law and it proved just as effective a fiscal argument in causing its reduction.

It is clear that the Senate was cognizant of the position of the "special interest groups" that they represented. Fully supported and represented by Dutch slave holders and pro-enslavement forces, the Senate was reluctant to eliminate the "subsidy" aspect of this law entirely. Nor were they willing to relinquish the services that they felt their supporters were entitled to as owners of "human property". Their position remained - *if slave holders were to give up their lifetime hold on these children, they should receive adequate restitution.*

However, even the Senate did not anticipate what would occur in the years following the enactment of the Gradual Abolition Law. In fact, for the period beginning 8 January 1802 to 8 January 1803, where Comptroller Jenkins had estimated expenditures of $2,500 for the maintenance of these abandoned children, the actual total expenditure listed under "Overseers of the Poor, for the support of children of slaves" began to increase at an alarming rate and totaled $10,552.76 in 1803.[11] In this one-year period, the expenditure for these abandoned children increased some six hundred and seventy-six percent (676%) from the first expenditure figure of $1,359.06 in 1802. This 1803 expense for the support and maintenance of abandoned slave children amounted to almost 3% of the entire State Budget for that year.

Consequently, Comptroller Jenkins, on 26 January 1803, informed the Legislature that his dramatic underestimation of expenses to the legislature for this subsidy provision of the Gradual Abolition Law was due to the fact that the Overseers of the Poor [in a variety of instances] "suffered the expenses to accumulate for two years before they presented their accounts for payment." He estimated that the number of registered abandoned children was 322, "which at 2 dollars per month will amount to 7,728 dollars per annum". He however, warned that, "There is probably a balance of about 3000 doll[ar]s due on accounts not yet presented; and the abandonments continue to be regularly made in several counties. It is probable, therefore, that a sum of ten thousand to twelve thousand dollars will be required for this object during the succeeding year." [12]

The Comptroller's projections proved correct for the succeeding fiscal year, 8 January 1803 to 8 January 1804, when the total expenditure for "Overseers of the Poor, for the support of children of slaves amounted to $12,898.18.[13] Notwithstanding his correct estimate, he now vigorously warned the legislature that, "A further increase of expense may be calculated on, if existing laws remain in force."[14] This alarming prediction led the legislature to repeal the abandonment aspect of the Gradual Abolition Act on 31 March 1804.[15]

When discussing the state funds appropriated to slave holders and localities, it is interesting to note the fact that during the period, January 8, 1804 to January 8, 1805, the cost for the maintenance and support of abandoned slave children in New York State had risen to $20,865.81[16] or 6.1% of the entire state budget of 1805, which amounted to $341,969.88. In 1806, this expenditure for the support and maintenance of abandoned slave children totaled $19,261.22, a sum again equal to almost 6% of the State's Budget and comparable to the total of the salaries of the Governor, Chancellor, Judges of the Supreme Court and the Attorney General.[17]

Vivienne Kruger in her dissertation, *"Born to Run"* gives a very detailed accounting of the expenditures made by the State of New York with respect to the maintenance and support of abandoned African descendant children taken from their mothers and families during the early 1800s. The following document entitled "Amounts and Proportions of the Total New York State Budget Spent on Abandoned Black Children, 1802 to 1824" is presented in its entirety, (doc. 46).

Document 46
Amounts and Proportions of the Total New York State Budget Spent on Abandoned Black Children [18]

1802 to 1824

AMOUNTS AND PROPORTIONS OF THE TOTAL NEW YORK STATE BUDGET SPENT ON ABANDONED BLACK CHILDREN, 1802 TO 1824

Date of Comptroller's Budget Report	Fiscal Period Covered	Dollar Amount Spent on Abandoned Children	Total State Budget	Proportion of State Budget Spent on Abandonment Program
January 28, 1802	January 8, 1801 - January 8, 1802	1,359.06	325,704.46	0.4
January 25, 1803	January 8, 1802 - January 8, 1803	10,552.76	367,497.67	2.9
January 31, 1804	January 9, 1803 - January 8, 1804	12,808.18	258,510.30	5.0
January 22, 1805	January 8, 1804 - January 9, 1805	20,865.81	341,969.88	6.1
January 28, 1806	January 9, 1805 - January 9, 1806	19,261.22	345,208.87	5.6
January 27, 1807	January 10, 1806 - January 9, 1807	15,310.65	437,624.55	3.5
January 26, 1808	January 9, 1807 - January 9, 1808	7,650.19	425,689.69	1.8
February 7, 1809	January 9, 1808 - December 31, 1808	2,214.08	883,118.98	0.3
January 30, 1810	January 1, 1809 - December 31, 1809	451.06	627,767.93	...
January 29, 1811	January 1, 1810 - December 31, 1810	188.69	606,157.22	...
January 28, 1812	January 1, 1811 - December 31, 1811	48.00	589,337.00	...
January 12, 1813	January 1, 1812 - December 31, 1812	258.00	755,384.30	...
January 25, 1814	January 1, 1813 - December 31, 1813	40.00	799,747.97	...
January 31, 1815	January 1, 1814 - December 31, 1814	104.00	...	...
February 27, 1816	January 1, 1815 - December 31, 1815	140.00	...	...
February 14, 1817	January 1, 1816 - December 31, 1816	99.12	...	...
February 12, 1818	January 1, 1817 - December 31, 1817	78.00	...	...
January 11, 1819	January 1, 1818 - December 31, 1818	94.00	...	...
January 26, 1820	January 1, 1819 - December 31, 1819	70.00	...	...
February 7, 1821	January 1, 1820 - November 30, 1820	130.00	...	...
January 21, 1822	December 1, 1820 - November 30, 1821	46.00	...	...
January 29, 1823	December 1, 1821 - November 30, 1822	50.00	...	...
January 25, 1824	December 1, 1822 - November 30, 1823	48.00	...	...
January 25, 1825	December 1, 1823 - November 30, 1824	168.00	...	...

SOURCE: New York State Comptroller's Reports, January 28, 1802 through January 25, 1825, Journals of the Assembly and Senate of New York State, Sessions 25-48 (1802-1825), New-York Historical Society.

NOTE: Comptroller's figures in the state budget reports for January 28, 1802 and January 27, 1801, indicated that no payments were made for abandoned children covering the two-year January 8, 1799 - January 8, 1801 fiscal period. Children born July 4, 1799 would first appear on overseer of the poor rolls on July 4, 1800. Local overseers of the poor held their 1800 support accounts and did not present them until they submitted bills for their 1801 poor expenditure. New York State continued to incur expenses under its abandonment program through the year 1824, when the last of the children born by March 1804 reached adulthood at age twenty-one. The State Comptroller's reports dated January 13, 1826, January 17, 1827, January 19, 1828, and January 14, 1829 (covering funds expended during the period December 1, 1824 to November 30, 1828) indicate that no further sums were spent by the state on the support of abandoned children of slaves. The abandonment program cost the State of New York a total of $92,055.02.

Document 46 chronicles these subsidy expenditure items both as separate expenditures and as a function of the state budget itself. The most compelling aspect of this information is the fact that the State of New York continued to appropriate funds for the maintenance of abandoned African descendant children long after the repeal of the "abandonment/subsidy provision" of the Gradual Abolition Act in 1804. The reasoning being that New York State was legally obligated and fiscally responsible for continuing the maintenance and support provisions for children abandoned between 1799 and 1804 until they reached the age of "emancipation" and those who were never bonded out to employers or outside individuals by the local Overseers of the Poor.

The total amount appropriated by the State of New York to underwrite the "abandonment/subsidy provisions" of the Gradual Abolition Act totaled over $92,000 by the time the last of these abandoned children reached adulthood. (Between 1802 and 1810 the State of New York spent the equivalent of $1.1 million in today's [2002] dollars on the bondage of African Descendant children)[19] However, this state appropriated total does not include the fiscal burdens that were placed on localities once the state abandonment /subsidy program was amended and later repealed. An example of this increase in local expenditures for the support of these abandoned children is highlighted in the Hebron Town Meeting Minutes of the first Tuesday of April 1802:

> *"Resolved that one hundred and fifty Dollars be passed for the support of the Poor the ensuing year."[20]*

A similar budgetary fiasco confronted the legislative body in the State of New Jersey, after they implemented a similar "abandonment/ subsidy program".

NEW JERSEY FOLLOWS NEW YORK

The slaveholder's persistent opposition meant that when abolition finally came to New York and New Jersey, it arrived laden with delay, compromise, and often outright opposition to African-American freedom.[21]

Once a part of the original Dutch colonies in New Netherland; the British established New Jersey after they acquired New Netherland in 1664. The British approach to enslavement in New Jersey was even more aggressive than that in the New York colony. The British offered sixty (60) acres of land, per slave, to any man who imported slaves to meet the labor shortage that plagued the further development of the New Jersey colony. By 1690, most of the inhabitants of the region owned one or more slaves.

The State of New Jersey was a late comer to abolition. The governor of New Jersey urged his legislature in 1778 to provide gradual abolition, but unlike other northern states abolition was aggressively opposed. New Jersey citizens believed that African descendants were unfit for freedom by their, "deep wrought disposition to indolence" and … "want of judgment."[22] The 1800 census listed 12,422 New Jersey enslaved African descendants, which made New Jersey second only to New York among the northern states after American Independence. New Jersey enacted a similar gradual abolition law in 1804 that required similar provisions for reporting as the 1799 New York State law. It provided that female slaves born after July 4th 1804, would be free upon reaching the age of 21 years of age, and males upon reaching the age of 25.

This law also included the registration of births and the "abandonment of responsibility" provision for their slave children which were recorded at the local level as illustrated in the following Document 47, "Certificate for Abandonment" from Piscataway, New Jersey.

In this document dated June 6, 1806, slave owner Mary Boice of Piscataway relinquished responsibility for the infant Sarah, born on November 16, 1805 to Boice's slave Judi. Because the child was born under the provisions of New Jersey's Gradual Manumission Act of March 1804, she was legally a free person. However, under the terms of that Act, slave holders were entitled to the services of the children of their slaves born after July 4, 1804, until these children were either 21 years old (for females) or 25 years old (for males) unless they chose to abandon their rights to that service. As this document shows, Boice abandoned her claim to Sarah's services and in so doing she also absolved herself of any legal or financial responsibility to care for the child. That responsibility for the child's support was then placed in the hands of the Overseers of the Poor of the town of Piscataway.

Document 47
Certificate of Abandonment, Piscataway Township New Jersey [23]

1806

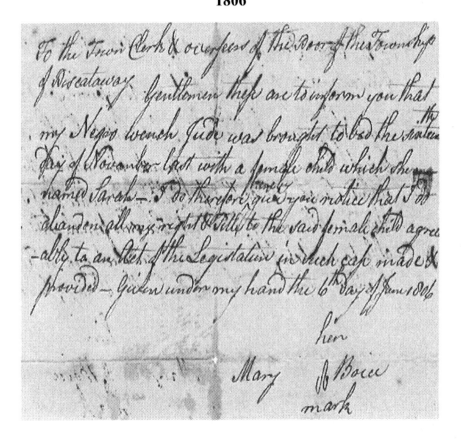

The subsidy provisions that existed in the New York State Gradual Abolition Law of 1799 were also included in the New Jersey Gradual Manumission Law of 1804. However, the New Jersey law provided support and maintenance subsidies to all slave holders who chose to maintain their rights with respect to these children born of their slaves. This provision in New Jersey established a "pure" "Compensated Abolition Program".

Two years after its passage, the New Jersey Legislature repealed the subsidy provisions of this law due to public pressure and the mounting financial crisis that it caused the state. New Jersey's implementation of this subsidy program produced expenditures that reached 30% of the state's budget (excluding prison and militia budgets) in fiscal year 1807 – 1808 and 40% in the following year.[24]

And, yet the cost to the States of New York and New Jersey, their localities and taxpayers represents only the fiscal toll of this fiendish plan.

ENDNOTES

1   Kruger, 840

2   Chapter 52 of the New York State Laws of 1802

3   Chapter 62 of the Laws of New York State of 1799, 388

4   **NOTE**: The yearly Journals of the Assembly, the Comptroller Report – "Audited accounts of payments made by "Overseers of the poor for support of children born to slaves, 1799-1820"; the Treasurer's Report – "Payment authorization to treasurer for support and maintenance of children born to slaves, 1807 and individual Town Minutes and Reports now afford individuals an opportunity to review these records themselves in the New York State Archives.

5   NY State Comptroller's Report, Series # B1718-00, NY State Archives

6   #100 Children of Slaves – Mamaroneck, NY, filed 19 July 1807, NY State Comptroller's Report, Series # B1718-00, NY State Archives

7   Journal of the Assembly of the State of New York , 1802, 17

8   Ibid, 21

9   Zilversmit, 184

10 Chapter 52 of the Laws of New York State of 1802

11 Journal of the Assembly of the State of New York, 1803, 22

12 Ibid, 25

13 Journal of the Assemblyof the State of New York, 1804, Comptroller's Report, 29

14 Ibid

15 Chapter 40 of the Laws of the State of New York of 1804

16 Journal of the Assembly of the state of New York, 1805, 43

17 Journal of the Assembly of the State of New York, 1806, 56

18 Kruger, 840

[19] **NOTE**: This figure represents the conversion of 1802-1810 dollars to year 2002 dollars.

[20] Hebron Town Meeting Minutes, 217

[21] Berlin, 234

[22] *"New Jersey Slave Trade and the beginning of the African American connection to the NJ Child Welfare Agency (DYFS)"*, NJ Slavery & DYFS, www.bpanj.org/slaverydyfs.htm

[23] Special Collections/University Archives, Rutgers University Libraries

[24] See Zilversmit, pg. 196-199 and Kruger, 851

CHAPTER VII

GRADUAL ABOLITION LAW HAS NO IMPACT ON THE STATUS OF ENSLAVEMENT

LAW HAS NO IMPACT ON ENSLAVEMENT

In New York and New Jersey, the largest enslaver states in the North, gradual emancipation left some black people locked in bondage or other forms of servitude until mid-century [19ᵗʰ] and beyond.[1]

GRADUAL ABOLITION MIRRORS ENSLAVEMENT

The Gradual Abolition Act of 1799 should in no way influence the reader to conclude that the institution of enslavement was in any way altered by the passage of this Act. As mentioned earlier, the Gradual Abolition Act did little to change the status of adult African descendants already imprisoned in this dehumanizing system of enslavement, for the law expressly stated that all African descendants already in bondage, prior to its July 4th, 1799 enactment, "would remain so for the remainder of their natural lives."[2] Ostensibly, the legislature included this provision to ensure that no investments incurred by New York State enslavers would be compromised or lost.

In fact by 1790, "there were still 35,900 slaves in the north because the Emancipation Laws had usually freed the children of slaves rather than the slaves themselves."[3]

It further had no impact on New York slave holders' propensity to continue to buy and sell more and more slaves. We have already observed the practices of Albany enslavers, who continued to buy and sell slaves without regard for the fact that the provisions of the Gradual Abolition Act were being debated and passed in their own back yard. This practice of buying and selling enslaved African descendants, however, was not isolated to upstate New York. Slave holders in the southern region of the state were just as highly invested. The following advertisement from the Suffolk Gazette, 13 May 1805, illustrates how sales of the enslaved continued, including the sale of "statutory slaves,' well into the period identified as "Gradual Abolition."

"FOR SALE: A Negro woman, in every respect suitable for a farmer -- she is 25 years old, and will be sold with or without a girl four years old."

This advertisement further exemplifies the under researched inhumanity of northern enslavement and places northern enslavement in direct relationship to its southern counterpart. Here we are presented with the age old criticism of southern enslavement that universally established its brutal and oppressive reputation – the separation of children from their parents. In this advertisement, the separation of mother and child was made available as an option to potential buyers.

Many other examples of the uninterrupted purchasing and sale of African descendants under New York's Gradual Abolition Act are recorded throughout New York State. One extraordinary representative of this practice of buying and selling enslaved African descendants during Gradual Abolition is embodied in the overly exuberant behavior of John Peter De Lancey, a farmer and political figure in Westchester County, who between 1790 and 1808, recorded the purchase of more than twenty enslaved African descendants in fifteen different transactions.[4]

There appears to have been little question on the part of New York enslavers that gradual abolition imposed few, if any, restrictions on their lives as buyers, sellers and merchants of "human flesh." The extended status of true enslavement to include "free" African descendant children born after the enactment of this law highlights the fact that in reality, the only discernable difference in the status of these "free born" children and their parents centered almost exclusively on the requirement that they be registered at birth with the local authorities. In other words, if their enslavers chose not to abandon their rights to these children's service as "statutory slaves," they were in fact treated no differently then their enslaved parents.

They could be sold, beaten, bartered, separated from family members and worked from sun up to sun down at the total discretion of their "registered" enslavers.

Theoretically, gradual abolition had been legislated in an effort to begin to move the state towards full emancipation and yet the reality was that slave holders paid little or no attention to this motive. They continued unimpeded in their lifestyles as holders of human property with little or no disturbance or interruption due to gradual abolition. Additionally, they extended, during the period of Gradual Abolition, the "freedom" to hire out or rent their "statutory slaves" as a means to increase their profits. One example of the hiring out of "statutory slave" children in the same manner as their ability to rent out their actual slaves is the case of Grace and her child Esther. Esther, the daughter of Grace was born "on or about the last of March last past" and according to the Gradual Abolition Act is registered and certified by the Town Clerk of Poughkeepsie on 25 December 1802. Esther's mother is recorded as being enslaved by one Smith Thompson. The relevance of this entry is that it goes on to state, **"which said wrench (Grace) and child have since been disposed of for a term of years to John Jacob Bush of Clinton Town in Dutchess County."** [5]

This is a prime example of the lack of distinction that slave holders held with respect to the enslaved and "statutory slave" during Gradual Abolition. Esther, born free, could be "disposed" of by her master Thompson, just as easily as her mother Grace, born enslaved. This entry clearly highlights the ability of slave holders to hire out or rent both their enslaved African descendants and their free-born "statutory slave" children without any restrictions. This observation is further supported by the fact that there exists no certification from the Overseers of the Poor with respect to this "disposal", leading one to believe that it was an action that legally could be undertaken by enslavers, although this practice is not provided for in the 1799 law. [6]

Another example of the misuse of these children of enslaved African descendants is a hire agreement receipt between Gerrit Van Zandt of Albany and an individual named van Schaick, **(d**oc. 48).

Document 48
Hire Agreement Bill For Negro Pete [7]

1801

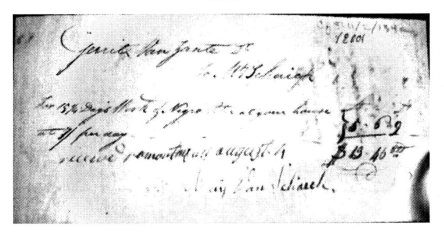

This receipt for the service of Gerrit Van Zandt's enslaved man named Pete for 15 ¼ days by Van Schiack at his house totals $13.45. Pete is hired out at a rate of less than $1 per day. The receipt also states, "Received amount in full August 4."[8]

This document, illustrates the unrestricted ability of slave holders to continue to hire out their "statutory slaves" in any way that they deemed necessary during Gradual Abolition. These hiring out practices, as mentioned earlier in this work, were designed to provide slave holders with a means to further profit from the forced labor of their enslaved African descendants and "statutory slaves," who were rented by enslavers and non enslavers, alike. This profit motivation on the part of New York enslavers was supported by the 'hire system", which was not addressed in the Gradual Abolition Act of 1799. This would seem to further support the contention that the Gradual Abolition Act of 1799 was not designed to eliminate enslavement, but on the contrary, it was developed as a mechanism to serve the needs of New York enslavers. It was developed to implement a compensated abolition program that would provided enslavers in New York State with the opportunity to continue to profit from the forced labor of their newly constituted "statutory slaves," while at the same time receive a financial subsidy for the maintenance of these "statutory slave" children from the state.

LIFE OF THE "STATUTORY SLAVE"

In much the same manner as slaves, "statutory slaves" created by the Gradual Abolition Act of 1799 were employed in agricultural work. It is sometimes incorrectly conjectured that slaves were not widely used on New York's farms. It is true that the smaller New York "plantations" could not support the huge-scale agricultural enslavement that was sustained by West Indian sugar, coffee, and cocoa plantations; Central American mahogany stands; tidewater Virginia and Rhode Island tobacco plantations; or later cotton plantations in the upland south. However, a difference in the scale of the economy meant only a difference in the numbers of slaves applied to agricultural labor, not its absence. The central feature of New York and northern enslavement was that most slaveholdings were small and contained only from one to five enslaved African descendants. Because of the small number of enslaved and "statutory slaves," family members were usually owned by separate enslavers and forced to live apart. While most enslaved New Yorkers and their "statutory slave" children fulfilled white society's need for domestic convenience, skilled trades, and hierarchical display, they unquestionably worked on farms. Enslavement and its continuance under Gradual Abolition created artificial demographic conditions for African descendants in New York: a small overall African descendant population, low population density, unbalanced adult sex ratios, and a random rather than familial distribution of those enslaved [and their children] into white households.[9]

In Rural Areas

Since enslaved African descendants and "statutory slaves" did not work in plantation gangs or live in communities with others of African descent, they would have had much less contact with other African descendants, and would have been largely integrated into the white community, albeit clearly as inferior and vulnerable members.

As a result, they lived and worked more closely with their enslavers in the north than in the south.

New York "statutory slaves" and their enslaved parents were typically housed in basements, the kitchens, or attics of their owner's homes or in outbuildings. They slept, according to Sojourner Truth's experiences, "on straw laid on loose floor boards, which in turn rested on an earthen floor. The floor was often wet, and water could be heard sloshing under the floor boards". Sojourner Truth further relates that "these damp, cold cellars of their owners housed slaves of all ages and genders, and noted the small windows that admitted little light, and loose and uneven wooden floorboards." [10]

They worked as field-hands, construction laborers, and as household servants. However, others, specifically men, became skilled craftsmen who were called upon to perform more specialized tasks such as caulking, blacksmithing, bricklaying, barrel-making, carpentry, and animal husbandry. Others worked as butchers, sawyers, millers, and even iron-workers. Men and women often worked at very different tasks, with men working mostly outdoors on the farms or buildings, or in workshops, while women chiefly worked in the kitchens and at other domestic chores, although sometimes they helped out with agricultural work as well. A. J. Williams-Myers writes in "Long Hammering" that, "Slaves and ["statutory slaves"] were involved in the production of almost every item used or consumed on the farm: from such simple items as brooms, ladles, and cords of firewood for use year-round to more elaborate ones such as barns and Dutch cellars in which roots, vegetables, cider, milk, butter, and meat were stored for preservation. Males and females who performed farm work, shared domestic chores but with a clear division of labor by gender. Women were often found in the kitchen cooking, cleaning house, washing, and caring for their owners' children as well as being integrally involved in the production of linens and woolens for home consumption and the colonial markets."[11]

The regular tasks of enslaved African descendants and "statutory slave" children on New York State farms also involved working at mowing grass, cutting hay, splitting firewood, mending fences, thatching roofs, butchering hogs, handling horses and oxen, threshing wheat, clearing fields, growing hemp and tobacco, and making shoes, canoes, nets, and paddles. Just dealing with the livestock required skills in herding and tending, breeding, training oxen to plough and horses to halter, hay making for winter fodder of fresh meadow and salt marsh hay, sheep shearing, wool washing, carding, spinning and weaving, butchering, smoking, salting and packing up beef and pork, rendering of tallow, candle making and soap making were some of the regular work requirements.

In the fields, skills included clearing land not already cleared, making and planting, harrowing, hoeing, and weeding of crops, harvesting, threshing, winnowing, carting, cleaning, milling, and storage of grains which included wheat, winter wheat, oats and Indian corn. They made lanes for oxen teams. They made fence railings and fences. They stocked the warehouse and loaded and unloaded vessels. They even made bricks and laid them.

Conversely, enslaved and "statutory slave" women worked beside their mistresses at the tasks characteristically assigned to farmwomen of that period. These involved the production of linen and woolen textiles, dairying, gardening, preserving, preparing, and serving food, doing endless household chores, and perhaps taking surplus garden produce by cart to sell at the market house. The kitchen and household demanded cooking, gathering of vegetables and eggs, butchering, plucking and hanging poultry, making pillows and featherbeds, desalting brined foods, grinding corn for bread, baking and yeast preservation, pickling, preserving and drying, preparation of medicines, laundry and ironing, sewing and mending.

In the Cities

In New York City and other larger communities service provided the largest of labor requirements for enslaved and "statutory slave" children. Many such African descendants, male and female, worked as domestics, often living in the homes of their enslavers. These enslaved African descendants and "statutory slave" children served in conjunction with "free" African descendants as assistants to white artisans, in the post-revolutionary period. Free artisans of African descent primarily served the African American community. "Over one- third of the male free African descendant heads of households in New York City in 1800 worked as carpenters, coopers, cabinetmakers, upholsterers, sail makers, butchers, and bakers."[12] African descendants were also able to make inroads in a few semiskilled, licensed occupations. Though still barred from carting, enslaved, "statutory slaves" and free African descents replaced whites in the lowest and the most menial of jobs as chimney sweeps and porters. They were also prominent as hackney coach drivers.

THE RATIONALE FOR GRADUAL ABOLITION

Proponents of Gradual Abolition in New York State's were primarily comprised of members of the Society of Friends and Episcopalians, or reconstituted Anglicans, the most paternalist denominations in the state. Methodists, who originally were anti-enslavement, began to shrink from emancipation by the 1790s. Those most vehemently opposed to emancipation were the Dutch Reformed farmers and large land owners of the mid-Hudson and southern portion of New York State. Also included in this group were the Huguenots of the Mid-Hudson Valley, where enslaved African descendants provided towns with an abundant supply of labor for use in their farms, mills, and homes.

Less than half of the white population provided the impetus for gradual abolition in New York State. It has been surmised that the early abolitionists created no general sentiment against [the immorality of] enslavement."[13] Its participants were the wealthy (socialite) land holders and a political minority not the common majority of lower and middle-class Americans in the North. The Pennsylvania Anti-Enslavement Society, itself, concurred. While addressing the National Anti-Enslavement Society, they admitted, "Those actively engaged in the cause of the oppressed Africans are very small." [14]

Gradual Abolition had been offered by abolitionists of the day as a means to an end - a way to address the issue of enslavement while at the same time allow enslavers to continue to own and profit from a system (gradual abolition) that was designed to protect their financial investment, first. The freedom of African descendants and their children seemed a secondary motivation for Abolitionists, like William Lloyd Garrison[15] and others.

During these years, abolitionists sought to transform enslavement from an unquestioned part of the status quo to a significant problem. The principal challenge facing them was arousing a conviction that enslavement was wrong. Like their non-abolitionist contemporaries, many white abolitionists were convinced of the racial inferiority of African descendants. Nevertheless, abolitionists acted forthrightly to correct what they perceived as a grievous wrong, but they could not wholly separate themselves from the assumptions and limitations of their time. It can be argued that these triumphs in the North including New York State, e.g. Gradual Abolition, were perhaps less an opposition to enslavement than a well orchestrated political strategy to protect the economic well being of their fledgling economy. The fact is that, "most white New Yorkers held racist attitudes and opposed immediate abolition."[16]

AFRICAN DESCENDANT VIEWS ON GRADUAL ABOLITION

Where, then, did the protest voices of people of African descent opposing this dehumanizing system of servitude come from? Who spoke about the hypocrisy in this gradual approach to emancipation? Where were the David Walkers, the Henry Highland Garnets, the Frederick Douglasses, or the Richard Allens? Who spoke for the African descendants caught in this fraudulent freedom?

If we consider this period of Gradual Abolition in New York State (1799-1827) in its historical context, we see that most of the individuals listed above were either enslaved themselves or were still a decade or two away from reaching their prominence as the vanguard of Abolitionists of African descent. David Walker didn't publish his Appeal until September of 1829, two years after Gradual Abolition. Henry Highland Garnet was enslaved during New York's Gradual Abolition period (1815-1824) and didn't stand before the delegates of the National Negro Convention in Buffalo, New

York until 1843, when he made his "Call to Rebellion" in which he encouraged enslaved African descendants to revolt against their masters.

During the Gradual Abolition period in New York State, Frederick Douglass was himself enslaved. In 1817, Richard Allen denounced the American Colonization Society's plan to return free African Americans in the United States to a colony in Africa but it wasn't until September, 1830 that Richard Allen and other free African descendants issued a call "on behalf of the Coloured Citizens of Philadelphia" and addressed it to their brethren throughout the United States. In fact, it wasn't until 1827 that Samuel Cornish joined John Russworm in editing the Freedom's Journal, which first appeared on March 16, 1827.

So during this period of gradual abolition, who spoke for the African descendants unwittingly caught in the throws of this legalized human bondage in New York State. We must search the archives and libraries for stories of the whole-life conditions of African descendants during gradual abolition. It is in the Narratives written by the enslaved and their "statutory slave" children who with great persistence survived this oppressive period of New York State history. It is important to this history of Gradual Abolition in New York that we avail ourselves of the human record that chronicles and expresses the traumatic effects of this Gradual Abolition period on the individuals, children and families. Their feelings of horror and helplessness are conveyed in some very compelling personal histories that chronicle the inner workings of gradual abolition. They also provide us with the best in a realistic and daunting view of how African descendants, trapped in the enslavement- like conditions of gradual abolition, persevered and survived their plight.

Herein lies the answer to these questions as to how African descendants viewed and perceived the experiences of Gradual Abolition. Four such Narratives follow that provide us with this personal and historical insight. The first addresses the consequences of a mother and her 'statutory slave" children struggling to survive during Gradual Abolition. The second depicts the story of a young enslaved African descendant brought to New York during Gradual

Abolition. The third depicts the story of a 'statutory slave' child born in the period identified as Gradual Abolition and how his perspective of it allows us to view this period in the same context as enslavement, itself. Lastly, we are confronted with the story of an enslaved family of African descent thoroughly focused on their survival as both individuals and as a family unit during Gradual Abolition.

Figure 20

Sojourner Truth[17]
1797/1800 -1883

NARRATIVE #1

"In process of time, Isabella (Sojourner Truth) found herself the mother of five children, and she rejoiced in being permitted to be the instrument of increasing the property of her oppressors! Think, dear reader, without a blush, if you can, for one moment, of a mother thus willingly, and with pride, laying her own children, the 'flesh of her flesh,' on the altar of slavery–a sacrifice to the bloody Moloch! But we must remember that beings capable of such sacrifices are not mothers; they are only 'things,' 'chattels,' 'property'."[18]

Sojourner Truth in her Narrative conveys her real and personal experiences with gradual abolition. In this context, Sojourner describes the broken promise of freedom made to her by enslaver and how this occasion of dejection is expressed clearly in the following:

"After emancipation had been decreed by the State, some years before the time fixed for its consummation, Isabella's master told her if she would do well, and be faithful, he would give her 'free papers,' one year before she was legally free by statute. In the year 1826, she had a badly diseased hand, which greatly diminished her usefulness; but on the arrival of July 4, 1827, the time specified for her receiving her 'free papers,' she claimed the fulfilment of her master's promise; but he refused granting it, on account (as he alleged) of the loss he had sustained by her hand. She plead that she had worked all the time, and done many things she was not wholly able to do, although she knew she had been less useful than formerly; but her master remained inflexible."[19]

Her feelings toward this act of betrayal are further expressed in the following statements:

'Ah!' she says, with emphasis that cannot be written, 'the slaveholders are TERRIBLE for promising to give you this or that, or such and such a privilege, if you will do thus and so; and when the time of fulfilment comes, and one claims the promise, they, forsooth, recollect nothing of the kind: and you are, like as not, taunted with being a LIAR; or, at best, the slave is accused of not having performed his part or condition of the contract'."[20]

She then sets out to rectify this denial of freedom.

"The subject of this narrative was to have been free July 4, 1827, but she continued with her master till the wool was spun, and the heaviest of the 'fall's work' closed up,

when she concluded to take her freedom into her own hands, and seek her fortune in some other place."[21]

Sojourner escapes with her youngest child to the nearby Wagoner farm and awaits the outcome of her freedom negotiations between the Wagoners and her former enslaver, John J. Dumont. Isaac S. Van Wagoner had not been involved in the practice of buying and selling enslaved African descendants and he did not believe in enslavement. However, rather than have Isabella (Sojourner) taken back by force, he decided he would purchase her services from Dumont for the balance of the year. Dumont taking full advantage, sets the price for Sojourner at twenty dollars, and additionally, sells her "statutory slave" child to the Wagoners for five dollars. The sum is paid by the Wagoners and Sojourner and her child are finally free of her enslaver.[22]

Ironically, on July 4th 1827, final abolition became a reality throughout New York State however, Sojourner, who was then legally free on that date, had been convinced by Dumont that she was required to serve him for another year in bondage before she could be freed. The Wagoners were also duped by Dumont and paid him for an enslaved woman who was already free.

Here again, we are presented with the buying and selling of "statutory slaves" (Sojourner's baby) in conjunction with or separate and apart from the sale of their parents. No provisions prohibiting the purchase or sale of "statutory slaves" were ever included in the Gradual Abolition Act of 1799. This experience is but one example of Sojourner Truth's despair and betrayal within the period of Gradual Abolition. For prior to her escape, her master John I. Dumont, of Ulster Park, NY choose to sell off one of Sojourner's five "statutory slave" children, Peter, who was born in 1821. Peter is sold several times throughout New York State before he is finally sold illegally out of state to an Alabama planter. Sojourner uses this ultimate act of betrayal for a mother as another reason to flee the Dumonts in 1827.

During Gradual Abolition it would appear that slave holders did not fear any penalty from the state or other authorities with respect to buying and selling their own "property," whether "free born" or enslaved. This unrestricted ability on the part of enslavers in New York State allowed them to place very little distinction on the differences in law of African descendants designated as either enslaved or "free born." As far as they were concerned, they were exercising their rights as property holders to handle their property or dispose of it as they saw fit. It is evident that the State of New York was exceedingly feeble in its willingness to exercise any authority that would cause these New York enslavers to act otherwise.

As noted earlier, this practice of selling "statutory slave" children was common in New York however, the practice of selling "statutory slaves" outside the state was illegal although not included in the provisions of the Gradual Abolition Act of 1799. In fact, the selling of slaves outside of the state had been declared illegal in legislation passed in 1788.[23] Upon learning of this miscarriage of justice, Sojourner proceeded to resolve this tragedy on her own.

"A little previous to Isabel's leaving her old master, he had sold her child, a boy of five years, to a Dr. Gedney, who took him with him as far as New York city, on his way to England; but finding the boy too small for his service, he sent him back to his brother, Solomon Gedney. This man disposed of him to his sister's husband, a wealthy planter, by the name of Fowler, who took him to his own home in Alabama."[24]

"This illegal and fraudulent transaction had been perpetrated some months before Isabella knew of it, as she was now living at Mr. Van Wagener's. The law expressly prohibited the sale of any slave out of the State,–and all minors were to be free at twenty-one years of age; and Mr. Dumont had sold Peter with the express understanding, that he was soon to return to the State of New York, and be emancipated at the specified time.

When Isabel heard that her son had been sold South, she immediately started on foot and alone, to find the man who had thus dared, in the face of all law, human and divine, to sell her child out of the State; and if possible, to bring him to account for the deed."[25]

It takes a lawsuit paid for by Ulster County Quakers for Sojourner to retrieve Peter from Alabama in 1828. However, unknown to Sojourner, he had been severely beaten; showing large welts on his back and scars all over his body.[26]

Sojourner's voice has informed us of the most cruel and barbaric practices of Gradual Abolition: the separation of families by sale of "statutory slaves" out of their families. As chronicled in this work, we now understand that she was not the only enslaved woman in New York during this period that experienced such tragedies.

Figure 21

Austin Steward[27]
(1793-1869)

NARRATIVE #2

A slave of William Helm in Virginia, Austin Steward was taken to Sodus and Bath, NY, when his master moved there from Virginia. Hired out by his master, Steward escaped, circa. 1815. He was advised by the Manumission Society in Farmington, NY that his hiring out made him free under New York law. His former master later attempted to kidnap him while he was in Palmyra, NY, unsuccessfully. For four years, he attended school in Farmington and worked on the farm of Otis Comstock.

A one-time resident (1831-1837) and president of the Canadian Wilberforce Colony of free slaves, Steward operated a meat and grocery businesses in Rochester (1817-1831). He also started a Sabbath school for African children. Returning to Rochester in 1837, he later moved to Canandaigua. There Steward played an active role in the 1847 "Emancipation Day" celebration that attracted nearly 10,000 people to the Academy grove on North Main Street. He died of typhoid fever and is buried in West Avenue Cemetery, Canandaigua.

In 1857, Steward published his autobiography, *Twenty-two Years a Slave, and Forty Years a Freeman*. Steward informs us that:

"While I was staying with my master at Bath, he having little necessity for my services hired me out to a man by the name of Joseph Robinson, for the purpose of learning me to drive a team. Robinson lived about three miles from the village of Bath, on a small farm, and was not only a poor man but a very mean one. He was cross and heartless in his family, as well as tyrannical and cruel to those in his employ; and having hired me as a "slave boy," he appeared to feel at full liberty to wreak his brutal passion on me at any time, whether I deserved rebuke or not; nor did his terrible outbreaks of anger vent themselves in oaths, curses and threatening only, but he would frequently draw from the cart-tongue a heavy iron pin, and beat me over the head with it, so unmercifully that he frequently sent the blood flowing over my scanty apparel, and from that to the ground, before he could feel satisfied.

These kind of beatings were not only excessively painful, but they always reminded me of the blows I had so often received from the key, in the hand of Mrs. Helm, when I was but a little waiter lad; and in truth I must say that the effect of these heavy blows on the head, have followed me thus far through life; subjecting me to frequent and violent head-aches, from which I never expect to be entirely free. Even to this day I shudder at the thought, when I think how Robinson used to fly at me, swearing, foaming, and seeming to think there was no weapon too large or too heavy to strike me with."[28]

Steward's Narrative tells of a similar atrocity with resent to the sale of his aunt Betsy Bristol and her "statutory slave" children to separate owners, while this enslaver kept her husband and the father of her children, Aaron Bristol, for his own needs.

> *"The Captain sold my aunt Betsy Bristol to a distinguished lawyer in the village, retaining her husband, Aaron Bristol, in his own employ; and two of her children he sold to another legal gentleman named Cruger. One day Captain Helm came out where the slaves were at work, and finding Aaron was not there, he fell into a great rage and swore terribly. He finally started off to a beach tree, from which he cut a stout limb, and trimmed it so as to leave a knot on the but end of the stick, or bludgeon rather, which was about two and a half feet in length. With this formidable weapon he started for Aaron's lonely cabin. When the solitary husband saw him coming he suspected that he was angry, and went forth to meet him in the street. They had no sooner met than my master seized Aaron by the collar, and taking the limb he had prepared by the smaller end, commenced beating him with it, over the head and face, and struck him some thirty or more terrible blows in quick succession; after which Aaron begged to know for what he was so unmercifully flogged."*[29]

Additional references are made in Steward's Narrative with respect to the hiring out and sale of enslaved African descendants and "statutory slave" children

> *"For some reason or other, Capt. Helm had supplied every lawyer in that section of country with slaves, either by purchase or hire; so when I thought of seeking legal redress for my poor, mangled sister, I saw at once it would be all in vain. The laws were in favor of the slave owner, and besides, every legal gentleman in the village had one or more of the Captain's slaves, who were treated with more*

or less rigor; and of course they would do nothing toward censuring one of their own number, so nothing could be done to give the slave even the few privileges which the laws of the State allowed them."[30]

NARRATIVE #3

Rev. Thomas James
1804-1891

We are also fortunate to have had African descendants tell their story of gradual abolition from the perspective of the "statutory slave" child. One such Narrative gives us further documentation with respect to the brutal and inhuman conditions of gradual abolition and its similarities with enslavement. In the *"Wonderful Eventful Life of Rev. Thomas James, by Himself"*, Rev. James recounts his experiences as a "statutory slave" in upstate New York in the first years of Gradual Abolition. He writes:

"I was born a slave at Canajoharie, this state [New York], in the year 1804. I was the third of four children, and we were all the property of Asa Kimball, who, when I was in the eighth year of my age, sold my mother, brother and elder sister to purchasers from Smith-town, a village not far distant from Amsterdam in the same part of the state. My mother refused to go, and ran into the garret to seek a hiding place. She was pursued, caught, tied hand and foot and delivered to her new owner. I caught my last sight of my mother as they rode off with her.

He continues;

While I was still in the seventeenth year of my age, Master Kimball was killed in a runaway accident; and at the administrator's sale I was sold with the rest of the property, my new master being Cromwell Bartlett, of the same neighborhood. As I remember, my first master was a well to do but rough farmer, a skeptic in religious matters, but of better heart than address; for he treated me well. He owned several farms, and my work was that of a farm hand. My new master had owned me but a few months when he sold me, or rather traded me, to George H. Hess, a wealthy farmer of the vicinity of Fort Plain. I was bartered in exchange for a yoke of steers, a colt and some additional property, the nature and amount of which I have now forgotten. I remained with Master Hess from March until June of the same year, when I ran away. My master had worked me hard, and at last undertook to whip me. This led me to seek escape from enslavement."[31]

Rev. James's first hand account represents an aspect of gradual abolition that has been virtually ignored and inexplicably neglected by numerous historians. Here we have Rev. James state emphatically that, "This [his treatment during gradual abolition] led me to seek escape from enslavement."[32] It is clear how this "statutory slave" perceived the conditions to which he was born and raised. In his mind and being, and by way of his experiences, if he was a participant in a form of emancipation, it clearly didn't represent anything other than enslavement to him.

Many historians, with their focus squarely placed on the option of eventual "freedom" that gradual abolition promised and the inevitable disappearance of enslavement itself, lost sight of the fact that gradual abolition was not emancipation. It was in fact and practice, the continuation of enslavement! Thousands of African descendant children in New York State, like Rev. James, were subjugated under this legalized system of enslavement, and have been completely forgotten in these "beautification" versions of history.

As illustrated above, life as a "statutory slave" under the "protection" of the Gradual Abolition Act belies any and all reference to this law as an opposition or deterrent to enslavement. Further, its portrayal as anything more then a "de jure" form of enslavement can be categorized as nothing more then propaganda. Graham Russell Hodges, himself, theorized that,

"Gradual emancipation insured that in rural societies ...where slavery remained popular, blacks would exist in the shadow of servitude."[33]

Similar abuses of the Gradual Abolition Act are recorded all throughout New York State, particularly instances where "statutory slaves" were taken by their holders to the south and sold as 'real' slaves. During Gradual Abolition, masters and enslavers , alike, began their nefarious practice of selling African descendants, who were about to be freed, to southern states where their bondage became permanent. Isaac Holmes, an English traveler, described large profits made by masters willing to sell slaves in New Orleans. New York slave holders evaded the 1788 law forbidding such sales by finding justices of the peace willing to agree that the slaves assented to their sale. [34]

Previous laws encouraged masters to accuse slaves of crimes, particularly those slaves they could not sell easily in the state because they were older or handicapped in some way. Those slaves would then be sold to traders, who would take them to other areas, particularly out of state, where their medical history was unknown. As is the case with most economic systems controlled by avaricious entrepreneurs, with the passage of the Final Abolition Act in 1817, the value of these 'statutory slaves' free labor increased considerably and enslavers, realizing the impending end of enslavement, offered these children's services to the highest bidder.

> **"Assured now of slavery's eventual demise, [slave] holders hastened to cut their losses. Many put their slaves on the market at once, and in spite of the ban on out-of-state sales it was soon being reported that the exportation of slaves to the West Indies had increased 'to an alarming magnitude,' often under circumstances of great barbarity."[35]**

NARRATIVE #4

The Silliman Family of Statutory Slaves

BACKGROUND

Gradual abolition statutes in New York were a carbon copy of the laws enacted throughout the northern states during this period. The lateness in the enactment of the Gradual Abolition Act in New

York allowed New York legislators the opportunity to model their impending legislation after similar statutes enacted in other northern states. Ironically, it also would have provided New York legislators with an opportunity to observe and familiarize themselves with the abuses inherent in such a system. It seems, however, that this knowledge was no match for the avaricious nature of New York enslavers. As expected, New York legislators made no attempts to modify or eliminate the brutal and criminal conditions that existed in Gradual Abolition laws in other northern states prior to implementing their own version in 1799. For example, in 1784 a gradual emancipation law was passed in Connecticut. This law like New York's was intended to slowly "phase out" enslavement. It would become the primary mechanism of abolition throughout New England and it served as the model for the New York State law.

THE SILLIMAN FAMILY

Chandos Michael Brown, biographer for Benjamin Silliman, the benefactor of Silliman College at Yale University, offers one example of how gradual emancipation laws were put into effect by a family of slave holders to the detriment of one particular family of African descent[36]. Benjamin Silliman's mother, Mary, was the largest owner of enslaved men and women in Fairfield County, Connecticut. In 1795, when it came time for Benjamin and his brother to attend Yale College, she sold two of their enslaved African descendants to help finance their education. After graduation, Benjamin Silliman returned to become the "overseer" of Holland Hill, the family farm, which included a "negro house" and six enslaved African descendants-Tego, Sue, Rose, Lowes, Peter, and old Job, together with their "statutory slave" children.

Beset by financial troubles the Silliman family began to liquidate their slave-holdings, "they were [now] faced with the problem of the "Negro children"[37], born at Holland Hill after the passage of the Gradual Abolition Law. This generation of African descendants had been "free" born as "statutory slaves." A few years later,

"a crisis was created when Benjamin's brother moved to Rhode Island and Cloe, one of their statutory slaves, objected to being taken out of state. She claimed that she belonged properly to Benjamin. Iago, presumably Cloe's husband [was] determined to prevent this removal of his wife it if at all possible. His hope was to appeal this action on the grounds of it being contrary to the Gradual Abolition law for slave holders to carry "statutory slaves" out of the state. Iago and Cloe appear to have won the day, for they stayed with Benjamin in Connecticut."[38]

During Gradual Abolition, however, Benjamin Silliman and his family also began leasing their 'statutory slaves' to their neighbors and receiving regular payments. For example, in 1803 Annise had four years left of statutory enslavement until she was to be legally emancipated at age 21. She was, however, leased for the final four years of labor for $100. In that same year, the Sillimans secured an even better deal regarding another one of their "statutory slaves", Ely. The Sillimans signed a contract leasing Ely to a Mr. Hubbel for 7 years. The contract stated: "We bound the boy till he should be 26." At the time, statutory slaves were to be legally freed at the age of 21, but apparently the Sillimans managed to get an extra 5 (five) years of service out of Ely. As Silliman's biographer, Brown puts it:

> *"Legally, the boy should be freed upon reaching twenty-one, but in practice the law was apparently elastic on this point. Silliman was ready to free Ely at the age of 25, but brother William settled with Hubbel that he should own the service of the boy an extra year. [Benjamin] Silliman agreed without much hesitation."[39]*

Under normal human circumstances, it would seem logical to assume that in the course of reviewing the Connecticut law that knowledge of or even rumors of these examples of abuses under Gradual Abolition would cause New York State legislators to alter the quality of their own Gradual Abolition legislation in some significant form -- ***But they didn't!***

ESCAPE AS AN ELEMENT OF GRADUAL ABOLITION

Runaways also tell an interesting story with respect to gradual abolition. The primary drive for freedom came from African descendants who did not restrict their push for freedom to politics and the courts but voted with their feet by flight from rural pietist farmers to the more liberal, if paternalist, world of New York City.[40] Dr. Kruger's study has shown that there were two major reasons that might motivate a slave to escape. First, enslaved African descendants often ran away when facing the prospect of major change in their ownership, frequently at the death of the master, or sale to another slave holder. Secondly, they also ran away to visit distant family members and loved ones. Sometimes both of these motives contributed to the decision to escape, particularly when the death of their enslaver resulted in the separation of family members. Other enslaved African descendants fled from particularly cruel enslavers, as well. [41]

In an interesting 'sidebar' of life for the African descendant under the provisions of Gradual Abolition, Shane White in "*Somewhat More Independent*" has chronicled the escape of some 1,232 enslaved during the period between 1771 and 1805 in New York State. If in fact the condition of African descendants in New York was significantly altered during this time- frame due to the impending implementation of gradual abolition or gradual abolition, itself – African descendants were not aware of it. They chose to respond to this period in their history in New York in the same manner that they had always responded to oppression and bondage – *escape*!

White further estimates that the average rate of thirty-five runaways per year, allowing for population differences, surpasses the numbers for escapes in the south during this same period! [42] The overall affect of this "individual-inspired" form of resistance to enslavement and gradual abolition is more definitively illustrated by the following two "Notices of Runaway Slaves," (docs. 49 and 50). The first notice chronicles the escape of an enslaved man named Will, who escaped from North-Castle in Westchester County, in 1774. The second notice addresses the escape of Jack from one Abel Whalon of Milton in upstate Saratoga County in 1809, ten years after the enactment of

Gradual Abolition. The occurrence of these two escapes some thirty –five years apart and in two geographically distant regions of New York (southern and northern, respectively) should serve to illustrate to the reader the far-reaching nature of this individualized form of resistance.

Document 49
Notice Of Runaway -- 26th Aug. 1774

NORTH CASTLE, WESTCHESTER COUNTY, NEW YORK

TEN DOLLARS Reward.

RUN AWAY on Friday the 26th of August 1774, from the subscriber, living in Middle-patent, North-Castle, Westchester county, and province of New-York,

A NEGRO MAN,

Named WILL, about 27 years of age, about five feet six inches high, somewhat of a yellow complexion, a spry lively fellow, very talkative; had on when he went away, a butter-nut coloured coat, felt hat, tow cloth trowsers; he has part of his right ear cut off, and a mark on the backside of his right hand.

Whosoever takes up said Negro and brings him to his master, or secures him in gaol, so that his master may have him again, shall have the above reward and all reasonable charges, paid by JAMES HANKS

N. B. Masters of vessels are hereby warned not to carry off the above Negro.   7t

Document 50
Notice Of Runaway -- 13th June 1809

From Abel Whalon, Milton, New York

(Printed By: William Child, at The American Press Co., Ballston Spa, NY)

A Runaway Negro.

RAN AWAY

From the subscriber on the night of the 11th inst. a Negro man, named

JACK,

About five feet eight or nine inches high ; stout, thick set, and well made. Had on, when he went away, a black Nap't Hat ; a butter-nut colour Sailor Coat ; had a small pack or bundle of clothes with him.

Any person who will secure said Negro in some gaol, or return him, shall be handsomely rewarded, and all reasonable charges paid, by the subscriber.

Abel Whalen.

Milton, 13th June, 1809.

BALLSTON SPA : PRINTED BY WILLIAM CHILD, AT THE AMERICAN PRESS

The act of escape constituted a direct challenge to a enslavers' authority. Dutchess County newspapers contain advertisements for 200 enslaved African descendants who escaped from their enslavers between 1785 and 1827. Likewise, during the period of the American Revolution, many African descendants in the Hudson River Valley had capitalized upon the anarchic situation of war by fleeing their masters, and African descendants continued to escape after the cessation of hostilities, although at a slower rate than that during the war years. While ads for sixty fugitives appeared in the local press between 1777 and 1783- an average of almost nine escapes annually, however, advertisements for only three fugitives per year appeared in the Poughkeepsie Journal between 1785 and 1799. During the decade and a half after the war, however, the number of escapes did noticeably increase while twenty-two (22) African descendants appeared in newspaper advertisements during the ten years between 1785-1799 (an average of 2.2 annually), twenty-four (24) fugitives escaped during the five years immediately preceding the adoption of the gradual abolition Act in 1799, or an average of almost five per year.

The adoption of gradual abolition seems to have been an important turning point in the history of resistance to enslavement by African descendants. The number of escapes appearing in the local press increased noticeably after 1799, doubling from an average of 3.1 runaways annually to 6.0 between 1800 and 1817. The number of escapes did decline slightly after 1817, when the state legislature essentially mandated the end of enslavement in New York within ten years. The passage of the 1817 Act, which freed all the enslaved born prior to July 4, 1799 in 1827, must have rendered servitude even more abhorrent to younger African Americans who were born after July 4, 1799; these "statutory slaves" were required to serve their masters until adulthood. Throughout the end of the eighteenth and the beginning of the nineteenth centuries, young adults and adolescents comprised the vast majority of escapes, and that proportion actually increased over time. Between 1785 and 1799, fugitives less than twenty-six years of age accounted for three out of every four escapes, while that proportion increased to 78.5 percent of all African descendants escapes during the eighteen years between 1800 and 1817. After 1817, nine of every ten escapes were twenty-six years of age or younger.[43]

The proof of New York slave holders' responses to these ever increasing escapes is the existence of newspaper advertisements offering rewards for runaway slaves in Ulster County. Their ads give testament to the fierce desire for freedom from their masters. In fact, the problem of escapes became so great during Gradual Abolition, that a group of enslavers in New Paltz banded together in 1810 to form the "The Society of Negroes Unsettled" which raised money to search for and apprehend escaped enslaved African descendants. Contained within this document are notes on the routes that escaped slaves were suspected to have taken. It is not surprising that many of the enslaved and "statutory slaves" escapees were thought to have gone to northern and western portions of the state, particularly the counties of Otsego, Yates, and Montgomery, although there is also suspicion of at least one heading northeast towards Vermont.[44]

Additionally, in Ulster County,

> **"A new mood of assertiveness among slaves manifested itself in the region. Residents of Ulster County organized the "Slaver Apprehending Society of Shawangunk" in response to the "uneasiness and disquietude" among local slaves, some of whom believed that the legislature had liberated them "and that they are now held in servitude by the arbitrary power of their masters."[45]**

In the year 1810, an escape occurred in the northern County of Ontario which seems to belie any supposition on the part of some historians that upstate and western New York was any less affected by escapes. This notice appeared in the *Geneva Gazette*, Aug. 1, 1810, (doc. 51).

Document 51
Geneva Gazette [46]
Aug. 1, 1810

6 Cents Reward.

RAN away from *James Dobbin,* about the 15th ult. a mulatto wench belonging to the subscriber, named MIMA, of a middle size. The public are cautioned against trusting her on account of the subscriber, and any person harboring her will be prosecuted according to law. Whoever will return said wench to the owner, shall receive the above Reward, but no charges will be paid. WILLIAM POWELL.

Geneva, August 1st. (59)

AFRICAN DESCENDANTS PROVIDE SAFE HAVEN

As was the case during New York's extensive period of enslavement, African descendants during Gradual Abolition assumed the role of liberator for their abandoned slave children and relatives' children. The opportunity for the survival of these children was considerably greater if their placement by local authorities was made with a relative, whether the authorities were aware of this relationship or not.

In addition to the well used option of escape, African descendants, themselves, provided a viable and secure haven of "freedom" during gradual abolition. It should be noted that the employer options outlined in the Gradual Abolition Law[47] did not exclude "free" African descendants, particularly, after the state legislature repealed the subsidy provisions of the Gradual Abolition Act of 1799. Free African descendants had the ability to serve as an employer location for abandoned slave children with local Overseers of the Poor. If a "free" African descendant become aware of the abandonment of certain slave children (including their own children with enslaved wives or the children of relatives) in their area, they could provide themselves as an option for placement for these abandoned children. Two such cases are documented in the Town of Flushing, in Queens County, New York between 1806 and 1809. Two abandoned "statutory slave" children classified as paupers by the authorities of the town are contracted out for service by the Overseers of the Poor to African descendants, who were probably their fathers or relatives.[48]

These opportunistic placements followed a pattern of struggle for African descendants to keep the unity of their families intact. As has been mentioned earlier in this work, the abandonment of these slave children was accomplished without any consultation or input of their enslaved parents. As was the case throughout enslavement in New York State, African descendants presented themselves as a vehicle for freeing their children and relatives from whatever the cycle of misery and despair they were subjected to by New York slave holders and governmental authorities.

ABOLITIONISTS RECANT ON GRADUAL ABOLITION

Irrespective of the efforts of white abolitionists, gradual abolition proved to be a failure primarily due to the fact that is was essentially an economic "solution" to a moral issue - human bondage. Therefore, it becomes evident that Gradual Abolition, despite the rhetoric of Abolitionists to the contrary, can best be viewed, for all intents and purposes, as less of an opposition to enslavement than:

1- **a "protectionist" attempt to preserve the existing profit centers of New York State economy –enslavement; or**

2- **a resolve by merchants and manufacturers to establish a more pure form of capitalism dependent on "free" wage labor.**

To attribute any moral or humanitarian purpose to this law would be to completely ignore the reality of the fact that gradual abolition did not constitute in any respect abolition or emancipation.

This position is evident in the statements of Northern abolitionists who initially supported the concept of gradual abolition but were later repulsed at the devastation and destruction it created. A perfect example of this reversal is William Lloyd Garrison, himself. Although originally an early advocate of gradual abolition by 1830, Garrison had denounced his earlier position and forcefully demanded immediate emancipation and the subsequent incorporation of freedmen into American society. In a column titled "To The Public" in *"The Liberator"* in 1831, Garrison states:

> *"In Park-Street Church, on the Fourth of July, 1829, in an address on enslavement, I unreflectingly assented to the popular but pernicious doctrine of gradual abolition. I seize this opportunity to make a full and unequivocal recantation, and thus publicly to ask pardon of my God, of my country, and of my brethren the poor slaves, for having uttered a sentiment so full of timidity, injustice and absurdity. My conscience is now satisfied."* [49]

A similar recantation from Garrison was published in the Genius of Universal Emancipation in Baltimore on September 1829. Other abolitionists were also morally persuaded to accept this view of gradual abolition. Elizabeth Heyrick, a Quaker abolitionist and women's rights advocate writes, in the "Immediate not Gradual Abolition", in 1824: [50]

> *"The slave holder knew very well that his prey would be secure, so long as the abolitionists could be cajoled into a demand for gradual instead of immediate abolition. He knew very well, that the contemplation of a gradual emancipation would beget a gradual indifference to emancipation itself."*

She further states:

"But this GRADUAL ABOLITION has been the grand marplot of human virtue and happiness; the very masterpiece of satanic policy. By converting the cry for immediate, into gradual emancipation, the prince of slave-holders 'transformed himself, with astonishing dexterity, into an angel of light,' -and thereby 'deceived the very elect.' -- He saw very clearly, that if public justice and humanity, especially if Christian justice and humanity could be brought to demand only a gradual extermination of the enormities of the slave system; if they could be brought to acquiesce, but for one year, or for one month, in the slavery of our African brother, -- in robbing him of all the rights of humanity, -- and degrading him to a level with the brutes; that then, they could imperceptibly be brought to acquiesce in all this for an unlimited duration. He saw, very clearly, that the time for the extermination of slavery was precisely, that, when its horrid impiety and enormity were first distinctly known and strongly felt."

"Had the labours of the abolitionists been begun, and continued on Divine instead of human reliance, -- immediate emancipation would have appeared just as attainable as gradual emancipation. But by substituting the latter object for the former, under the idea that its accomplishment was more probable, less exposed to objection; and by endeavoring to carry it, through considerations of interest, rather than obligations of duty; they have betrayed an unworthy diffidence in the cause in which they have embarked; -- they have converted the great business of emancipation into an object of political calculation; --they have withdrawn it from Divine, and placed it under human patronage; -- and disappointment and defeat, have been the inevitable consequence."

ENDNOTES

1   See Zilversmit, 196-199 and Kruger, 228, 851

2   Chapter 62 of the Laws of New York State of 1799

3   See Mc Colley, Robert, Slavery in Jeffersonian Virginia, 2nd ed., Urbana, 1978, 163-8,

4   Hodges, 165

5   "Town Minutes Poughkeepsie" 1799-1807

6   Ibid

7   Van Zandt Collection, CJ541/Box 2 –item 134, Albany Institute of History and Art,

8   Ibid

9   Kruger, abstract.

10   "The Narrative of Sojourner Truth" (1850), dictated by Sojourner Truth (ca.1797-1883); edited by Olive Gilbert

11   Williams-Myers, A.J. Long Hammering: Essays on the forging of an African American presence in the Hudson River Valley to the early twentieth century. (Trenton, NJ: African World Press, Inc., 1994), 25

12   Graham Russell Hodges, Root & Branch: African Americans in New York & East New Jersey, 1613-1863, (Chapel Hill Publishing, North Carolina) 178

13   Quarles, Black Abolitionists, also see Zilversmit

14   An Historical Memoir of the Pennsylvania Society for the Abolition of Slavery; Relief of Free Negroes Unlawfully Held in Bondage and for Improving the Conditions of the African Race, 1848, by Edward Needles – 64 as quoted in Quarles, 13; McManus, 182-184

15   Garrison's opinion of Gradual Abolition will be examined later in this Chapter.

16   See Benjamin Quarles

17   www.mala.bc.ca/~mcneil/truth1.htm

18 "The Narrative of Sojourner Truth" (1850), dictated by Sojourner Truth (ca.1797-1883); edited by Olive Gilbert

19 The emancipation referred to in the preceding quote speaks to the Final Abolition legislation passed by the New York State Legislature in July 1817 yet with the curious caveat that it would not take effect until July 4th 1827.

20 "The Narrative of Sojourner Truth" (1850)

21 Ibid

22 Ibid

23 Chapter 39 of the Laws of 1788 of New York State

24 "The Narrative of Sojourner Truth" (1850)

25 Ibid

26 Ibid

27 Austin Steward, Twenty-Two Years a Slave, and Forty Years a Freeman, facing Title page, http://raims.com/education/SlaveryIssueAug04. htm

28 Austin Steward, 92-93

29 Austin Steward, 99

30 Ibid

31 Rev. Thomas James, by Himself, "The Wonderful Eventful Life of Rev. Thomas James", (Post-Express Printing Co., Rochester, NY: 1887); 1-4

32 Ibid

33 Hodges, "Slavery and Freedom", 136

34 Hodges, "Root & Branch",191

35 Burrows, Edwing and Wallace, 349

36 Chandos Michael Brown, "Benjamin Silliman: A Life in the Young Republic",: (Princeton University Press, 1989); http://www. yaleslavery.org/WhoYaleHonors/silliman.html

[37] Ibid

[38] Ibid

[39] Ibid

[40] Hodges, "Root & Branch", 186

[41] See Kruger dissertation

[42] Shane White, Somewhat More Independent the end of slavery in New York City, 1770-1810, (Athens: Athens Press-University of Georgia) 140-141

[43] Michael E. Groth, The African American Struggles Against Slavery in the Mid- Hudson Valley, 1785-1827, The Hudson River Valley Institute, www.hudsonrivervalley.net

[44] Untitled document concerning Runaway slaves in New Paltz, 1810. Roelof J. and Ezekiel Elting Family Papers. Unpublished MSS Collection, Huguenot Historical Society of New Paltz, NY, Inc.

[45] The African American Struggle Against Slavery in the Hudson Valley, 1785-1827, The Hudson Valley Institute, www.hudsonvalley.net/afrAmerLesson/struggle.php

[46] Geneva Gazette, Aug. 1, 1810; Also see Local Slave Records, The Evils of Slavery Duly Recorded, http://raims.com/historian/NLTAUG04.htm

[47] Chapter 62 of the Laws of 1799, the section states: "these same [slave] children shall be the servant of the legal "owner" of his or her mother until such child, if a male, reaches the age of twenty eight years and, if a female, the age of twenty fi ve. It further states: should the slave owner of the mother choose to abandon his/her rights to the child's service, he/she was required to notify the town clerk. Lastly, it stipulates: town clerks would declare an abandoned child a pauper thus allowing the Overseers of the Poor in that town to bound out the child to any interested parties.

[48] Kruger, 842;

NOTE: Kruger sights the cases of William, page 6, bound out to William Hottentot and Nancy, age 4, to Michael Moses found in the Records of Flushing, Work Projects Administration, 1:51-52, 56-57.

49   Cain, William Lloyd Garrison and the Fight Against... Bedford Books/
      St. Martin's Press. Inc.

50   Elizabeth Heyrick, "Immediate not Gradual Abolition; or, an inquiry
      into the shortest, safest and most effectual means of getting rid of West
      Indian slavery", (London: 1824), 15-18, 35-6.

CHAPTER VIII

FINAL ABOLITION IN NEW YORK STATE

FINAL ABOLITION

"Final Abolition" presented former slaves with a myriad of proscriptive statutes and discriminatory practices, as white lawmakers limited the legal rights of former slaves, and as white employers created new forms of subordination that kept African descendants dependent." [1]

Regarding the actual abolition of enslavement in New York, the New York State Legislature passed in 1817 "An Act relative to slaves and servants." This law was New York State's emancipation statute. It became effective on 4 July 1827.[2] Essentially, it extended emancipation to those "slaves" born before July 4, 1799 who were not included under the provisions of the Gradual Abolition Law of 1799, and it stipulated that these "slaves" were to become free as of July 4, 1827. It should be noted that the effective date of this final abolition legislation in New York State, July 4, 1827, was exactly twenty-eight years after the passage of the Gradual Abolition Act of 1799. This occurrence was not a coincidence. The effective date of this law guaranteed that slaveholders would receive a full twenty-eight years of service from male slave children who were born in the year 1799 under Gradual Abolition.[3]

Enslavement, however, was still not entirely repealed in New York State. This new emancipation law allowed at least two exceptions to the total abolition of enslavement in New York State. First, it allowed nonresidents to continue their slaveholding practices for up to nine months. Secondly, it allowed part-time residents to maintain their slaves in the state temporarily. This provision remained in state law until it was repealed in 1841.

Notwithstanding the final abolition of enslavement in New York after 200 years of unrestricted practice, African descendants in New York demonstrated a remarkable sense of political acumen by choosing not to celebrate "their emancipation" on the 4th of July in conjunction with the celebration of American Independence. After the first few years of emancipation, African descendants chose this course of action in a conscious effort to demonstrate their conflict with "the disparity between rhetoric and reality, between their country's high professions of liberty and equality and the existence of enslavement [in the South] and the high wall of color [that persisted in the United States as a whole]."[4] African descendants had also become acutely aware of the potential dangers inherent in participating in or celebrating near white crowds during the 4th of July. Since numerous instances of violence towards African descendants were reported on that date. Instead, these newly freed African descendants chose to celebrate either the 5th of July or August 1st, the anniversary of the unconditional freedom of "slaves" in the British West Indies, as their "Emancipation Day."[5]

William Steward in his narrative, tells us of the reaction of newly freed African descendants in Rochester, New York.

> *"...the Emancipation Bill had been passed, and the colored people felt it to be a time fit for rejoicing. They met in different places and determined to evince their gratitude by a general celebration. In Rochester, they convened in large numbers, and resolved to celebrate the glorious day of freedom at Johnson's Square, on the fifth day of July. This arrangement was made so as not to interfere with the white population who were everywhere celebrating the day of their independence - " the Glorious Fourth," - for amid the general and joyous shout of liberty- prejudice had sneeringly raised the finger of scorn at the poor African, whose iron bands were loosed, not only from English oppression, but the more cruel and oppressive power of Slavery."[6]*

THE JIM CROW STATUS OF "FREED" AFRICAN DESCENDANTS AFTER EMANCIPATION

"Free Negroes were brutalized by ruffians and excluded from skilled employment by the hostility of white workers. Indeed, free Negroes in the nineteenth century remained as much a class apart as in the days of slavery." [7]

BACKGROUND

With the abolition of enslavement in 1827, whites began to establish a societal barrier that legally, economically, and socially designated people of African descent as a separate, dependent, and unequal group within the New York State community. Of greater significance was the fact that the passage of this law abolishing enslavement was accompanied by the emergence of a virulent form of racial hatred. The status of "free" African descendants in New York State was epitomized by their relegation to second-class even third class citizenship. This can be attributed to the fact that under the institution of enslavement they were "trained to pursue a great variety of crafts and occupations, while under the status of freedom they were virtually abandoned and systematically pauperized."[8] Consequently, the difference between being enslaved and being "free" was largely one of perception rather than one of practice. As an example, an account kept by Ann Bevier of Marbletown, New York shows that freed slave laborers "were given just enough compensation to cover their room and board expenses." [9]

In this manner, enslavement existed in practice longer than it did in legislation. Many more freed African descendants found themselves in county poorhouses and almshouses all across the state. These locally managed houses for paupers, indigents, travelers and abandoned "statutory slaves" offered nothing but sickness, death, and misery for most of their inhabitants. As an example, the Poorhouse, which had been constructed in New Paltz in the late 1820s to deal with the growing destitute population, offered its inhabitants only impoverished living conditions, with minimal provisions of food and water, inadequate medical attention, and ill treatment by overseers.[10]

"New York's emancipation laws were defined to free slaves carefully and thus control and contain free blacks."[11]

Discrimination policies relegated the status of "free" African descendants in New York State to the lowest rung of society. This reduction in status was also directly related to the massive influx of white immigrants into New York State during the nineteenth century. Alexis De Tocqueville wrote that "anti-Negro feelings were greatest in those states where slavery has never been known."[12] Historian Edgar J. Mc Manus also speaks to the issue of white resentment of these third- and sometimes fourth-generation African descendants when he states, "as the working class grew and the wage rate fell, **negrophobia,** became the anodyne of lower class [white] frustration."[13]

A classic example of this second- and third-class citizenship transpired in New York City with the passage of the "Freemanship Laws" which required local residency and enabled citizens in New York to protect their occupations against "outsider". In New York City, outsiders included "freed" African descendants who were further excluded from the privileges of citizenship. This relegation of "free" African descendants was designed to exclude them from all but the most menial trades while white applicants easily found work.[14]

Prior to the mass emigration of whites from Ireland, Germany, French Canada and other parts of Europe, African descendants held a monopoly on jobs like: coachmen, barbers, whitewashers, washerwomen, and other generally defined domestic positions. The evidence seems to suggest that during the Revolutionary and Confederation years there was a sharp increase in the number of free African descendants in the state. Census data for 1790 shows 21,329 enslaved African descendants in the state and 4,654 free African descendants, roughly 18 percent of the overall African descendant population.[15] We can surmise that some were freeman from before the war, some were freed because of their service during the war, and some had been manumitted in other parts of the country and state and had migrated to New York City after the war. Surprisingly, few of these "free" African descendants were formerly enslaved in New York City who had been manumitted by slaveholders who caught the abolitionist spirit in the wake of the Revolutionary War.[16]

Even before the law took effect, however, the percentage of "free" African descendants in the state rose precipitously and continued to rise over the next three decades. In 1800, the number of free African descendants doubled over the previous ten years: there were 8,573 free blacks and 15,602 enslaved in New York at that time. By 1810 the "free" African descendant population had surpassed the enslaved population, 25,333 to 15,017. On the eve of the Constitutional Convention of 1821, there were 22,332 'free' African descendants and 7,573 enslaved in the state.[17]

Thus, in the opening decades of the nineteenth century, we see the same phenomenon in New York that occurred in other Northern states that passed gradual abolition laws in the late eighteenth century - namely, that African descendants were emerging from enslavement en masse over a relatively short period of time.

And yet, while relatively few in number, an increasing 'free' African descendant population became more visible in every way, particularly in the bustle of an urban center like New York City. In the latter days of enslavement, most African descendants in New York City worked as domestics in the houses of the old (Federalist) aristocracy. As laborers, they were not in competition for jobs with whites at the lower end of the economic ladder. As "citizens", they were utterly invisible, both in the political and social sense. Most lived in white-headed households rather than their own communities on the one hand, and all but a few were disqualified from the vote on the other. With abolition came wrenching political, social, and economic changes that brought with them a backlash against African descendant communities just uplifted from enslavement. Economically, African descendants were perceived by working class whites as a potential threat to jobs.

THE POLITICS OF DISCRMINATION

Politically "free" African descendants were seen by Republicans politicians seeking office as a dangerous voting block. Anthony Gronowicz in *Race and Class Politics in New York City Before the Civil War* asserts that Irish Republican fervor contributed heavily to the development of the Democratic Republican ideology well before the War of 1812, and that New York Republicans drew upon the competition between Irish and African American labor for political support.[18] In short, Tammany Hall taught the Irish that they could climb the ladder of success by shunning any contact with African descendants while Tammany leaders rode the wave of this hostility to political power.[19]

The politics of race began to again raise its ugly head as early as 1804, when Republican newspapers such as the *American Citizen* published parodies of black speech patterns in which "Zambo" degraded himself by comparing his skin to the rough rind of a coconut.[20] In 1799, the *New York Journal and Patriotic Register* pointed out not only the Federalist detestation of the Irish, but also its enthusiasm for "the black ones of Santa Domingo."[21] Republican newspapers also never hesitated to remind their readers that "nineteenth-twentieths" of all African descendant voters voted the Federalist ticket.[22]

In the decades after the final abolition of enslavement, due to this influx of European whites into New York City and the state, whites began to move into the so-called "Negro" jobs. By the Reconstruction period, these racial labor practices resulted in a wholesale displacement of African descendants.[23] The exclusion of African descendant workers soon extended to include industrial jobs where white inclusion and the exclusion of workers of African descent became the reality of New York State's employment landscape.

Despite the level of skill African descendants possessed, they were increasingly relegated to the most menial jobs and persistently forced to the bottom rung on the economic and social ladder. White immigration to the state made matters worse, but economic downturns were another factor. President Thomas Jefferson's Embargo of 1804, the depression that followed the War of 1812, and the Panic of 1819 all hit the African descendant community the hardest, as white immigrants flooded into the domestic service industry in the 1810s and 1820s, a field predominantly African American since colonial days. According to Herman Bloch in "The Circle of Discrimination" the number of Irish filing for employment with the New York Society for the Encouragement of Faithful Domestics in the late 1820s was more than three times that of African descendants. Even the number of other 'whites' filing for employment surpassed African descendants.[24]

As a consequence of these factors, many newly freed New Yorkers of African descent had no choice but to continue to live as dependent workers in white households after emancipation. This reality forced them to continue to separate themselves from their families, as expectations born under enslavement that African descendant families would live apart survived among this first generation of freedmen. While many freedmen found it difficult to support themselves, they, either lived with whites, relied on their old owners for help, or became paupers. Others successfully established their own households and reunited their families. A population that had functioned well throughout society found sudden unemployment and job discrimination once free.[25]

"Free" African descendants in the North also faced sweeping protests from white workers, a ban on the ownership of private property, land and homes, segregation in public accommodations, segregated schools, economic discrimination, poverty, disease and horrendous living conditions,[26] as well as increasing degrees of disenfranchisement. The North had become to resident African descendants and newly arriving fugitives from the "slavocracy" of the South a hierarchical white supremacist world of separation and degradation.

DISENFRANCHISEMENT

The right to vote for citizens of African descent had been established in 1777, when the first New York Constitutional Convention was held and the predominately abolitionist drafters made a conscious point of not mentioning race, creed, or previous condition of servitude as an impediment to suffrage. The suffrage qualification was offered to "every male inhabitant of full age" who met the property and residence requirements.

However, New York State under the control of Republican politicians on a number of occasions leading up to final abolition attempted to impose conditions on African descendants that would in effect disenfranchise them of the right to vote in the state's elections. Even as early as 1785, Republicans in the New York State Legislature sought to disenfranchise African descendants with the introduction of legislation that would grant gradual abolition but eliminate the ability of newly freed African descendants to exercise

their preexisting right to vote.[27] This legislation mandated a recurring theme in Northern abolition laws of the period. They allowed for the "freedom of slaves" after a period of what amounted to "statutory servitude" but denied "freed" African descendants the right to vote, hold public office, intermarry with white persons and testify against white defendants in court.

In 1811 and again in 1814, Republican politicians consolidated their gains in statewide elections and moved to destroy the impact of African descendant voters in New York City. In 1811, the state legislature passed a harsh law entitled a "Bill to Prevent Frauds at Elections, and For Other Purposes." Essentially this law sought to legalize what Republican inspectors in New York City had accomplished by force in previous elections. The main provision of the law was as follows:

> **"Whenever any person of color, or black person shall present himself to vote at any election of this state, he shall produce to the inspectors, or persons conducting such an election, a certificate of freedom under the hand and seal of one of the clerks of the counties of this state, or under the hand of a clerk of any town within this state."[28]**

The provisions of this law proved regressive and made compliance for voters of African descent exceedingly difficult. In order to receive the required certificate, a potential voter of African descent had to obtain the services of a lawyer and appear before a Supreme Court judge, at which court appearance their proof of freedom could be obtained in writing. The total cost to prospective voters of African descent attempting to certify their rights as a free citizen included attorney fees, court costs and county clerk filing fees for the certificate. In addition, each voter had to take an oath saying he was the person listed on the certificate.

The Federalist-led Council of Revision of the New York State once again stepped in on the side of the voters of African descent and vetoed the legislation. In its objections, the Council offered several reasons for its rejection, ranging from the feasibility of carrying out the law, to questions dealing with the scientific basis for the law, and finally to a deep skepticism of its moral underpinnings. The Council first argued that the description of "persons of color" offered in the bill was too vague for inspectors to follow accurately considering the fact that the 'races' had been mixed since their initial encounters centuries ago. The Council questioned whether inspectors were to judge voters of African descent based on differences presented to the eye, or the "quality of the blood." It emphasized the possibility that an inspector would have difficulty determining which voters were of African descent and which were not. It would seem that the Council was suggesting that a science of racial identification was nearly impossible.

We must keep in mind that this racial identification clause in the early nineteenth century may represent the first modern attempts to construct a "scientific racism." Moreover, the emergence of a science of race that placed African descendants in a subordinate position to whites formed the basis of much of the rhetoric that justified the disenfranchisement of African descendants in the first place.

The Council of Revision relied upon a natural rights argument for most of its objections, stating that, the bill selects certain persons who, "under the constitution and laws of the state, are entitled to the elective franchise, many of whom were born free." It also stipulated the fact that this legislation violated the rights of African descendants whose ancestors have uninterruptedly enjoyed the elective franchise under the colonial as well as state government. The Council further concluded that this right to vote had been transmitted with their freeholds. The bill was not passed over the Council's veto.

With the advent of the elections of 1813, African descendants again voted the Federalist ticket in the spring elections. Consequently, in 1814, the Republican-led legislature put forth a bill similar to the one proposed in 1811, in an effort to suppress the voting power of African descendants and stymie any future Federalists gains. This later version also stipulated that African descendants were to present a certificate of freedom upon voting. Interestingly enough, however, the bill only applied to New York City where Federalist election victories had been secured by the votes of citizens of African descent.

Once again, the Council of Revision vetoed it. But this time the Republican-led legislature overrode the veto. A year later, new amendments and new restrictions were added to a bill passed on April 11, 1815.[29] This bill exempted African descendants that had obtained prior certificates from the disenfranchisement provisions of the 1814 bill. This new law, however, forced African descendants to register to vote five days prior to the election and deliver their affidavits to the mayor for inspection.[30]

Finally, in 1821, with the election of the Martin Van Buren-led Bucktail Republicans, the State of New York instituted what proved to be its most successful effort to disenfranchise voters of African descent. This regressive and discriminatory law required that the State of New York impose a property qualification of $250 for voters of African descent. This racist restriction on voters of African descent was levied at the same time that the state eliminated all such requirements for white voters. The law essentially denied African descendants the right to vote unless they owned land valued at $250.

"Prior to this act, a single qualification for voting (owning property valued at $100) had applied equally to men of both races." [31]

Edward S. Abdy in *"Journal of a Residence and Tour in the United States"* relates the absurdity of this newly enacted law.

"In New York State, colored men of the qualified age, and possessed of 250 dollars in freehold estate, are entitled to the elective franchise. It is singular, that, where no political privileges are connected with property, an exception should be made in favor of those with whom vice, not virtue, is supposed to be hereditary; and that the parchment on which

the pedigree is written is the skin of the claimant. Equality of civil rights is granted where equality of social rights is denied; and the same man who is admitted to the ballot-box, is thrust out of the dining room. Let the "African" carry off the palladium of the constitution; but he must not disturb the digestion of its friends. Plutus must be highly esteemed, where his rod can change even a negro into a man. If 250 dollars will perform this miracle, what would it require to elevate a monkey to this enviable distinction?"[32]

This action, in effect and intention, eliminated the ability of African descendants to exercise their franchise in New York State. Our curiosity as to the purposes of these legislative actions on the part of the white majority tends to become jaded after a period, especially when we discuss these outright actions of institutional racism. The State of New York had abolished enslavement in 1827 and yet, it denied the right to vote to African descendants who were enthusiastic in their effort to exercise their full rights as citizens.

One theory for the passage of this 1821 legislation suggests that in 1813 the Federalist Party obtained the majority in the legislature, by way of the free African descendant electorate in New York City. The resulting victory of the Federalist Party was more than likely the reasoning behind the Republican action in 1821 to impose property eligibility qualification on African descendants. In 1821, after the victory of the Bucktail Republicans, the Republicans represented the majority of the legislature when the new state constitution of 1821 was formed.

However, not all of the Republican politicians of the day toed the "party line" with respect to this obvious attempt at legalized racial discrimination. Republican State Assemblyman R. Clarke was among those who came to the defense of these disenfranchised citizens. He was courageously willing to assert his dismay at the inclusion of this property requirement in the following terms:

"It is haughtily asked", said he, "who will stand in the ranks, shoulder to shoulder, with a negro? I answer, no one in time of peace: --no one when your musters and trainings

are looked upon as mere pastimes. But when the hour of danger approaches, your 'white' militia are just as willing that the man of color should be set up as a mark to be shot at by the enemy, as to be set up themselves. In the war of the Revolution, these people helped to fight your battles by land and by sea. Some of your States were glad to turn out corps of colored men, and to stand 'shoulder to shoulder' with them. In your late war [1812], they contributed largely towards some of your most splendid victories. On Lakes Erie and Champlain, where your fleets triumphed over a foe superior in numbers, and engines of death, they were manned in large proportion with men of color.

He further states:

And in this very House, in the fall of 1814, a Bill passed, receiving the approbation of all the branches of your Government, authorizing the Governor to accept the services of a corps of 2000 free people of color. . . They were not compelled to go, they were not drafted, they were volunteers --yes, Sir, volunteers to defend that very country from the inroads and ravages of a ruthless and vindictive foe, which had treated them with insult, degradation, and slavery."

I never knew a man of color that was not an anti-Jackson man. In fact, it was their respectability, and not their degradation, that was the cause of their disfranchisement. The Albany Camarilla limited the suffrage to the blacks, and opened it to the Irish; --a pretty good proof that the former were not likely to be their tools."[33]

To a large extent, the Republican members of the legislature had finally achieved the goal they set out to accomplish as early as 1785 – the disenfranchisement of people of African descent.

Notwithstanding the extraordinary efforts against them, African descendants persevered. They worked diligently to meet the requirements of this law as illustrated in the Introduction of this work as well as through the individual struggles and efforts of African descendants like Solomon Northup as related in his narrative: *"Twelve Years a Slave"*. While recounting the working conditions of his "free" father Northup states,

"Besides giving us an education surpassing that ordinarily bestowed upon children in our condition, he acquired, by his diligence and economy, a sufficient property qualification to entitle him to the right of suffrage."[34]

NEW YORK STATE CONSTITUTION OF 1821

In keeping with this disenfranchisement strategy and to further limit the participation of African descendants in the privileges of full citizenship, New York State ratified a new state constitution in 1821 which significantly limited the voting rights of freed African descendants. Subsequently, proposed amendments to the constitution designed to restore the voting rights of African descendants were rejected by the voters of New York State in 1846 and again in 1860. Citizens of African descent who had suffered the traumatic centuries of enslavement and discrimination in the cities and towns of New York State continued to suffer after emancipation at the hands of a white political and social hierarchy that placed them in a fully legalized position of second or third citizenship. These actions mirrored in much the same way those of the southern states of America after the Civil War.

This new system of "Jim Crow" discrimination and disenfranchisement existed for another fifty years until the federal government passed the Fifteenth Amendment to the United States Constitution which was ratified in 1870. It should be noted that while citizens of African descent waited for this relief from the federal government, New York State continued on its path of "Jim Crow" by enacting laws in 1841 and again in 1864 that authorized separate public schools for children of African descent.

A PERSPECTIVE ON THE POLITICS OF ENSLAVEMENT AND ABOLITION IN THE UNITED STATES

It has been the opinion of many historians including Benjamin Quarles, that the abolitionist movement of the Federalist era must be viewed as a failure. The reality is, "The Northern states had all but abandoned slavery, it is true, but the chief reason had been the availability of a free labor supply which made bonded labor unprofitable."[35]

The Northern states were beginning to prosper with the growth of diversified manufacturing as part of the worldwide Industrial Revolution. Immigrants and the institution of free labor employment boosted the North's population and economic prosperity while the south became the principal provider of raw materials. Southern farms shipped agricultural products such as cotton to Northern mills, which sent finished goods back to the South and Europe.

Southern prosperity based on cotton production relied on enslaved labor. Enslaved workers were considered capital resources, used in the production of raw materials. This became a source of significant friction between the North, which paid its workers wages (normally as little as possible given the abundant supply of labor that existed) and the South, which "owned" its workers. Growing concerns among groups in the north regarding the immorality of enslavement led to political moves to outlaw enslavement. Slaveholding Southerners felt threatened by what they perceived as the destruction of their (human) capital resources. In an attempt to end enslavement peacefully, congressmen drafted many compromises that proposed compensating slaveholders for their "property" (just such a proposal was included in a preliminary version of Abraham Lincoln's Emancipation Proclamation) but they encountered consistent opposition by abolitionists.

On the international front, by 1832, most of Europe and Mexico had abolished enslavement. And great international pressure was placed on the United States to follow suit. However, the South held fast to states' rights, a principle that was grounded in the maintenance of their enslaved agricultural workforce. Given the fact that they relied on their enslaved workers for their livelihoods, Southern planters elected congressional representatives who would support the right of self-determination for each state and oppose the annexation of anti-slavery territories. Due to the fact that ante-bellum industrial development was concentrated solely in the north, white Southerners maintained their political and economic control in a primarily agricultural South, unaffected by the problems of wage labor. The unwillingness of these opposing regions to reach a compromise ultimately led to the Civil War.[36]

The Great Compromise

Ironically, one of the fateful compromises made at the United States Constitutional Convention of 1787 played a significant role in the issue of enslavement, its abolition and the Civil War. This compromise was directly responsible for the forthright rejection of the idea of "one man, one vote" contrary to the "vision" of American democracy. At the convention that eventually produced the document ratified by nine of the thirteen colonies in 1788, one of the last issues to be resolved was how to elect a president, according to Roger A. Burns in *A More Perfect Union: The Creation of the United States Constitution*.[37]

While Southerners opposed the enfranchisement of slaves, the Southern delegates enthusiastically supported the counting of slaves within their populations, thus increasing the region's political clout and voice in the selection of the presidency, due to their increased numbers in the Electoral College. The Northern states, of course, objected to this proposal and to the disproportionate advantage the inclusion of the Southern slave population would have in the overall outcome for representation in Congress.

Hence, the Great Compromise, the notorious "three-fifths of a man" clause, that permitted enslavement to continue in the United States and thus, struck an unhappy medium between Northern and Southern states by permitting those enslaved and people of color to be counted as three-fifths of a white person when setting the number of the seats in the House of Representatives due each state. The compromise was instrumental in giving the southern states an advantage in their representation in Congress. In fact, between the presidencies of George Washington and Abraham Lincoln, fifty (50) years of slaveholders ruled the White House. Southern white slaveholders had become the governing force of the United States. They wrote, adjudicated, and enforced the laws of the nation. Consequently, the United States truly was a slaveholding republic.

"By 1850, a growing number of northerners were convinced that slavery posed an intolerable threat to free labor and civil liberties. Many believed that an aggressive Slave Power had seized control of the federal government, incited revolution in Texas and war with Mexico, and was engaged in a systematic plan to extend slavery into the western territories."[38]

Document 52
Population Of The State Of New York, ca. 1800[39]

STATEMENT, Shewing the Aggregate Number of PERSONS in each of the Wards of the City of New-York, and in each of the Counties in this State, including, however, no more than three-fifths of the whole number of Slaves.

A STATEMENT,

Shewing the Aggregate Number of PERSONS in each of the Wards of the City of New-York, and in each of the Counties in this State, including, however, no more than three-fifths of the whole number of Slaves.

	Free Persons.	Three fifths of Slaves.	Aggregate.
City and county of New-York,			
First Ward,	3,903	250	4,153
Second do.	4,622	327	4,949
Third do.	6,068	168	6,236
Fourth do.	9,514	252	6,766
Fifth do.	8,878	222	9,100
Sixth do.	12,779	178	12,957
Seventh do.	14,857	322	15,179
	57,621	1,719	69,349
County of Richmond,	3,888	405	4,293
Suffolk,	18,578	531	19,109
Queens,	15,365	918	16,283
Kings,	4,261	888	5,149
Westchester,	26,169	756	26,925
Rockland,	5,802	330	6,182
Orange,	28,208	687	28,395
Ulster,	22,598	1,353	23,951
Dutchess,	46,166	966	47,132
Columbia,	33,851	882	34,733
Delaware,	10,212	9	10,221
Green,	12,064	312	12,376
Rensselaer,	29,552	534	30,086
Albany,	32,235	1,086	33,321
Washington,	35,494	48	35,542
Clinton and Essex,	8,456	35	8,491
Saratoga,	24,125	216	24,341
Schoharie,	9,454	213	9,667
Montgomery,	21,234	279	21,513
Herkemer,	14,418	36	14,454
Oneida,	21,997	30	22,027
Onondaga,	7,395	6	7,401
Otsego,	21,588	27	21,615
Chenango,	15,650	9	15,659
Tioga,	6,862	9	6,871
Cayuga,	15,818	32	15,850
Ontario,	15,161	33	15,194
Steuben,	1,766	12	1,778
Total,	565,988	12,362	578,349

ENDNOTES

1   Berlin, 228

2   Chapter 188 of the Laws of 1817 of New York State

3   Chapter 62 of the Laws of 1799 of New York State. This law stipulated that, "… these same children shall be the servant of the legal "owner" of his or her mother until such child, if a male, reaches the age of twenty eight years and, if a female, the age of twenty five."

4   Quarles, 122

5   Ibid

6   Austin Steward, 150

7   Williams-Myers, 139-141

8   Morris, Foreword, *A History of Negro Slavery in New York*, pg. ix; also see Thomas Archdeacon, *New York City, 1664-1710, Conquest and Change,* (Tthaca, NY: Cornell University Press, 1976)

9   Account Book, Ann Bevier, 1802-1812, *Philip Dubois Bevier Family Papers (1685-1910).* Unpublished MSS Collection, Huguenot Historical Society of New Paltz, NY, Inc

10   Eric J. Roth, The Society of Negroes Unsettled: The History of Slavery in New Paltz, NY, May 2001, Huguenot Historical Society Library and Archives, www.hhsnewpaltz.net/library_archives/topics_of_interest/slavery.htm

11   Leslie M. Harris, In the Shadow of Slavery: African Americans in New York City, 1626-1863, (Chicago: University of Chicago Press, 2003) 5

12   Timothy Crumrin "Back to Africa?" The Colonization Movement in Early America, 5. Presumably, he was referring to the northern states.

13   See McManus quoted in A. J. Williams-Myers, Long Hammering, 139-141.

14   Graham Russell Hodges, 5-6

15   Census of New York State, 1855, .xi.

[16] See Shane White, *Somewhat More Independent: The End of Slavery in New York City, 1770-1810* (Athens, GA: University of Georgia Press, 1991), pp.28-30. According to White, only seventy-six manumissions occurred in New York City between 1783 and 1800, not a particularly high number considering the high profile New York Manumission Society.

[17] Rhoda Golden Freeman, *The Free Negro in New York City in the Era before the Civil War* (New York: Garland Publishing, 1994), 6.

[18] Anthony Gronowicz, *Race and Class Politics in New York City Before the Civil War* (Boston: Northeastern University Press, 1998), 30

[19] On Tammany Hall, see for instance, Gustavus Myers, *The History of Tammany Hall* (New York: Burt Franklin Press, 1917); Jabez D. Hammond, *History of Political Parties in the State of New York* (Buffalo: Phinney and Company, 1850), vol.1, ch. xvii; Alfred E. Young's *The Democratic Republicans of New York: The Origins, 1763-1797* (Chapel Hill: University of North Carolina Press, 1967)

[20] Gronowicz, 32

[21] *New York Journal and Patriotic Register*, March 16, 1799

[22] Gronowicz, 32

[23] Williams-Myers, 142-143

[24] Herman D. Bloch, *The Circle of Discrimination: An Economic and Social Study of the Black Man in New York* (New York: New York University Press, 1969), 26. The numbers are as follows: 8,346 Irish, 3601 white, and 2,574 colored Americans

[25] Roth, Ibid

[26] *Narrative of Sojourner Truth,* 1850, Boston, 14-15; Liwack, 97

[27] Journal of the Assembly of New York State, 1785, 53

[28] *Journal of the Senate of the State of New York*, 1811, 143

[29] *New York Spectator,* April 19, 1815

[30] *Ibid*

31 Katherine Butler Jones,, "They called it Timbucto",_Orion Magazine_, Winter 1998, 29

32 Edward S. Abdy, "Journal of a Residence and Tour in the United States", Vol. 2, (London, 1835)

33 Ibid, INDEX

34 Solomon Northup, *"Twelve years a slave. Narrative of Solomon Northup, a citizen of New-York, 1853"*, (London: Sampson Low, Son & Company, 47 Ludgate Hill., 1853) 19

35 See Quarles, *Black Abolitionists*

36 Dr. Henry McCarl, Beyond Face Value, Economic Environment, *(www.cuc.lsu.edu/economics)*

37 Roger A. Bruns, A More Perfect Union: The Creation of the United States Constitution, published for the National Archives Trust Fund Board.

38 See Gilder Lehrman, *The Origins and Nature of New World Slavery*, Abolition

39 GLC08893, Population of the State of New York, ca. 1800,The "Three-Fifths Clause", Archive of Past Documents, The Gilder Lehrman Institute of American History, The Gilder Lehrman Institute of American History,The Collection- Newly Discovered Documents.

CHAPTER IX

CONCLUSION

CONCLUSION

Whether slavery is characterized as "mild"... or "harsh"... the modern institution rests on economic and political assumptions that deny not merely the equality but indeed the humanity of the enslaved.[1]

The Historical Background

The preceding documentation and testimony chronicles the involvement of state and local government in the organization, administration and fiscal support of chattel enslavement and the forced bondage of children of African descent in New York State. Additionally, it clearly and unequivocally illustrates to any discerning reader that enslavement and its institutionalized hybrid, gradual abolition, were not haphazard occurrences, regardless of where they were practiced in the United States, whether North or South. Enslavement was a calculated, government-initiated and/or government-supported action on the part of Western "civilized" nations designed to gain a worldwide economic advantage. At the same time, this work exposes both Europe and America's efforts to consciously institute a racial system of inferiority and subjugation that would result in the ultimate goal of implementing a "New World Order." This paradigm was accomplished by establishing a monopoly on trade, and the execution of the colonization of Africa and the New World. The result of these policies and actions was the inevitable destruction of and the forced subjugation of the ancient and extraordinarily culture and resource rich civilizations in Africa and the New World.

Corporate development, economic superiority and world dominance were the byproducts of the institutions of the slave trade and enslavement. However, the birth of the United States and the elevation of New York City and New York State to their status as the centerpiece of the New World economy were undeniably the results of calculated and ruthlessly evil acts and crimes perpetrated against people of African descent.

Enslavement's existence in New York State could not have subsisted for as long as it did nor could it have sustained or benefited the state as much as it did without the full and complete involvement and active participation of its public and private governing bodies. This culpability of these governmental entities has been proven by the preceding documentation and testimony, beyond any reasonable doubt.

Much has been discussed and written, for that matter, of the horror and depravity of enslavement in the southern United States and yet, as we now know, New York State implemented and benefited immeasurably from the *exact same system* of institutional enslavement and racial discrimination. Slave codes, whippings, murders, the breakup and separation of families, disenfranchisement and brutality were all aspects of New York State enslavement and its hybrid bondage during gradual abolition. Likewise, the fact that financial support was appropriated by both local and state governments to perpetuate the bondage of men, women *and* children, is inescapable.

In addition, it has been established that public policy in New York State was designed and manipulated in a conscious effort to benefit the slaveholder and aristocratic classes. New York State slaveholders were granted reimbursement by the state for their "property" losses from the executions of rebellious and runaway slaves. Additionally, they were allocated taxpayer-generated dollars for the implementation and subsistence of a legalized program of bondage called gradual abolition that legally enslaved and provided maintenance for the support of African descendant children (compensated emancipation).[2]

The Results of Gradual Abolition

During this period of the forced bondage of African descendant children, the New York State Legislature affirmed their financial responsibility for the maintenance of thousands of abandoned slave children beginning in 1799 and continuing through 1827, when it passed its final abolition law.[3] The real cost of gradual abolition however, was the effect that it had on the African descendant babies, children, mothers and families. Under the guise of protecting "property rights," a devastatingly destructive and unprecedented plan of *"de jure"* enslavement was inflicted on innocent African descendant children. The fact remains that African descendant children were summarily ripped from the arms of their mothers without regard to human rights or adherence to any standards of human decency, and placed in a system of state-sponsored and state-funded human bondage.

Under this Act, families were forced to give up their children within a year of birth and legally barred from developing any type of family bond. These "abandoned" children, abandoned not by their mother's choice but through the power of the State, were sentenced by this Act to provide free labor to designated individuals. They were also forced to live in separate households often far removed from the care and nurturing of their family members. As late as 1820, almost half of the African descendant children in the state under the age of fourteen lived in these white households. After the advent of "Final Abolition" in 1827, which "freed" their parents and other relatives, these children remained in human bondage until their legally established sentence of bondage was completed.

In practice, New York State had created its own legal hell for African descendants during the 1800s. Not quite enslavement but certainly not the "freedom" promised in the Gradual Abolition Act which stated in 1799 that any child born of a slave within the state after July 4, 1799 "should be deemed and adjudged to be born free." The cost of these legalized actions of institutional enslavement upon the future development and prosperity of these children and the African descendant community, in general was the devastation and destruction of the African descendant family. The broader cost is still being calculated to this very day.

Through the legislative authority of the Gradual Abolition Act, the State of New York never allowed these children who were "freed" by statute to experience any semblance of a secure and protected childhood. They were placed in the custody of local Overseers of the Poor at the age of one year and were subsequently bonded out by the age of four to white masters as "free labor" until they reached adulthood.

It is understandable how these children would suffer from both despair and an insidiously high mortality rate. The fact that their "unexpired" sentence could be sold from one slave holder to another at any time had to also contribute to a constant state of fear and vulnerability. Most assuredly, the greatest harm caused to the African descendant family by this Act was that it was self-perpetuating. Once taken from their families and forced to provide free labor for others until adulthood, these children now adults were faced with the same difficulties of establishing a stable family as their enslaved parents had experienced in New York State. Still under the forced obligation of bondage, if they chose to marry they would be forced to live in separate residences if their partner was "free." Unable to control their own destiny, they would always have to face the possibility that they could be resold by their masters away from their marriage and children. These legally designated masters had complete control over every aspect of their lives, personal and otherwise and the complete control of their freedom of movement from one day to the next.

Employment opportunities that presented themselves to the "free" partner meant the breakup of the marriage or prolonged separation. Children of these unions would also be forced to experience the life of bondage, constantly under the threat of the hiring out of their bonded parent. And so this vicious cycle continued, but this time - *it was created and financed by the State of New York.*

The history of New York State is replete with examples of artificially created circumstances that either led to or were designed to ensure the constant instability of African descendants and their families. These instances of private or public subjugation inspired conditions not of these families choosing, but conditions that were imposed on them by both private greed and public protectionism. In fact, whether imposed by the institution of enslavement or the legal mandates of gradual abolition, the survival of the African and African descendant family was a consequence of factors outside the control of the individuals themselves. This statement can be applied to the entire period that Africans and African descendants "resided" in New York beginning in 1625 with the introduction of the first enslaved African to New Amsterdam.

Consider the fact that it wasn't until the mid-1870s in New York State (when bonded women born shortly before July 4, 1827 ended their childrearing years) that an entire generation of African descendants began to be born, **none** of whose parents had ever been the victims of enslavement or the mandates of gradual abolition's legalized bondage in their youth.[4]

Poverty and illiteracy, despair and hopelessness, disease and deprivation, high infant and adult mortality, dysfunctional and displaced families, this is the baggage that African descendant families were forced to carry into the twentieth century. This cruel and unusual form of government-subsidized bondage provided for in the Gradual Abolition Act of 1799, was designed for the express purpose of the ***"bondage of children."*** At the very least, its enactment and the continued existence of the institution of chattel enslavement in New York State provides testament to and further demonstrates the complicity on the part of the State of New York in the exploitation and subjugation of men, women, and children of African descent.

The Remedy Available to African Descendants

We all should learn through the study of history, one of life's truer lessons, that ignoring the facts does not change the facts! This work's purpose has been to demonstrate New York State's complicity in and direct responsibility for the extended duration of enslavement through the legalized bondage of gradual abolition. In addition, the State of New York has been found both legally and morally culpable for the subjugation, bondage and enslavement of Africans and African descendants by means of both public policy and financial (taxpayer) support. Therefore, by virtue of its callous and inhumane policies and laws, New York State is thereby charged with committing "crimes against humanity" during both the periods of enslavement and gradual abolition.

This determination is based on the fact that enslavement and the legalized bondage of children has been labeled and repudiated by numerous worldwide sanctioning bodies including the Nuremberg Tribunal and the World Conference against Racism, Racial Discrimination, Xenophobia and Related Intolerance (WCAR) as "crimes against humanity". The Charter of the Nuremberg Tribunal defines "crimes against humanity" as:

> **"murder, extermination, enslavement, deportation, and other inhumane acts committed against any civilian population.... whether or not in violation of the domestic law of the country where perpetrated."[5]**

The World Conference against Racism, Racial Discrimination, Xenophobia and Related Intolerance (WCAR), having met in Durban, South Africa, from 31 August to 8 September 2001 declared that:

> **"We acknowledge that slavery and the slave trade, including the transatlantic slave trade, were appalling tragedies in the history of humanity not only because of their abhorrent barbarism but also in terms of their magnitude, organized nature and especially their negation of the essence of the victims, and further acknowledge that slavery and the slave trade are a crime against humanity and should always have been so, especially the transatlantic slave trade and are among the major sources and manifestations of racism, racial discrimination, xenophobia and related intolerance, and that Africans and people of African descent, Asians and people of Asian descent and indigenous peoples were victims of these acts and continue to be victims of their consequences."[6]**

These two world-sanctioned assemblies, even though occurring over a half-century apart, arrived at the same conclusions - that "enslavement" and "bondage" are internationally recognized as "crimes against humanity. In this context, the atrocities of gradual abolition perpetuated by the State of New York would constitute a profound "crime against humanity."

The enactment of the policies of gradual abolition by the State of New York, as documented throughout this work, would also support litigation for recovery against New York State for these "crimes against humanity." This "recovery" would assume the form of restitution and/or reparations" as outlined in the WCAR Report. The WCAR urges as a remedy for past "crimes against humanity" that states be required to:

> **"Reinforce protection against racism, racial discrimination, xenophobia and related intolerance by ensuring that all persons have access to effective and adequate remedies and enjoy the right to seek from competent national tribunals and other national institutions just and adequate reparation and satisfaction for any damage as a result of such discrimination."[7]**

FINDINGS

These revelations are an aspect of New York State history that should shock and horrify any civilized citizenry. At the very least, it should provoke a new awareness and understanding of the efforts now being undertaken by Africans and African descendants to advocate for reparations for these "crimes against humanity" perpetrated by the United States, in general and the State of New York, in particular. When a government participates in "crimes against humanity" and benefits from them, then that government is obliged to make the victims whole. This is now a recognized principle of international law, the Law of State Responsibility, under which a state may be liable for certain harmful acts.

The issues elaborated on and detailed in this work would justifiably set the groundwork for a case for reparations against the State of New York. This effort would be in keeping with the WCAR Report that stipulates:

"We acknowledge and profoundly regret the untold suffering and evils inflicted on millions of men, women and children as a result of slavery, the slave trade, the transatlantic slave trade, apartheid, genocide and past tragedies. We further note that some States have taken the initiative to apologize and have paid reparation, where appropriate, for grave and massive violations committed."[8]

ENDNOTES

1   Hodges, *Slavery and Freedom,* xii

2   **NOTE**: This practice was not restricted to New York State. In Washington, D.C. in 1862, Congress abolished enslavement in the district and paid cash compensations to the holders of enslaved Africans who established claims within a specified period. See Wilson, 18

3   Chapter 188 of the Laws of 1817 of New York

4   Kruger, 865

5   *Charter of the International Military Tribunal,* Nuremberg Trial Proceedings Vol. 1; II. JURISDICTION AND GENERAL PRINCIPLES Article 6

6   Report of the World Conference against Racism, Racial Discrimination, Xenophobia and Related Intolerance;; Sources, causes, forms and contemporary manifestations of racism, racial discrimination, xenophobia and related intolerance; Durban, 31 August - 8 September 2001; hereafter referred to as WCAR Report.

7   Ibid

8   WCAR Report, "Provision of effective remedies, recourse, redress, and compensatory and other measures at the national, regional and international levels", # 100, 21

RECOMMENDATION

A CASE FOR REPARATIONS
AGAINST THE STATE OF NEW YORK

THE MORAL ISSUE OF REPARATIONS

"In our legal tradition we have 'inherited" liabilities along with our assets. Assets are bequeathed, but most liabilities must be honored and creditors satisfied before assets can be distributed to heirs. Slavery was legal for a long time; and economic discrimination, though largely illegal, has been widespread. Thus, we might object that, even if we do benefit from past economic injustices, those practices were accepted at the time. Making restitution so late is ex post facto and violates legal and constitutional principles. Depending on its ideological composition, an appeals court might find that perspective technically correct. Thus, the concept might not prevail in such a court in a formal adversarial proceeding.

However, as a practical and moral matter, we cannot have it both ways. If past practices are now seen as unacceptable and offensive, the benefits are illegitimate."[1]

A CASE FOR REPARATIONS AGAINST NEW YORK STATE [2]

"...there is nothing remarkable in ... redressing injuries attributable to acts thought to be legal when committed, if they are condemned by a later change in legal or constitutional doctrine."[3]

THE CASE FOR REPARATIONS

The case of reparations to people of African descent in New York State is rooted in fundamental justice; a justice that encompasses every struggle and campaign waged by African people to assert their human dignity. These iniquities perpetrated against African people today in New York State are the continuing consequences. The "damages" as legal experts would say, flowing from the 200 years long atrocity of the slave system, and the bondage of innocent children of African descent. It has been documented and recorded in this work and others that these crimes were perpetrated and enforced by the State of New York against men, women, and children of African descent.

If this were merely an appeal to the conscience of the State of New York, it would be misconceived and ignored. For decades, there have been many committed individuals and movements of solidarity in the State of New York and yet, its political and economic power centers have evidenced a ruthless lack of conscience when it comes to African peoples and their cause for justice. It is, therefore, essential to locate "A Case for Reparations against New York State" within a framework of law and justice. It is only then that forms of legal redress that may not have existed before have been devised.

Our own history in New York reminds us about how this occurs. For example, it used to be perfectly legal in New York State for employers or landlords to put up notices, which read, ***"NO COLOREDS NEED APPLY."***

Today, any employer or landlord who discriminates on racial grounds can be required by the courts to pay compensation. At an international level, apartheid in South Africa used to be regarded as an internal affair, although regrettable. Over the years, however, apartheid became recognized as a "crime against humanity" and a threat to peace, so that international sanctions could be imposed.

This is not to say that the achievement of legal sanctions brings automatic justice. This has not happened either in the United States, New York, or South Africa. Nevertheless, these examples show that the demand for justice and legality is an essential element in the struggle for a just cause. It is likewise with "A Case for Reparations against the State of New York." Once the truth of the following four propositions is accepted, then, the justice of "A Case for Reparations against the State of New York," will be proven beyond reasonable doubt.

1- **That the mass enslavement of Africans and the "forced bondage" of children of African descent was a calculated and government sponsored criminal act against humanity;**

2- That no compensation was ever paid by any of the perpetrators to any of the sufferers;

3- That the most culpable potential defendants are the state and municipal governments, which do not have the same sovereign immunity as the federal government; and,

4- That the consequences of the crime continue to be massive, both in terms of the enrichment of the descendants of the perpetrators, and in terms of the impoverishment, discrimination, deprivation, and economic and social subjugation of African descendants.

To those who may say that this is all very true in theory, but that in practice there is no mechanism to enforce the claim or no willingness on the part of New York State to recognize it, we would suggest that - *where there is a wrong, there must be a remedy!*

Once the claim is grounded in legal principle in New York State, as it is recognized in the International community, remedies and mechanisms will be found. Given the unique and multi-faceted nature of the claim, it is imperative that impartial and independent, possibly international jurists will be needed in order to show corresponding creativity and imagination.

New York State law has never been static; witness the volume of issue specific legislation passed into law each year by the New York State Legislature. Historically, new structures have often been devised to give effect to newly recognized principles. The Nuremberg War Crimes Tribunal is an example of new legal thinking, which brought a measure of justice following the atrocities of Nazism. The International Court of Justice, where states could settle disputes with each other by law rather than by war, was unknown at the start of this century. Neither was the International Criminal Court which was ratified by 100 nations; however, the United States, is conspicuously absent from the roster of supporters of the tribunal which was created to prosecute individuals who commit genocide or crimes of war. The court, which came into existence in 2002, was created by a treaty negotiated by 120 nations at a conference sponsored the United Nations in Rome in 1998. President George W. Bush has rejected U.S. participation.[4]

Nevertheless, the premise of this work is an attempt to conceptualize a legal framework for the formulation and prosecution of "A Case for Reparations against the State of New York.

It is argued by reference to seven fundamental propositions:

1. **The enslavement of Africans and African descendants and the forced "bondage" of African -descendant children by the State of New York were crimes against humanity;**

2. **International law recognizes that those who commit crimes against humanity must make reparation;**

3. **There is no legal barrier to prevent those who still suffer the consequences of crimes against humanity from claiming reparations, even though the crimes were committed against their ancestors;**

4. **The claim would be brought on behalf of all African descendants in the State of New York who suffer the consequences of the crime, through the agency of an appropriate representative body;**

5. **The claim would be brought against the government of the State of New York, local governments, corporations, and individuals who promoted and were enriched by the African slave trade, the institution of enslavement and the state government's sponsored and financially supported forced "bondage of African descendant children";**

6. **The amount of the claim would be assessed by experts in each aspect of life and in each region of the state, affected by the institution of enslavement and the**

forced "bondage of African descendant children";
and,

7. The claim, if not settled by agreement, would
   ultimately be determined by a special commission or
   tribunal recognized by all parties.

THE HISTORY OF REPARATIONS

Lord Anthony Gifford of Jamaica cites in his presentation "The
legal basis of the claim for Reparations" that the right to reparations
is well-recognized in international law and has been defined by the
Permanent Court of International Justice (the predecessor of the
International Court of Justice) in these terms:

> "The essential principle contained in the actual notion of
> an illegal act - a principle which seems to be established by
> international practice and in particular by the decisions
> of arbitral tribunals - is that reparation must, as far as
> possible, wipe out all the consequences of the illegal act.
> [It must, in addition] re-establish the situation which
> would, in all probability, have existed if that act had
> not been committed. Restitution, in kind or, if this is not
> possible - payment of a sum corresponding to the value
> which a restitution in kind would bear ... the award, if
> need be, of damages for loss sustained which would not
> be covered by restitution in kind or payment in place of it.
> Such are the principles which should serve to determine
> the amount of compensation due for an act contrary to
> international law." [5]

He also states that the leading textbook on international law by
Schwarzenberge described the recognition of the right to reparation
as a process:

> International judicial institutions have slowly groped
> their way towards the articulate formulation of the rule
> that the commission of an international tort (wrong)
> entails the duty to make reparations.[6]

Most of the case law on reparations concerns the compensation for specific losses such as the destruction of property, buildings, ships etc. Nevertheless, the principle is just as valid in the case of illegal actions on a larger scale, which affect whole peoples. Indeed there are direct precedents for the payment of reparations in such cases:

- In 1952, the Federal Republic of Germany reached agreement with Israel for the payment of $822 million following a claim. Israel was limited to the costs of resettling 500,000 Jews who had fled from Nazi-controlled countries.

- In 1990, Austria made payments totaling $25 million to survivors of the Jewish holocaust.

A number of agreements have been made under the British Foreign Compensation Act of 1950. Lump sum settlements were made by Bulgaria, Poland, Hungary, Egypt, and Rumania, and a tribunal was set up to make awards from the sums made available, so as to do justice as between many thousands of claimants whose property had been expropriated. A "U.S.-Iran Claims Tribunal" was set up in 1981 for a similar purpose. Japan has made reparation payments to South Korea for acts committed during the period of invasion and occupation of Korea by Japan. And most recently, the United Nations Security Council passed a resolution, binding in international law, requiring Iraq to pay reparations for its invasion of Kuwait.

It is, therefore, clear that the concept of reparations is firmly established and actively pursued by states, on behalf of their injured nationals, against other wrongdoing states. Litigation will show what enslavement and gradual abolition meant, how it was profitable and how the issue of white privilege is still with us.

In addition, one can identify a second category of reparation, which is of greater relevance. This is where a state has accepted the responsibility to make restitution to groups of people within its own borders whose rights had been violated, not just to other states. The following actions represent United States precedents for reparations to individuals for crimes against a group.

1-- In 1988, the United States Congress passed the Civil Liberties Act, which was designed to make restitution to Japanese Americans. This restitution was made in respect of losses brought about by "any discriminatory act of the United States Government based upon the individual's Japanese ancestry during the wartime period when Japanese Americans were interned in great numbers." A commission was set up to investigate claims. The U.S. Congress appropriated a total of $1.2 billion, or $20,000 for each claimant.

This Act began by stating the basis for reparations in clear terms, which could be applied with the greatest relevance to the claims of African descendants in New York State. Some of the more relevant sections of this Act include:

(1) Acknowledge the fundamental injustice of the evacuation, relocation and internment of United States citizens and permanent resident aliens of Japanese ancestry during World War II;

(2) Apologize on behalf of the people of the United States;

(4) Make restitution to those individuals of Japanese ancestry who were interned...; and,

(7) Make more credible and sincere any declaration of concern by the United States over violations of human rights committed by other Nations.[7]

2-- In 1988, Canada made similar restitution to Canadians of Japanese descent totaling $230 million.

3-- Similar provision were made for restitution to the Aleut residents of various Alaskan islands "in settlement of US obligations in equity and at law, for injustices suffered and unreasonable hardships endured while those Aleut residents were under US control."[8]

4-- Additionally, some steps have been taken to recognize the rights to restitution of indigenous peoples whose land was plundered and occupied, and whose people were decimated, especially in the United States, Canada, and Australia. Each of these countries has made land rights settlements and/ or financial payments to these indigenous peoples. This restitution took the forms as outlined in Table 10.[9]

**Land Settlements and Financial Payments
to Indigenous People**

DATE	COUNTY	REPARATIONS	INJURED PEOPLES
1988	Canada	Land-250,000 Sq. Miles	Indians & Eskimos
1986	USA	$32 million 1836 Treaty	Ottawas of Michigan
1985	USA	$31 Million	Chippewas of Wisconsin
1985	USA	$12.3 million	Seminoles of Florida
1985	USA	$105 million	Sioux of South Dakota
1980	USA	$81 million	Klamaths of Oregon
1971	USA	$1billion plus 44 million acres	Alaska Natives Land Settlement

These are woefully inadequate gestures, given the atrocities committed in these countries against indigenous peoples and their own citizens. However, they represent recognition of the fact that the surviving generations of aggrieved people have the right to a measure of reparation for the crimes committed against their ancestors.[10] It also serves to establish a precedent that recognizes that there is *no* statute of limitations with respect to the issue of reparations for "crimes against humanity" particularly in the United States.

It should also be remembered that the federal government benefited directly from the practice of chattel enslavement, particularly with respect to the use of enslaved African descendants in the building of public works. One such example is the utilization of "slaves" in the building of the United States Capitol in Washington, D.C. The "owners" of these innocents received five dollars a month for their slaves' labor.

THE "CASE FOR REPARATIONS FOR INDIVIDUALS OF AFRICAN DESCENT AGAINST THE STATE OF NEW YORK" SHOULD RECEIVE NO LESS CONSIDERATION!

ENDNOTES

[1] Richard F. America, Paying the Debt: What White America Owes Black America, (Westport, CT:-Praeger Publishers, 1993)

[2] Adapted from several sources including WCAR Report; Brother Kojo Adimu, "Report from Durban, South Africa", Association for the Study of Classical African Civilizations Newsletter; Lord Anthony Gifford, "The legal basis of the claim for Reparations" April 27-29, 1993, First Pan-African Congress on Reparations, Abuja, Federal Republic of Nigeria; Oscar Beard, "Notes on Overcoming Black People's Objections to Black Reparations", 1998, Atlanta, GA.; "Made a Chattel Slave", (www.ncobra.com/documents); Tamar Levin, "Calls for Slavery Restitution Getting Louder", College Times/The New York Times, 4 June 2001, Tamu T. Henry, "'Is it Payback Time?", Africana. com, 2001;Desmond Tutu, "R100 million for Apartheid Reparations is a Significant Step", (www.woza.co.za/budget98) ;"The Genealogical Calculus of Reparations, (www.msstate.edu/listarchives/afrigeneas) and The Civil Liberties Act of 1988.

[3] Boris Bittker, *The Case for Black Reparations*, (New York: Random House, 1972)

[4] Helen Thomas, *"Review Nuremberg Lessons"*, Times Union newspaper, March 7, 2005

[5] Chorzow Factory Case, Germany v Poland: Impact of Supranational and International Law, 9.INT.15. PCIJ, Judgment No. 13, 13 September 1928, Factory at Chorzów (Merits) (Germany v. Poland). Chorzów Factory, 9.3. Case-Law of International Courts and Arbitral Tribunals; also see (http://www.law.kuleuven.ac.be/casebook/tort9.php)

[6] Gifford, "The legal basis of the claim for Reparations"

[7] The Civil Liberties Act of 1988, *Redress for Japanese Americans,* US Department of Justice, Civil Rights Division (*www.usdoj.gov/crt/ora/ main.html*)

[8] Title 50, Appendix--War and National Defense Restitution for World War II internment of Japanese Americans and Aleuts, pub. l. 100-383, Aug. 10, 1988, 102 stat. 903, Sec. 1989

9   Dorothy Benton-Lewis, BRC, Black Reparations Now!, Part 1 "40 Acres, $50.00 and a Mule"

10   **NOTE:** On March 2005, the United States government settled claims with the families of Hungarian Holocaust victims whose treasures were plundered by U. S. Army officers during World War II. This settlement totaled $25.5 million dollars. Report: Holocaust Damage Cost Up to $330B, Diversity Inc., April 2005 www.diversityinc.com/public/13788print.cfm

SELECTED BIBLIOGRAPHY

BOOKS

Abdy, Edward *Journal of a Residence and Tour in the United States of North America, from April, 1833 to Oct., 1834,* London: J. Murray, 1835

Bahn, Gilbert S., *Slaves and Nonwhite Free persons in the 1790 Federal Census of New York,* Baltimore: Clearfield Press, 2000

Berlin, Ira, *Many Thousand Gone,* 1998, Harvard University Press

Blackbure, Robin, *The Overthrow of Colonial Slavery, 1776-1848*, 2000, Verso (London/New York)

Davis, Thomas J., "A Rumor of Revolt: The 'Great Negro Plot' in Colonial New York, 1985, Free Press, NYC, (Macmillan Inc.)

Foote, Thelma Wills, *Black and White Manhattan: The History of Racial Formation in Colonial New York City,* 2004, Oxford University Press

Gellman, David N. and Quigley, David, eds., *Jim Crow New York: A Documentary History of Race and Citizenship, 1777-1877*, 2003, New York University Press

Gibbs, C.R., *Black Explorers,* 1992, Three Dimensional Publishing Co.

Greene, Evanrt and Virginia Harrington, *American Population before the Federal Census of 1790*, 1932, Columbia University Press

Goodfriend, Joyce D., *Before the Melting Pot,* 1992, Princeton University Press

Harris, Leslie M., *In the Shadow of Slavery: African Americans in New York City, 1626–1863*, The University of Chicago Press, 2003

Hart, Simon, ed. *The Prehistory of the New Netherlands Company: Amsterdam Notarial Records of the First Dutch Voyages of the Hudson*, City of Amsterdam Press, 1959

Heyrick, Elizabeth, *"Immediate not Gradual Abolition; or, an inquiry into the shortest, safest and most effectual means of getting rid of West Indian slavery"*, London, 1824

Hodges, Graham Russell and Alan Eward Brown,eds. *"Pretends to be Free": Runaway Slave Advertisements from Colonial and Revolutionary New York and New Jersey* (New York and London: Garland Publishing,1994

Hodges, Graham Russell, *Root & Branch: African Americans in New York and East Jersey, 1613 – 1863,* 1999, The University of North Carolina Press

Hodges, Graham Russell, *Slavery and Freedom in the Rural North* , 1997, Madison House Publishers, Inc.,

Kim, Sung Bok *Landlord and Tenant in Colonial New York,* 1978, The University of North Carolina Press

Kroger, Larry, *Black Slaveowners: Free Black Masters in South Carolina*, 1985

Kruger, Vivienne L. *Born to Run: the Slave Family in Early New York, 1623-1827*, PHD, 1985, Columbia University, University Microfilms International

McManus, Edgar J., *Black Bondage in the North,* 1973, Syracuse University Press

McManus, Edgar J. *A History of Negro Slavery in New York,* 1966, Syracuse University Press

Melish, Joanne Pope, *Disowning Slavery: Gradual Emancipation and 'Race' in New England*, 1780-1860, 1998, Ithaca: Cornell University Press

Northup, Solomon *"Twelve years a slave: Narrative of* Solomon Northup, *a Citizen of New-York,"* London: Sampson Low, Son & Company, 47 Ludgate Hill, 1853

O'Callaghan, E.B. *The Documentary History of the State of New York.* 4 volumes. Albany, NY: Weed, Parsons & Co., Public Printers, 1850

Ottley, Roi and William J. Weatherby, eds. *The Negro in New York: An Informal Social History,* 1967, Oceana Publications

Rink, Oliver A. *Holland on the Hudson: An Economic and Social History of Dutch New York*, 1986

Robinson, Randall, *"The Debt: What America Owes To Blacks",* 2000, Dotton Publishing

Smith, Venture, *"A Narrative of the Life and Adventures of Venture, A Native of Africa: But refident above fixty years in the United State of America.* Related by Himself, New London: printed by C.Holt, at the BEE-Office, 1798

Steward, Austin *Twenty-Two Years A Slave and Forty Years a Freeman* Rochester: Wm. Alling, 1857

Thomas, James Rev., by Himself, "The Wonderful Eventful Life of Rev. Thomas James", 1887, Post-Express Printing Co., Rochester, NY (*African American Perspectives: Pamphlets from Daniel A. P. Murray Collection, 1818-1907*)

Truth, Sojourner *Narrative of Sojourner Truth*, 1850, Boston

White, Shane, *Somewhat more independent: the end of slavery in New York City, 1770-1810*, Athens Press-University of Georgia

Williams, Oscar, *African Americans and Colonial Legislation in the Middle Colonies*, 1998, Garland Publishing

Willaims-Myers, A. J., *Long Hammering*, 1994, Africa World Press

Wilson, Sherrill D., New *York City's African Slaveowners: A Social and Material Culture History,*1994, Garland Publishing

Woodson, Carter G., *Free Negro Owners of Slaves in the United States in 1830, 1924,* Negro University Press

Zilversmit, Arthur *The First Emancipation: The Abolition of Slavery in the North,* 1967, The University of Chicago Press

ARTICLES

Albany County *"Register of Manumitted Slaves, 1800-1829"*, Records Series, County Clerk's Hall of Records

American Minerva Newspaper, 6 & 8 February 1796

The Argus Newspaper, 23 January 1796

Benton-Lewis, Dorothy, BRC, *Black Reparations Now!* Part 1 *"40 Acres, $50.00 and a Mule"*

Chamberlin's Records, *City of Albany Records,* 1783-1815, Albany County Hall of Records

David, Thomas J., "New York's Long Black Line: A note on the Growing Slave Population, 1626-1790, *"Afro-Amweicans in New York Life and History*, 2 (January 1978)

Goodfriend, Joyce D., Black Families in New Netherland, *Selected Rensselaerswijck Seminar Papers*

Morgan, Edwin Vernon, "Slavery in New York: The Status of the Slave under English Colonial Government", *Harvard Historical Review, 5 January 1925*

Mc Manus, Edgar J., "Antislavery Legislation in New York", *The Journal of Negro History,* vol. XLVI, October, 1961

New York Gazette and Weekly Post Boy Newspaper, March 26, 1749 and July 20, 1747

New York Gazetteer Newspaper, February 4, 1785

New York Journal Newspaper, April 15th, 1784

Report of the World Conference against Racism, Racial Discrimination, Xenophobia and Related Intolerance; Durban, 31 August - 8 September 2001

Strickland, William, *"Journal of a Tour of the United States of America 1794-1795"*, ed. J. E. Strickland, 1791, *New York Historical Society*

Yoshpe, Harry P. "Records of Slave Manumission in New York During the Colonial and Early National Periods", *Journal of Negro History,* vol. XXVI, 194

INTERNET SITES

Colonial Albany Social History Project, Albany County, *nysed.gov/Albany/ albanycounty.html*

New Netherland Project, (*www.nnp.org*)

1790 United States Census Data, *1790 County Level Census Data – Sorted by State/County Name*, (*http://fisher.lib.virginia.edu/cgi-local/censusbin/census/cen. pl*)

INDEX

A

Abandoned children 139, 146, 237,
    240, 243, 247, 253, 257, 259,
    272, 273, 277, 278, 281, 316
  abandonment rate 201, 202, 223,
    224
  maintenance and support of 202,
    237, 243, 247, 273, 278, 279
Abandonment 138, 139, 143, 144,
    146, 148, 153, 157, 187, 201,
    202, 211, 216, 223, 224, 236,
    243, 247, 249, 266, 267, 270,
    278, 281, 282, 283, 316
  abandonment provisions 144, 146,
    157
  intention to abandon 146, 211
Abolition xx, xxi, xxv, xxvi, xxvii,
    xxx, 64, 87, 99, 102, 106, 123,
    125, 127, 128, 130, 136, 138,
    139, 140, 141, 142, 144, 146,
    148, 149, 150, 157, 160, 161,
    164, 165, 168, 178, 181, 183,
    184, 185, 192, 193, 197, 198,
    199, 201, 202, 217, 219, 237,
    243, 244, 245, 247, 266, 270,
    273, 274, 277, 278, 281, 283,
    288, 289, 290, 291, 292, 295,
    296, 297, 300, 301, 302, 305,
    306, 307, 308, 309, 310, 311,
    314, 315, 316, 317, 324, 343,
    347, 348, 350, 367, 369
  abolition movement 102
  Dutch freedom policies 112
Abolitionists 87, 89, 102, 296, 316,
    343
  abolitionists recant gradual abolition
    316
Adams, Thomas 168, 169, 170
Africa xxiii, xxxii, 2, 3, 7, 8, 9, 13,
    14, 22, 29, 31, 42, 52, 55, 58,
    65, 74, 75, 82, 90, 297, 341,
    346, 351, 357, 365, 368, 369

Africans xxvii, xxviii, xxx, 9, 13, 14,
    18, 19, 20, 22, 24, 25, 26, 27,
    28, 29, 31, 34, 35, 36, 37, 38,
    39, 40, 41, 42, 43, 46, 47, 49,
    50, 51, 52, 53, 55, 56, 61, 62,
    63, 64, 65, 66, 68, 72, 73, 74,
    76, 82, 84, 86, 87, 89, 90, 98,
    100, 112, 113, 114, 116, 117,
    118, 124, 131, 166, 174, 295,
    350, 351, 352, 354, 357, 359
African culture 47
African descendant family 270, 348,
    349
African gangs 55
African Slaveholders 58, 86, 90, 94,
    130
Agriculture 9, 13, 24, 29, 34, 38, 113,
    114, 121
  farms 26, 40, 163, 292, 293, 295,
    305, 337
  farm workers 28, 38
Akan-Asante society 52
Alaskan islands 362
Albany xiv, xix, xx, 2, 3, 6, 13, 38,
    43, 44, 46, 56, 64, 68, 81, 82,
    83, 86, 87, 88, 92, 93, 94, 109,
    110, 111, 127, 130, 184, 186,
    188, 189, 192, 193, 197, 198,
    199, 201, 202, 211, 216, 217,
    219, 223, 224, 227, 232, 233,
    237, 238, 240, 243, 266, 274,
    288, 290, 335, 368, 369, 370
  Common Council of Albany 46
  payments to slave holders 240
  slave codes xxvi, 42, 46, 68, 109
Albany Argus 127
Albany Committee of Safety 44
Albany County Hall of Records 233,
    243, 369
Albany Institute of History and Art
    xiv, 93, 186, 188, 189, 219,
    232, 233

American Citizen 329
American Convention of Abolition
    Societies 99
American Loyalists 100
American Minerva 127, 133, 369
American Revolution 19, 99, 100,
    124, 312
Amsterdam 3, 4, 6, 13, 17, 19, 20, 22,
    25, 26, 27, 31, 39, 40, 56, 57,
    81, 83, 113, 114, 115, 116, 117,
    131, 266, 305, 350, 367
Anglicans 295
Anglo-Dutch war 31
Angola 22, 29, 114, 115, 117
An Act for preventing the Conspiracy
    of Slaves 48
An Act relative to slaves and servants
    141, 324
Atlantic Creoles 14, 18
Atlantic Ocean 13, 14

B

Baltimore, MD xxxii, 86
Bank of New York 72, 124
Bath, NY 302
Benoit 123, 132
Bethlehem, NY 224, 225, 228
Beverwyck 3, 6, 11, 13
Big Manuel 114, 117
Bill to Prevent Frauds at Elections,
    and For Other Purposes 331
Bleecker family 216
Bondage 132, 185, 368
Boston, MA 82
Boston News- Letter 49
Brazil 19, 31, 51
British xxvii, 23, 27, 31, 32, 34, 35,
    36, 41, 42, 43, 44, 47, 52, 74,
    82, 88, 99, 100, 101, 104, 117,
    118, 282, 325, 361
Bucktail Republicans 333, 334

C

"Call to Rebellion" 297
Canajoharie, NY 305

Capitalism 75, 121, 316
Caribbean, The 13, 19, 24, 51, 82
Catskill, NY 197
Census data 327
Charles II of England 31
Children of slaves 139, 148, 240, 247,
    257, 259, 262, 277, 278, 288
Children follow the condition of their
    mothers 108
Church, The 41
Civil rights 127, 334
Clarke, John Henrik xxxii
Clinton De Witt 276
Colbert, Lloyd 165
Colonial America xxvii, 19, 24, 53,
    61, 86
Colonial Assembly 35, 43, 48, 49,
    51, 75
Colonial New York 41, 43, 62, 75, 81,
    84, 85, 86, 87, 89, 94, 99, 185,
    227, 367, 368
Colonial Records of New York 19, 83
Columbia County 266
Compensated Abolition Program 283
    compensating slave holders 136
    compensation scheme 272
Comptroller Jenkins 72, 276, 277,
    278
Congo, Simon 114
Connecticut 15, 60, 99, 128, 175, 308,
    309
Conspiracies (Slave) 56
Continental Congress 101
Cornbury, Edward Lord Viscount 48
Cornish, Samuel 297
Council of Appointments 103
Council of Revision 106, 129, 332,
    333
Crimes against humanity xxx, 136,
    270, 350, 351, 352, 359, 364
culpability of New York State 253

D

Davis, T. J. 55, 87, 89
Deer River 15

Delaware 4, 15, 31, 81, 99, 174
de Gerrit de Reus, Manuel 114
De Lancey, Peter 289
Director General of New Netherland 11, 61
Discrimination 326, 329, 342, 351, 354, 370
Disenfranchisement xxi, xxvi, 106, 330, 332, 333, 335, 336, 347
Domestic service 40, 329
Douglass, Frederick 297
Down, Volkert A. 199
Duane, James 126
Dumont, John J. 300
Dutchess County 76, 150, 151, 152, 153, 187, 266, 290, 312
Dutch East India Company 2
Dutch farmers 98, 120
Dutch trading firms 27
Dutch West India Company 2, 3, 6, 9, 11, 25, 34, 36, 61, 112, 113, 116, 117

E

Easton, NY 92
Economic importance of slavery 146
Edgar J. Mc Manus 327
Egbert Benson 104
Electoral College 338
Ellison, Rev. Thomas 216
Emancipation 87, 128, 130, 185, 186, 288, 303, 317, 325, 337, 368, 369
Emancipation Day 303, 325
Employers 66, 67, 281, 324, 357
English colonies 22
English Manor 12
English Navigation Act of 1651 31
Escape 43, 49, 300, 306, 310, 312, 314, 315
  escaped slaves 55, 213, 314
Euro-Americans 104
Europeans 18, 24, 28, 34, 40, 121
Export duty 26, 28

F

Fairfield County, CT 308
Farmington, NY 302
Federalist Party 334
Final Abolition (New York State) 323
Fire of 1911(Albany-Capitol) 243, 266
Flatlands, NY 271
Fonda, Eloise 211
Forbiding intermarriage 106
Forms of legal redress (Reparations) 357
Fort Orange 3, 6, 9, 11, 12, 13, 31, 38, 81, 86, 114
Fort Plain 306
Francisco, Jan 114
Francisko 18
Franklin, Benjamin 124
Freedom's Journal 297
Freeholds 332
Freemanship Laws 327
Freemen 50
Free artisans of African descent 294, 295
Free Coloureds xxi
Free labor xxix, 40, 67, 80, 307, 337, 339, 348, 349
Free workers 26, 34, 122
French 3, 43, 44, 327
Fugitive Slave Law 173, 174
Fur trading 13, 29

G

Gambling in public (prohibition) 50
Garcia 114
Garnet, Henry Highland 296
Garrison, William Lloyd 317, 322
Geneva Gazette 314, 315
Germany 327, 361, 365
Gomez, Esteban 15, 16
Gradual Abolition xx, xxi, xxv, xxvi, xxvii, xxx, 64, 106, 123, 125, 127, 136, 138, 139, 140, 141, 142, 144, 146, 148, 149, 150,

157, 160, 161, 164, 165, 168,
178, 181, 183, 184, 192, 193,
197, 198, 199, 201, 202, 217,
219, 237, 243, 244, 245, 247,
266, 270, 273, 274, 276, 277,
278, 281, 283, 288, 289, 290,
291, 292, 295, 296, 297, 300,
301, 302, 305, 306, 307, 308,
309, 310, 311, 314, 315, 316,
317, 324, 347, 348, 350, 367
politics of 136, 328, 337
slave life 29
Gradual Abolition Act xx, 64, 123,
127, 136, 139, 141, 144, 147,
149, 150, 157, 161, 164, 165,
168, 178, 181, 183, 184, 192,
197, 198, 199, 201, 202, 217,
219, 237, 243, 244, 270, 273,
274, 276, 278, 281, 288, 289,
290, 291, 292, 300, 301, 306,
307, 315, 324, 348, 350
provisions of xxi, 141, 144, 146,
149, 157, 158, 160, 164, 198,
201, 202, 219, 237, 282, 284,
288, 301, 310, 315, 324, 326,
331, 333
subsidy xvii, 138, 139, 146, 202,
216, 237, 238, 240, 241, 243,
244, 245, 247, 253, 266, 267,
270, 271, 272, 276, 277, 278,
281, 283, 284, 292, 315
Gradual Abolition Act's impact on
slavery 269
Great Compromise 127, 338
Great Negro Plot 52
Greenwich Village 83, 116, 130
Guyana 4

H

Half-slaves 26
Hallet, William Jr 48
Hamilton, Alexander 75, 101, 123,
128
Harlem 55
Henry Hudson 2, 3

High mortality rate 349
Hire market 69, 72
Hire system (Profitability) 66, 291
Holland Hill, CT 308
Howell, Nathanial 165, 166
Hudson River 2, 3, 6, 15, 17, 112,
227, 312
Hudson Valley xxix, 29, 39, 64, 295
Huguenots 295
Human property 75, 112, 199, 211,
213, 254, 277, 290
Human rights 105, 348, 362

I

Illegal importation and exportation of
slaves 124
Immediate abolition 105, 120, 125,
296, 317
Immigration 29, 62, 65, 73, 121, 329
Indentured servitude 142, 143
indentured servants 19, 34, 40, 142,
143
Inhuman treatment 46
International Criminal Court 358
Investment management 69
Irish 55, 328, 329, 335, 342
Israel 361

J

"Jim Crow" xxvi, 336
James, Rev. Thomas 305
Japanese Americans 362, 365
Jefferson. Thomas 329
Jenkins, Elisha 72, 276
Jewish Holocaust 361
John Jay 100, 101, 104, 122, 123,
126, 128, 132, 133
Journal of Negro History 58, 90, 129,
140, 186, 369, 370

K

Killing of slaves 49
King, Rufus 101
Kingston, NY 3, 43, 56, 76, 266

Kings County xxix, 48, 61, 63, 243, 244
King Charles I of Spain 15
Kissam, Daniel Whitehead 143, 144, 145
Koromantine 52

L

Land grants 7, 116
Land rights settlements 363
Laurens, Colonel Henry 101
Law of State Responsibility 352
Legalized oppression 118
Liberalism 122, 125
Lincoln, Abraham 337, 339
  compensated abolition xxix, 139, 143, 238, 266, 273, 291
Little Anthony 114
Little Manuel 114
Livingston, Robert 106
Lord of the Manor 227
Loss of property (slave) 44

M

Maafa 22
MAAT xxxi
Madagascar 36
Mamaroneck, NY 275, 276, 285
Manhattan 3, 6, 17, 18, 27, 33, 36, 52, 55, 62, 81, 84, 116, 120, 131, 367
Manumission 90, 102, 118, 122, 123, 124, 126, 133, 139, 168, 180, 183, 186, 192, 282, 283, 302, 342, 370
Maranda, John 58
Marbletown 326
Marbletown, NY 326
Maroons 48, 55
Maryland 4, 15, 16, 32, 42, 63, 77, 78, 99, 166, 167
Mason /Dixon line xxvii, 62
Massachusetts 25, 89, 128, 139, 171
Mayken 115

Merchants 76, 81, 84, 94
Methodists 295
Mexico 75, 337, 339
Middle Colonies 19, 61, 81, 83, 84, 369
Middle Passage 22
Military service (slaves) 100
Milton, NY 312
Monopoly Game of Colonization 31
Monopoly on trade 26, 346
Montgomery County 184, 213, 266
Morris, Lewis 101, 103, 122
Mulattoes 68
Multilingual 29
Murray, John Jr 124

N

"New Age Slave-Traders" 272
Narratives 81, 82, 84, 231, 297
Native Americans 6, 10, 17, 18, 25, 50
Negroes 19, 20, 25, 29, 36, 43, 46, 51, 53, 56, 68, 80, 95, 106, 109, 113, 314, 325, 341
Negrophobia 327
New Amsterdam 3, 6, 13, 19, 20, 22, 25, 26, 27, 39, 40, 56, 57, 81, 113, 114, 115, 116, 117, 131, 350
New England 16, 27, 44, 62, 98, 120, 186, 308
New Englanders 120
New Jersey xxvii, 4, 27, 43, 46, 58, 62, 88, 91, 99, 167, 185, 281, 282, 283, 284, 286, 288, 367
New Netherland 2, 3, 4, 6, 7, 9, 11, 12, 13, 14, 18, 19, 22, 25, 26, 27, 28, 29, 31, 32, 34, 36, 39, 40, 51, 62, 65, 81, 82, 83, 84, 85, 90, 112, 114, 117, 130, 131, 227, 282, 367, 369, 370
New Paltz, NY 321, 341
New World 2, 6, 7, 9, 13, 14, 20, 22, 24, 29, 31, 32, 53, 65, 82, 121, 343, 346

discrimination xxi, 139, 330, 334,
336, 347, 351, 352, 354, 356,
358
maintenance workers 26
New York's commercial prosperity 73
New Yorks commercial prosperity 73
New York City xxvii, xxviii, xxix,
xxxii, 6, 13, 19, 26, 34, 38, 39,
42, 46, 49, 50, 51, 52, 53, 56,
57, 58, 62, 63, 64, 65, 68, 69,
72, 73, 74, 83, 86, 89, 90, 91,
92, 94, 100, 116, 118, 122, 123,
127, 130, 132, 185, 192, 201,
294, 310, 327, 328, 329, 331,
333, 334, 341, 342, 346, 367,
369
New York Colony 36, 62, 282
New York Gazetteer 122, 132, 370
New York Journal 104, 129, 329, 342,
370
New York Manumission Society 102,
122, 123, 124, 126, 342
New York Society for the Encouragement of Faithful Domestics
329
New York State xiv, xix, xx, xxi, xxii,
xxv, xxvi, xxvii, xxviii, xxix,
xxx, 6, 44, 50, 56, 63, 64, 66,
67, 72, 76, 82, 94, 98, 99, 101,
102, 104, 105, 109, 112, 114,
120, 121, 122, 124, 125, 127,
128, 129, 130, 132, 133, 136,
137, 138, 140, 146, 151, 157,
159, 165, 174, 184, 185, 186,
188, 189, 192, 201, 202, 219,
229, 230, 231, 237, 238, 240,
243, 244, 245, 265, 266, 267,
271, 272, 273, 275, 278, 279,
280, 281, 282, 283, 285, 288,
289, 291, 293, 295, 296, 297,
300, 301, 306, 307, 308, 309,
310, 316, 324, 326, 329, 330,
332, 333, 334, 336, 341, 342,
346, 347, 348, 349, 350, 352,
354, 356, 357, 358, 362

case for reparations xxx, 357, 359
crimes of xxiv, 359
remedy xvii, 352, 358
New York State Budget Spent on
Abandoned Black Children,
1802 to1824 279
New York State Legislature xx, 105,
122, 127, 192, 272, 320, 324,
330, 347, 358
New York State Senate 185
Nicoll, Caesar 228, 231
Nicoll, Rensselaer 228
North-Castle, NY 310
Northeast, NY 381
Northup, Solomon 77, 94, 174, 188,
336, 343, 368
North America xxxiii, 3, 6, 14, 15, 17,
18, 19, 40, 52, 66, 81, 89, 95,
121, 130, 131, 132, 185, 367
North Hempstead, NY 145
Nuremberg Tribunal 351
NY State Comptrollers Report 285

O

Ontario County 163, 165, 166, 167
Overseers of the Poor 138, 139, 144,
146, 147, 150, 151, 157, 158,
159, 165, 181, 202, 217, 225,
238, 243, 244, 245, 247, 249,
251, 253, 257, 259, 271, 273,
274, 277, 278, 281, 283, 290,
316, 348

P

Patriotic Register 329, 342
Patroons 7, 19, 227
Patroonship 7, 9, 12
Paupers 146, 316, 326, 330
Pawpaw 52
Peggy Pruy (Van Vranken) 180
Pennsylvania 4, 62, 88, 98, 104, 128,
295
Permanent Court of International
Justice 360

376

Pernambuco 20
Philipse, Adolphus 36
Phillipsburg Manor 36, 86
Piscataway, NJ 282
Plantations 14, 24, 38, 39, 292
Poor House xxi
Poor Master 138, 139, 144, 146, 147,
     148, 149, 150, 151, 157, 158,
     159, 165, 181, 184, 202, 217,
     225, 238, 243, 244, 245, 247,
     249, 251, 253, 257, 259, 271,
     273, 274, 277, 278, 281, 283,
     290, 316, 321, 348
Population 87, 92, 343, 367, 369
Portuguese, Anthony 114, 117
Port of New York 121
Posting of a bond 140, 149
Poughkeepsie Journal 313
Privateers 36, 116
Private or public subjugation 349
Profits (slavery) 2, 6, 9, 25, 26, 28,
     34, 36, 68, 74, 79, 85, 116, 117,
     122, 290, 307
Property rights 105, 112, 116, 126,
     143, 348
Property rights advocates 112, 116
Protests for freedom 114
Protests from white workers 330
Puels, Anabel xix

Q

Quakers 99, 124, 161, 163, 302
Quasi-freedom xxviii
Queens County 48, 273, 275, 316

R

Race in New York State 104
Rebellions 47, 49, 50
Records of Negro Children Born to
     Slaves 161
Regular tasks of slaves 293
Rensselaerswyck 82, 94
Rensselaer County xix, 168, 178, 180,
     183, 184, 266

Reparations xxx, 357, 359, 360, 365,
     366, 369
Republicans 136, 137, 186, 328, 330,
     333, 334, 342
Request for reimbursement 251, 253
Returning runaways 61
Revisionist history xxiii
Revolt of 1712 (NYC) 50
Revolutionary leaders 100, 101, 104
Revolutionary plot 53
Rhode Island 99, 128, 139, 292, 309
Right to vote xx, xxi, xxvi, 105, 106,
     107, 330, 331, 332, 333, 334,
     335, 336, 347
Rochester, NY 93, 368
Rockaway Native American 17
Rodrigues, Jan 17
Root, Erastus 123, 127
Royal African Company 34
Russworm, John 297

S

Salem, NY xxi
Sale of slaves 72
Salisbury, Sylvester 227, 228
Santomee, Peter 114
Schagticoke, NY xix
Schuyler, Philip 122, 193
Schuyler, Stephen 168
Science of racial identification 332
     scientific racism 332
Segregation 330
     public accommodations 330
     schools 330, 336
Separation of families xxvi, 270, 302,
     347
Serving on juries 105
Silliman family 308
Slave-owning class 8, 9, 39
Slavery 83, 84, 85, 86, 87, 88, 89, 91,
     92, 94, 112, 128, 129, 130, 132,
     133, 185, 186, 187, 188, 286,
     325, 341, 342, 343, 354, 356,
     365, 367, 368, 369
     slavery in New York 83, 84, 85, 88,

91, 129, 185, 341, 342, 368, 369

under the Dutch xxvii, 47

Slaver Apprehending Society of Shawangunk 314

Slaves xxxiii, 32, 40, 43, 48, 49, 51, 66, 67, 83, 86, 88, 91, 93, 94, 95, 109, 122, 130, 133, 159, 161, 162, 182, 186, 201, 224, 232, 233, 249, 267, 285, 293, 307, 310, 340, 367, 369

gradual abolition xx, xxi, xxv, xxvi, xxvii, xxx, 64, 106, 123, 125, 126, 127, 136, 138, 139, 140, 141, 142, 144, 146, 147, 148, 149, 150, 157, 160, 161, 164, 168, 178, 181, 183, 184, 192, 193, 197, 198, 199, 201, 202, 217, 219, 236, 237, 243, 244, 245, 247, 266, 270, 273, 274, 276, 277, 278, 281, 283, 288, 289, 290, 291, 292, 295, 296, 297, 298, 300, 301, 302, 305, 306, 307, 308, 309, 310, 311, 314, 315, 316, 317, 319, 322, 324, 347, 348, 350, 367

New Netherland 2, 3, 4, 6, 7, 9, 11, 12, 13, 14, 18, 19, 22, 25, 26, 27, 28, 29, 31, 32, 34, 36, 39, 40, 51, 62, 65, 81, 82, 83, 84, 85, 112, 114, 117, 130, 131, 227, 282, 369, 370

population 87, 92, 340, 343, 367, 369

Slave Book of the Town of Lloyd, New York 150

Slave Codes xxvi, 42, 46, 68, 108, 109

Slave holders 90, 108, 137, 146, 288

payments to 240, 266

Slave labor 98

Slave market 34, 76

Slave Narratives 231

Slave ownership 122

Slave ship 76

Slave trading 9, 41

Slave unity 47

Slavocracy 330

Small Pox 72

Smith, Venture 368

Society of Friends and Episcopalians 295

Society of Negroes Unsettled 314, 341

Southerners 337, 338

Southern colonies 50, 73

Southern planters 38, 338

South Africa 351, 357, 365

South Carolina 46, 63, 90, 101, 368

Spanish Negroes 53

Specialized labor 24

St. Peters Church 216

Stake in society 106

State Assemblyman R. Clarke 334

Statute of limitations 363

Statutory Servitude 105, 331

statutory slaves 142, 150, 183, 202, 270, 288, 289, 290, 291, 292, 293, 295, 300, 301, 302, 307, 308, 309, 313, 314, 326

Stereotypes 52

Steward, Austin 368

Strickland, William 370

Stuyvesant, Peter 11, 61

Suffolk Gazette 288

Suffrage 103, 107, 330, 335, 336

Surrogate parents 115

T

"Three-fifths of a man" 338

Tamandar'e 19, 20

Tammany Hall 328, 342

Ten Eyck family 216

The Liberator 317

The rights of property 125

Tobacco and cotton revolutions 62

Trading posts 117

Treaty of Breda 31

Triangle Slave Trade 7

Troy, NY 178

Truth, Sojourner 293, 298, 299, 300, 319, 320, 342, 369

U

Ulster County 42, 43, 56, 76, 87, 88, 94, 140, 186, 266, 302, 313, 314
Ulster Park, NY 300
United Nations Security Council 361
United States Constitution 99, 230, 336, 338, 343
United States Federal Census xxix, 92
Uprisings 47

V

Vanderhyden, Dirck Y 180
Van Bergen, Peter 68
Van Buren, Martin 65, 333
Van Derheyden family 216
Van Rensselaer, John 223
Van Rensselaer, Killiaen 9, 12, 227
Van Rensselaer, Phillip 216
Van Vranken, Johannes xix, xx, xxi
Van Vranken family xi
Van Wagoner, Isaac S. 300
Van Zandt, Gerrit 193, 194, 196, 197, 198, 199, 232, 290, 291
Veeder, Peter 223
Vendue 69, 72, 93, 159
Vermont xx, 98, 128, 314

W

Wall Street 25, 34, 73
Washington, George 339
Washington County xx, xxi, 65, 92, 146, 149, 184, 186, 187, 266
Way, Frisbee 175, 176, 177
Westchester County 3, 99, 161, 247, 289, 310
West Africa 31, 47, 48, 55, 74
West Indies 3, 17, 24, 29, 42, 46, 51, 53, 55, 65, 73, 114, 229, 307, 325
Whipper 50

Whippings xxvi, 229, 347
White House 78, 79, 339
White immigrant workers 65, 66
Williams, Prince 171, 172, 173, 175
Wiltwyck 3
Working class whites 328
World Conference against Racism, Racial Discrimination, Xenophobia and Related Intolerance (WCAR) 351

Y

Yale University 308
Yorktown, NY 187

ABOUT THE AUTHOR

L. Lloyd Stewart, the second of six children, is a third generation native of Albany, NY and an eighth generation native of New York State. His Ancestors on his father's side are Yoruba from Nigeria, West Africa and on his mother's side his Ancestors are Tikar from Cameroon, West Africa. Mr. Stewart is the father of six children, the oldest four of whom he raised as a single parent. He is also blessed with nine Grandchildren, who are the lights of his life.

In 1984, Mr. Stewart founded and served as President/CEO of Stewart Associates, a lobbying and consulting firm. As Principal, Mr. Stewart became the first registered independent African-American lobbyist in New York State history. He presently serves in that capacity.

In 1993, Mr. Stewart was appointed President/CEO of the Urban League of Northeastern New York, Inc. by its Board of Directors. During his tenure, he was directly responsible for increasing the agency's operating budget from $116, 000 to $1.7 million. In 1996, he left his position with the Urban League to realize a lifelong dream to live and work in Africa. While living in South Africa, Mr. Stewart secured the position of Manager of Economic Development for the City of Midrand's Development Corporation, MidDev.

Mr. Stewart has participated in extended "study-tours" to Egypt, Ghana and Zimbabwe and has visited a number of other African countries. He has written several articles, editorials and papers on African and African American history and the African Diaspora. He is presently the African American history writer for the Urban Voices Newspaper of the Capital Region (New York). He also serves on the Executive Committee and Board of Directors of the African Reflections Foundation (Albany, NY and Tanzania, East Africa).

Mr. Stewart attended Columbia University on a scholarship and, later transferred to the State University of New York at Albany, as a Van Slyke scholar, where he received his Bachelor of Arts degree in History with a minor in African American History. After graduation, he accepted a Graduate Assistantship in that University's African American Studies Department.

Printed in the United States
43721LVS00003B/58-135

9 781420 883657